The Real North Korea

The Real North Korea

Life and Politics in the Failed

Stalinist Utopia

ANDREI LANKOV

OXFORD
UNIVERSITY PRESS

Oxford University Press is a department of the University of Oxford.
It furthers the University's objective of excellence in research,
scholarship, and education by publishing worldwide.

Oxford   New York
Auckland   Cape Town   Dar es Salaam   Hong Kong   Karachi
Kuala Lumpur   Madrid   Melbourne   Mexico City   Nairobi
New Delhi   Shanghai   Taipei   Toronto

With offices in
Argentina   Austria   Brazil   Chile   Czech Republic   France   Greece
Guatemala   Hungary   Italy   Japan   Poland   Portugal   Singapore
South Korea   Switzerland   Thailand   Turkey   Ukraine   Vietnam

Oxford is a registered trade mark of Oxford University Press
in the UK and certain other countries.

Published in the United States of America by
Oxford University Press
198 Madison Avenue, New York, NY 10016

Library of Congress Cataloging-in-Publication Data
Lankov, A. N. (Andrei Nikolaevich)
The real North Korea : life and politics in the failed Stalinist utopia / Andrei Lankov.
   pages;   cm.
Includes bibliographical references and index.
ISBN 978-0-19-996429-1 (hardback : alk. paper)
1. Korea (North)—Politics and government—1994–
2. Korea (North)—Foreign relations. I. Title.
DS935.774.L36   2013
951.9304—dc23   2012046992

9 8 7 6 5 4 3 2 1

Printed in the United States of America
on acid-free paper

CONTENTS

CHAPTER 3 The Logic of Survival (Domestically) 109

CHAPTER 4 Survival Diplomacy 145

**INTERLUDE The Contours of a Future: What Might Happen
to North Korea in the Next Two Decades 187**

CHAPTER 5 What to Do about the North? 203

ACKNOWLEDGMENTS

The present book would have been impossible without the support and encouragement of many individuals with whom I have discussed the numerous issues dealt with in the book. Among many others, I would like to mention Rüdiger Frank, Scott Snyder, John Park, Stephen Haggard, Nicolas Eberstadt, Marcus Noland, Fyodor Tertitsky, Tatiana Gabroussenko, Kim Yŏng-Il, Kim Sŏk-hyang, Yu Ho-yŏl, Nam Song-uk, Yu Kil-chae, Kim Byŏng-yŏn, and Zhu Feng.

I am especially grateful to Peter Ward, who typed most of the manuscript while correcting my less than perfect English and also providing me with advice on both style and subject matter, as well as with valuable critiques of my ideas and arguments.

When it deals with the issues of the recent social and economic developments, the book draws on the result of the research that was supported by a grant from the National Research Foundation of Korea (NRF-2010-330-B00187). I also would like to express my deep gratitude to "Moravius" who allowed me to use some photos from his extensive collection.

What does the average Westerner think when North Korea is mentioned? In all probability a number of oft-repeated phrases straight from the media will spring to mind. "A mad country," "the world's last Stalinist regime," "nuclear brinkmanship," and other similar clichés dominate popular understanding of North Korea. Above all, North Korea is said to be "irrational." This is, allegedly, a country whose actions are unpredictable, defying common sense and perhaps even the laws of physics.

But there is one problem with these clichés: they are largely wrong. North Korea is not irrational, and nothing shows this better than its continuing survival against all odds. North Korea is essentially a political living fossil, a relic of an era long gone. Similar regimes either changed out of recognition or disappeared long ago and are now remembered with disdain, if at all. Meanwhile, the regime in Pyongyang still remains in full control of its country. This is a remarkable feat, especially if we take into consideration that it has to operate in a highly—and increasingly—unfavorable environment.

North Korea is a small country with few resources and a moribund economy. In spite of all this, however, it has managed to survive and successfully manipulate larger players, including an impressive number of the great powers. You simply cannot achieve this by being irrational. North Korea's alleged penchant for irrational and erratic behavior is illusionary: the North Korean leaders actually know perfectly well what they are doing. They are neither madmen nor ideological zealots, but rather remarkably efficient and cold-minded calculators, perhaps the best practitioners of Machiavellian politics that can be found in the modern world.

And what of other descriptions: Is North Korea really "driven by an insane ideological zeal"? Is it "unpredictably aggressive"? Indeed, the grotesquely bellicose and often nonsensical rhetoric of the North Korean official media and the country's occasional armed provocations and nuclear weapons program might seem like a confirmation of its alleged aggressiveness. However, a deeper look into Pyongyang's decision making should make us skeptical of such claims. Pyongyang's brinkmanship indeed appears risky at times, but so far North Korea's leaders have known where to stop, how not to cross the red line, and how not to provoke an escalation of tensions into a full-scale war. They have employed saber rattling for decades as part of a shrewd (and highly rational) manipulative strategy that has succeeded—in most cases, at least.

This book is, first of all, about the inner logic of North Korean behavior. This logic is defined by the peculiarities of North Korean society, which in turn are the results of long-term developments. I have written this book in order to explain how North Korea has come to be an international problem, and I also attempt to explain why North Korea's leadership has had no option but to try to remain a pariah.

The book starts with a sketch of North Korean history, which is important since familiarity with the history of the North is vital for anybody who wants to understand the current predicament facing the North Korean leadership. The Kim family regime began as a bold experiment in social engineering. This experiment was led by the elite, whose efforts were much encouraged—and often directly controlled—by Stalin's Russia, but they also enjoyed considerable support from below.

However, the initial rosy expectations and popular enthusiasm were sadly misplaced and soon North Korean society found itself saddled with an increasingly inefficient and unsustainable economic model that had become dependent on the constant infusion of foreign aid. Matters were made worse by the nature of the North Korean elite, which had become hereditary and almost impossible to challenge or change. As time passed and with no apparent way out of the predicament, the economic and po-litical position of North Korea changed from acceptable to difficult before becoming disastrous.

Sadly and strangely, the major problems faced by North Korea's decision makers were created by the staggering economic success of North Korea's twin state—the Republic of Korea. Even though it was impossible to know in 1945, South Korea chose a path that, at the end of the day, proved to be far more efficient and promising than the choices made by (or partially forced on) North Korea's decision makers. However, the existence of the highly successful South Korean state has created continuous and nearly insurmountable problems for the North Korean elite.

Thus, when things moved from bad to worse around 1990 after Soviet aid suddenly dried up, the North Korean elite and the Kim family decided that they should avoid reform, keep the situation under control as best as possible, and use diplomacy (backed, when necessary, by a bit of nuclear blackmail) to extract foreign aid, which remained vital for the survival of their economy. This decision led to a massive famine, not to mention countless deaths in prison camps, but it has worked so far: unlike other Communist regimes, the North Korean state has survived against seem-ingly impossible odds.

As we shall see, the North Korean elite are neither zealous ideologues nor irrational sadistic killers—even though they occasionally look like (and indeed want to look like) both of these. As a matter of fact, some of these people might be quite nice human beings who, from time to time, feel sorry about the suffering that their policies have inflicted upon their people. But given the present situation, they simply do not see how else they can stay in control and protect not only their property (quite meager by current international standards) but, more importantly, their freedom to act and their lives (as well as the freedom and lives of their loved ones). Their approach is often described as paranoid, but I will argue that there may be no alternative to the current North Korean policies if judged from the prospects of the regime's survival, which is the supreme goal of North Korean policy makers. Their current survival strategy might inflict con-siderable suffering on ordinary people, make genuine economic growth impossible, and generate significant international security risks. However, this strategy also ensures that a small hereditary elite keeps enjoying power and (moderate) luxury. And, sadly, there is no alternative that would be acceptable to the decision makers.

It has often been suggested that Chinese-style, market-oriented reforms are the solution to the North Korean problem. Some people believe that North Korean decision makers can be lured or blackmailed into starting reforms, while others hope that they will finally come to their senses and do the right thing for their people as long as the outside world stops meddling in their affairs. However, as we shall see, there is a sound logic behind the stubborn unwillingness among the North's decision makers to follow the Chinese way. Their fears might be exaggerated, to be sure, but they are by no means unfounded.

This book might appear to be quite pessimistic. Even though I argue that there are ways to mitigate the problems and control the damage, it seems that there are no silver bullets or magic potions that can solve the North Korean problem instantly, easily, and painlessly.

Just as the book was going to print a new leadership has begun to emerge in North Korea. As one might expect, the emergence of this new leadership has been accompanied by expectations and hopes for a better future for North Korea. As we will see, however, the country's past gives little ground for optimism, but it is not impossible that the plump and jolly-looking young new Kim may well seek to break with the past and reform the country. He is still surrounded by the advisers and senior lieutenants of his father, but he might not agree with the logic of their survival strategy. There is a distinct possibility that he will attempt to improve the situation. Such attempts might even succeed, but it is also possible that the old guard is right, and that tampering with the system will aggravate the situation and lead to an uncontrollable implosion of the regime—a nightmarish scenario for North Korea's many neighbors.

At any rate, we might be on the brink of some serious changes, and even a transformation in North Korea. Taking into account the earlier experiences and sad present of this country, one should not expect a miracle. On the contrary, if past precedent is anything to go by, changes are likely to be painful and dangerous, even if they remain preferable to the current sorry state of affairs.

Indeed, it might be that the worst is still yet to come—both for the North Koreans and outsiders. Hungarians are known to say: "What is worse than Communism? The things which come after it." It is not impossible that one day, North Koreans will recycle this joke, saying, "What is worse than the Kim family regime? The things that come after it." We do not know the final outcome, but it seems that the eventual transformation of North Korea is not going to be easy or unproblematic. I discuss some potential scenarios at the end of the book, and readers will see that some of these solutions might be more palatable than others. However, all are less than perfect.

The North Korean regime might be annoying and occasionally dangerous for the outside world—largely thanks to its nuclear brinkmanship and proliferation threats—but its major victims are the North Koreans themselves, the vast majority of some 24 million people who inhabit this unlucky country. They are the primary victims of the regime, but also victims of history. North Korean rulers do what they are doing not because they are "evil" or driven by some delusionary ideologies, but rather because they sincerely believe that their current policy has no alternatives, and that any other policy choice will bring ruin to them and their families. Unfortunately, their assumption and worries might be well founded, so the concerns of the "top ten thousand people" (as well as a million or two of their henchmen, big and small) are understandable. Nonetheless, it does not bring any relief to the vast majority of the North Korean population whose lives have been—and continue to be—ruined by the regime.

TRANSCRIPTION

The transcription of Korean personal names has always been a challenge. The book generally follows the McCune-Reischauer system, but in the case of people whose names are frequently spelled differently in the mass media, the established spelling is used instead (this being the case with Kim Il Sung, Kim Jong Il, Kim Jong Un, Kim Jong Nam, and other members of North Korea's top leadership).

CHAPTER 1

The Society Kim Il Sung Built
and How He Did It

One cannot understand modern North Korea without having a look at its past. North Korea never experienced "reform," that is, a government-initiated and government-controlled chain of systematic changes. But this by no means implies that North Korea has not changed. The North Korea of Kim Jong Il's era was dramatically different from the North Korea of the 1953–1994 period. Nonetheless, what happened under Kim Il Sung has determined many of the features of modern North Korean society.

The North Korea of the Kim Il Sung era was a very peculiar place indeed—arguably, one of the most idiosyncratic places in the entire world. It was established as a Soviet client state but with a great deal of support, enthusiasm, and hope. Soon, it evolved into the archetypal National Stalinist regime, and in this form it managed to survive all outside challenges and exist without much change until the early 1990s. It was a time when the Kim family regime grew and matured, and it was also a time when it learned how to survive and manipulate an utterly hostile environment.

CAPTAIN KIM RETURNS HOME

On some autumn September day of 1945 (the exact date is still in dispute, but it seems to be the 19th of September) a group of Asian-looking men, all clad in Soviet military uniform, disembarked from the Soviet steamer *Pugachev* at the Korean port city of Wonsan, then recently taken over by the Soviet forces. Among the arrivals there was a slightly stout man in his early 30s, with the insignia of a Soviet Army captain. To his comrades he was known as Kim Il Sung, commander of the 1st (Korean) battalion of the 88th independent brigade of the Soviet Army.

This young Soviet captain was soon to become the supreme leader of the emerging North Korean state, but in 1945 he came back home after almost two decades spent overseas. In the 1930s Kim Il Sung was a guerrilla field commander in Northeastern China, and in the early 1940s he became a battalion commander in the 88th Brigade of the Soviet Army. Nonetheless, he was a native of the city of Pyongyang, which in late August became the headquarters of the Soviet forces in Korea.[1]

By late August 1945, after a short, intense, and successful military campaign, the Soviet Army found itself in full control of the northern part of the Korean peninsula. Had the Soviet generals only wished, they would have probably taken the southern part as well, but at that stage Moscow was still inclined to respect the agreements made with Washington. One such agreement envisioned a provisional division of the Korean peninsula into two zones of occupation. It took half an hour of deliberation by two US colonels (one of whom eventually became a US secretary of state) to draw what they saw as the provisional demarcation line between the Soviet and US zones of operations. Neatly divided by the 38th parallel, the two zones were almost equal in territory, but vastly different in population size and industrial potential: the South had twice as many people, but its industry was seriously underdeveloped (essentially, in the pre-independence days, southern Korea was an agricultural backwater).[2]

When the Soviets found themselves in control of northern Korea, they had only a dim understanding of the country's political and social realities. Suffice to say that when the Soviet troops entered Korea in August 1945, they had no Korean-speaking interpreters, since they were prepared to fight the Japanese army and hence all their interpreters spoke Japanese. Only in late August did the first Korean-speaking officers (almost exclusively Soviet citizens of Korean extraction) arrive in the country.

Newly declassified Soviet documents seem to indicate that until early 1946, Moscow had no clear-cut plans about the future of Korea. However, the wartime alliance between the United States and Soviet Union proved to be short-lived, with the Cold War setting in. In this new era of hostile relations between the superpowers, neither side was willing to compromise. So by early 1946 the Soviet Union was increasingly inclined to establish a friendly and controllable regime in its own zone of occupation (arguably, the United States had similar plans in regard to the southern part of the peninsula). Under the circumstances of the era, such a regime could only be Communist. But there was one problem: there were no (well, almost no) Communists inside North Korea.

The native Korean Communist movement emerged in the early 1920s, and Marxism was much in vogue among the Korean intellectuals of the colonial era. Nonetheless, due to the harshness of the Japanese colonial regime, a majority of the prominent Korean Communists in 1945 operated outside the country. Those few Communists who in 1945 *could* be found in Korea proper, meanwhile, were overwhelmingly in Seoul, outside of the Soviet zone. Therefore, from late 1945, Soviet military headquarters began to bring the Communist activists to North Korea from elsewhere. Some of them were Soviet officials and technical experts of Korean extraction who were dispatched to North Korea by Moscow; others came from China, where a large number of ethnic Koreans were active in the Chinese Communist Party since the 1920s. A third group consisted of those Communist activists who fled the US-controlled South, where in 1945–1946 the Communist movement experienced a short-lived boom, only to be driven underground and suppressed in the subsequent years. There were also the people who came back with Kim Il Sung, the former guerrillas who spent the war years in the Soviet Union.[3]

It was the latter group that would have by far the greatest impact on Korea's future, but initially it appeared to be the least significant. Those former guerrillas were survivors of a heroic but small-scale and ultimately futile armed resistance to the Japanese occupation of Manchuria in the 1930s. After the resistance collapsed around 1940, the survivors fled to the Soviet Union, where they were enlisted into the Soviet Army and retrained for a future war against Japan. Ironically, the victory against Japan was so swift that these people could not directly participate in the last decisive battle with the Japanese empire. Nonetheless, even after the sudden end of the hostilities, the Soviet military authorities found a good use for these men (and few women). The Chinese and Korean ex-guerrillas were sent home on the assumption that they would be useful advisers and intermediaries serving the Soviet occupation forces.

Kim Il Sung was one of these former guerrillas. Efforts of North Korean propaganda-mongers and the power of hindsight have combined to ensure that historians tend to exaggerate his political significance in the years prior to 1945. Nonetheless, by the time of Korea's liberation, Kim Il Sung was probably already seen as an important leader—in spite of his young age and, admittedly, somewhat unheroic looks (a participant of the 1945 events described to the present author his first impression of the would-be Sun of the Nation and Ever-Victorious Generalissimo in less than flattering terms: "He reminded me of a fat delivery boy from a neighborhood Chinese food stall").

The events of 1945–1946 are a convoluted story, but to simplify it a bit we can say that Kim Il Sung was finally chosen by the Soviet military as the person to head the Communist regime that was to be built in North Korea. The reasons behind this decision may never be known with complete certainty, but Kim Il Sung seemingly had a combination of biographical and personal traits that made him seem a perfect choice to Soviet officials. He was a reasonably good speaker of Russian and his military exploits, though grossly exaggerated by propaganda of later days, were nonetheless real and known to many Koreans. It also helped that Kim was a native of North Korea and was never related to the crowd of Comintern professional revolutionaries and ideologues whom Stalin despised and distrusted.

Kim Il Sung was born in 1912 (on the day the *Titanic* sank, April 15) under the name Kim Sŏng-ju—he adopted the nom de guerre Kim Il Sung much later, in the 1930s. In their attempts to create a perfect biography for the Ever-Victorious Generalissimo, Sun of the Nation, North Korean official historians tried to gloss over some inconvenient facts of his family background and to present him as the son of poor Korean farmers. This is not quite true: like the majority of the first-generation Communist leaders of East Asia (including, say, Mao Zedong), the future North Korean dictator was born into a moderately affluent family with above-average income as well as access to modern education. Kim's father, a graduate of a Protestant school, made a modest living through teaching and practicing herbal medicine while remaining a prominent Christian activist.

Kim Il Sung himself graduated from high school—an impressive level of educational attainment for a Korean of his generation (only a small percentage could afford to take their education that far). Most of his childhood was spent in Northeast China, where his family moved in 1920.

With his good education, Kim Il Sung could have probably opted for a conventional career and become a well-paid clerk, businessman, or educator. He made another choice, however: in the early 1930s he joined the Communist guerillas who fought the Japanese invasion of Manchuria.

The North Korean narrative always plays down the Great Leader's foreign connections, so it remains silent on his decade-long membership in the Chinese Communist Party and his actual position as a junior officer in the essentially Chinese guerrilla force. Instead, the official narrative insists that the Dear Leader created a Korean guerrilla army at the age of 20 (we should not be surprised: if this narrative is to be believed, he became the supreme leader of all Korean Communists at the tender age of 14). Actually, until 1945 Kim Il Sung's military career was spent entirely under Chinese and/or Soviet command, albeit usually in ethnic Korean units.[4]

What made young Kim Sŏng-ju choose the arduous and harsh life of a guerrilla, and what kept him in this dangerous pastime for over a decade? Obviously, he was an idealist, a fighter for (and believer in) a Great Cause—in his case, it was the cause of Communism. However, one should keep in mind how the ideology of Communism was understood in East Asia. While in Europe aspiring Communists were motivated, above all, by the desire to ameliorate social injustices, the East Asian version of Communism had both social and nationalist dimensions. In the 1920s and 1930s, in the era when Kim Il Sung, Mao Zedong, and Ho Chi Minh were young idealists, Communism in East Asia was widely seen as a shortcut to the national revival and modernity, a way not only to solve social problems but also to leapfrog past stages of backwardness and colonial dependency.

In the last years of his life, Kim Il Sung would confess that he was both a Communist and a Nationalist. Frankly, the same could be said about a majority of East Asian Communists of his generation.

Even though initially installed in power by the Soviet military, Kim Il Sung had no desire to be Moscow's puppet—or, for that matter, anybody's puppet. In the 1940s the young ex-guerrilla probably still sincerely believed in the cause of international Communism but he, as well as a majority of his supporters, did not want to sacrifice Korea's national interests in the name of other countries, however progressive or revolutionary these countries said they were. If judged from the Soviet perspective, the Soviet officers in 1945–1946 made a poor choice: they decided to promote a shrewd man who was probably more Nationalist than Communist in his worldview. In due time this made him a serious thorn in the side for the Moscow (and, for that matter, Beijing) diplomats. However, taking into account the situation of late 1940s Korea, had the Soviet officials chosen someone else the eventual outcome would have probably been quite similar. Subsequent events demonstrated that Korean Communist leaders (and, for that matter, other Communist leaders of East Asian countries) made bad puppets—not least because of their deeply ingrained Nationalist convictions. Surprisingly, the leaders' stubborn adherence to the spirit of national independence was not always good news for their subjects: the post-Stalin version of the Soviet Communism that the East Asian strongmen so decisively refused to emulate in the late 1950s was remarkably softer on the common people than locally grown varieties of this revolutionary doctrine.

However, all these complexities became obvious only later. Whatever were Kim Il Sung's secret thoughts, between 1945 and 1948 the nascent North Korean regime operated under the complete control of the Soviet supervisors. The Soviet advisers drafted the above-mentioned land reform law and Stalin himself edited the draft of the 1948 North Korean Constitution. The Soviet military police arrested all the major opponents of the emerging Communist regime, who were then sent to prison camps in Siberia—no North Korean penitentiary system existed as yet.

Even the relatively mundane actions of the North Korean government on that stage needed approval from Moscow. The most important speeches to be delivered by the North Korean leaders had to be first pre-read and approved in the Soviet Embassy. For more important decisions, an approval had to be received from higher reaches of authority. The Soviet Politburo, the supreme council of the state, approved the agenda of the North Korean rubber-stamping parliament and even formally "gave permission" to stage a military parade in February 1948, when the establishment of a North Korean army was formally announced.[5]

My favorite story in this regard occurred in December 1946, when the first elections in the North were being prepared. On December 15 Colonel General Terentii Shtykov, then responsible for the political operations in Korea, discussed the future composition of the North Korean proto-parliament with two other Soviet generals. The Soviet generals (not a single Korean was present) decided that the Assembly would consist of 231 members. They also decided the exact distribution of seats among the parties, the number of women members, and, more broadly, the precise social composition of the legislature. If we have a look at the actual composition of the Assembly, we can see that these instructions were followed with only minor deviations.[6]

Guided and assisted by the Soviet advisers, between 1946 and 1950 North Korea quickly went through a chain of reforms that were standard for nascent Communist regimes of the era. In the spring of 1946 radical land reform led to the redistribution of land among peasants, while also sending a majority of former landlords fleeing South. Around the same time, all industries were nationalized, even though small independent handicraftsmen would still be tolerated until the late 1950s. In politics the local incarnation of the Leninist Party, known as the Korean Workers' Party (KWP), began to exercise increasingly thorough control over society.

In spite of the Christian family background of Kim Il Sung and many other Communist leaders, Christians were persecuted with great ferocity. Like landlords, many former entrepreneurs and Christian activists chose to flee South across the badly guarded demarcation line. Nobody bothered to collect exact statistics, but the number of North Koreans who had fled

South between 1945 and 1951 was approximately 1.2 to 1.5 million, or some 10–15 percent of the entire North Korean population. Among other things, this exodus meant that the potential opposition exiled itself, inadvertently making the emerging regime more homogenous.

At first glance the North Korean state of the late 1940s appears to be a nearly perfect specimen of what the cold warriors once described as a "Soviet satellite regime." But such a view, while not unfounded, is incomplete: North Korea might have been a puppet state, but this does not necessarily mean that the new regime was unpopular and lacked support from below.

In the late 1980s the Marxist and semi-Marxist Left reemerged in South Korea as a political and intellectual force, and soon afterward the nature of the early North Korean regime became a topic of hot (and largely ideology-driven) debate in Seoul intellectual and academic circles. The left-leaning historians and journalists usually present the events of 1945–1950 as a home grown popular revolution that might have been triggered and assisted by the Soviet presence, but generally developed spontaneously and independently. It is not surprising that South Korean leftist historians have demonstrated a remarkable ability to ignore newly published documentary evidence if it shows the true extent of Soviet control and hence undermines their cherished fantasies.

At the same time, the South Korean Right remains strangely obsessed with the desire to prove that Syngman Rhee's regime in South Korea was the "sole legitimate government of the entire Korean peninsula." Therefore, the right-leaning historians seem to be unwilling to pay attention to ample evidence for the genuine popularity enjoyed by Kim Il Sung's government in its early days.[7]

This argument, being essentially ideological in nature, sometimes turns vitriolic and is likely to continue for years if not decades. Nonetheless, it seems to be based on a false dichotomy, since the events of the late 1940s were *both* a foreign occupation and a popular revolution. The Soviet authorities and the then accepted Communist orthodoxy to a very large extent determined the shape of the emerging North Korean society and its institutions. Nonetheless, the promise of the Communist project generally coincided with what many North Koreans sincerely wanted at the time.

The dream of universal equality and affluence, enforced by the watchful but benevolent state, was difficult to resist—particularly when a blueprint of such a society was presented in the "modern" and "scientific" jargon of Marxism-Leninism and supported by the seemingly impressive success of the Soviet Union. After all, in those days, everybody knew that the USSR made good fighter jets and had the world's best ballet while almost nobody knew that a few million Soviet farmers had starved to death in the 1930s. So, the government initiatives, even imposed by the Soviet advisers, often met with enthusiastic response from below.

WAY TO WAR

By late 1946 the division of the country had become a fact of life, and in 1948 two Korean states formally came into being: on the 15th of August, the Republic of Korea (ROK) was proclaimed in Seoul, and on the 9th of September, the Democratic People's Republic of Korea (DPRK) was declared in Pyongyang. Neither state recognized the other; each government claimed itself to be the only legitimate authority on the entire Korean peninsula. This still remains technically the case now, six decades later.

Sometimes both sides went to slightly comical extremes to emphasize their fictional control over Korea in its entirety. For example, until 1972 Seoul (not Pyongyang!) was constitutionally the capital of the DPRK. Concurrently, the ROK government still appoints governors to the provinces of North Korea. Incidentally, the joint offices of these five governors are located not far from the university where this book was being written— and these offices are bustling with bureaucratic activity every time I visit. Both Korean states claimed—and still claim—that the national unification is their paramount political goal. Nowadays, as we will see below, such claims are increasingly shallow and disingenuous, but back in the late 1940s both Pyongyang and Seoul meant what they said.

Both Right and Left were willing to use force for the unification. The Seoul government, however, was engaging in bellicose rhetoric without doing much of substance to prepare for war. Meanwhile, the North Korean leadership kept petitioning Moscow for permission to invade the South and "liberate" its allegedly long-suffering population from the yoke of the US imperialists and their puppets. Kim Il Sung—and, for that matter, other Korean Communist leaders—assured Stalin that the victory would be quick, with America having neither time nor will to intervene. Kim Il Sung cited the reports of the South Korean Communists, who insisted that the entire people of South Korea would rise up against the hated pro-American clique of Syngman Rhee at the first news about the North Korean tanks rolling across the border.[8]

Stalin was initially unenthusiastic about the bellicose mood of his Korean appointees: he didn't want to get plunged into a full-scale confrontation with the United States, then the world's sole nuclear power, by the excessive nationalist zeal of some third-rate Communist leaders. However, by late 1949 things changed: in August, the Soviet Union successfully tested its first nuclear device and soon afterward, in October, Communists took power in China. Finally, the Soviet intelligence reports seemingly confirmed that the United States did not see Korea as vital for their own strategic interest. In this new situation, the Korean gamble looked less risky, and Kim Il Sung kept pressure on.

So, in early 1950, Stalin gave in. On January 30 Ambassador Shtykov met Kim Il Sung and told him of Stalin's approval. As the ambassador's cable to Stalin says, "Kim Il Sung received my report with great satisfaction . . . Kim Il Sung, apparently wishing once more to reassure himself, asked me if this means that it is possible to meet with Comrade Stalin on this question." Indeed, it was possible: in April 1950 Kim rushed to Moscow, where he spent a few weeks discussing the operational plans. He repeated his assurances of swift victory. As a Soviet memo says, he pledged to Stalin: "The attack will be swift and the war will be won in three days: the guerrilla movement in the South has grown stronger and a major uprising is expected." So, the Soviet generals were dispatched to Pyongyang to draw up the operational plans, and by June 1950 everything was ready for a liberation of the South.

The war began on June 25, 1950. Initially, everything went according to the optimistic expectations of the Pyongyang leaders. The anticipated mass uprising in the South never happened, but by early August 1950 the North controlled some 95 percent of the Korean peninsula. However, the United States finally decided to join the war, this decision turning the tide.

A massive American intervention began in September 1950. In a couple of weeks, the North Korean forces were all but annihilated and the North Korean leadership had to flee to the Chinese border. In turn, China decided to intervene and in late November of that year staged a massive counterstrike that probably became the most successful large-scale operation in China's recent military history.

After much fighting and bloodshed, the front line hardened and stabilized by the spring of 1951, even though trench warfare and intensive bombing campaigns continued for another two years. The final front line ran almost exactly where the initial demarcation was drawn in 1945. In 1953 the Armistice Treaty was signed and the front line became the DMZ, a border between two Korean states. Millions died, but the war ended in a nearly perfect draw.

The Korean War greatly strengthened Kim Il Sung's personal power. Before the war he was one of many North Korean Communist leaders, merely a primus inter pares in Pyongyang—one whose slightly special standing was largely, or even exclusively, derived from Soviet support. After the war, Kim emerged as the undisputed national leader; people who joined the Korean Workers' Party during the war and who remained the core of the North Korean bureaucracy for decades to come were joining the Party of Kim Il Sung. He was the only leader they knew. Understandably, he also used this opportunity to promote his guerrilla friends to positions of power.

The Soviet decision not to get involved in land warfare in Korea was also of great help to Kim Il Sung. From that time, the influence of the Chinese could be relied on to counter the influence of the Soviets—more so since the relations between Beijing and Moscow were never as good as official rhetoric implied. The two Communist great powers began to drift toward open hostility in the late 1950s, and this shift gave the North Korean leadership ample opportunities to exploit the contradictions between its two major sponsors. Indeed, from 1953 the Soviet control, so omnipresent in the late 1940s, greatly weakened, and Kim Il Sung began to take cautious measures that were aimed at reducing the ability of the "great Soviet Union" to mingle in North Korea's internal affairs. Some prominent pro-Soviet officials were ousted from their jobs, and the leader of the pro-Moscow group was first demoted and then found dead in his house (officially this was ruled a suicide).

However, on that stage the purges largely targeted the "domestic" Communists, those who had been involved with the Communist underground of the colonial era. In 1953–1955, a majority of these Communist zealots were purged, with some prominent leaders subjected to show trials and others shot or imprisoned without much attention to the legal niceties. The accusations were standard for the Stalinist regimes: the founders of the Korean Communist movement were asserted to be spies and saboteurs, on the payroll of the Americans and Japanese (as usual, the accusations were often comically inconsistent, but who cared?). In most cases, purge meant the death of the major culprits and permanent imprisonment of his/her family, including even distant relatives.

In 1956, however, Kim Il Sung faced a major and unexpected political challenge. His unabashedly Stalinist ways provoked dissatisfaction among the top officials, much influenced by the ongoing de-Stalinization in Moscow. Some of these high-ranking party dissenters obviously wanted to use this opportunity for their own career advancement while others might have felt genuine compassion about the plight of common people who bore the major burden of Stalinist policies. The pro-Soviet and pro-Chinese factions within the North Korean leadership conspired to move the country toward a more moderate political line, akin to the policy of the post-Stalin Soviet leadership (then briefly supported by China as well). To make this possible, they wanted to remove Kim Il Sung from power. The Soviet and Chinese governments were aware and mildly supportive of the scheme. In August 1956, during a Central Committee meeting, the opposition openly challenged Kim Il Sung and his policies.

This challenge was crushed, largely because the younger generation of the officials, deeply Nationalist, hardened by war and eager to see their country less dependent on Moscow, saw no need in the proposed

WITH FRIENDS LIKE THESE . . .

One of the sad facts of Communist history is that most of the founding fathers of Communist states perished at the hands of their own comrades, becoming victims of the machine they had themselves created. North Korea was no exception. If anything, the founders of the North Korean state fared worse than their Chinese or, for instance, Hungarian counterparts.

To confirm this, one has to look at the subsequent fate of the members of the North Korean Politburo in 1949. In Communist countries the Politburo was the supreme executive committee of the party and state, superior to any other institution, including the Cabinet of Ministers. The 1949 North Korean Politburo was technically the first executive board of the unified party. Before that there had been two independent parties, one operating in the North and the other in the South.

The 1949 Politburo had ten full members. It was headed by Kim Il Sung, the Party chairman, who remained the North Korean dictator until his death in 1994. He had two vice chairmen, Pak Hŏn-yŏng and Hŏ Ka-i.

Pak Hŏn-yŏng, the leader of the Korean Communist underground in the colonial era, was for a long time the chairman of the South Korean Workers' Party. After the merger of the two parties, he became second in command in the unified Party, and was also given the post of foreign minister in the DPRK government. However, in 1953 he was ousted from his position and soon arrested. In 1955 he faced a kangaroo court and was executed as an "American spy."

The other vice chairman, Hŏ Ka-i, was a seasoned Soviet bureaucrat of Korean extraction who was dispatched to North Korea to develop the local government and party machinery. In 1949 he was also the Party's first secretary. His close connection with Moscow made him the first target when Kim Il Sung decided to distance the North from its one-time Soviet sponsors. Hŏ Ka-i was accused of "political mistakes" in 1951, and in 1953 he was shot dead in his home. Official reports claim that Hŏ Ka-i committed suicide, but it is possible that he was assassinated on Kim Il Sung's orders. We may never know.

(continued)

Another member of the 1949 Politburo, Yi Sǔng-yǒp, a prominent leader of the South Korean Left, was, at that time, responsible for the guerrilla movement in the South. In 1953 he became a major defendant at the largest show trial in North Korean history. Yi Sǔng-yǒp was said to be an American spy who was planning to stage a coup in the North that would pave the way for a large-scale American landing in Wonsan. Broken, Yi Sǔng-yǒp delivered an expected penitence and was sentenced to death.

Only two of the ten members of that initial Politburo were killed by their enemies rather than by their comrades. Kim Sam-yong, a leader of the Communist underground in the South, was arrested by the South Korean police and hastily executed in the first days of the Korean War. Kim Ch'aek, once a guerrilla fighter in Manchuria, was killed in an American air raid in January 1951.

Of the four other members, Kim Tu-bong was probably most prominent. In 1949 he was the North Korean head of state. This was a largely ceremonial position that well suited the character of this outstanding scholar, a founder of modern Korean linguistics. He tried to distance himself from daily politics. This did not help: in 1957 Kim Tu-bong was purged, subjected to public humiliation, and disappeared from public view. We do not know whether he died in prison or was killed.

Another 1949 member, Pak Il-u, the then minister for the interior, suffered a similar fate. He was purged in 1955 and then disappeared. His fate remains unknown to this day.

Pak Chǒng-ae, the only female in the 1949 Politburo, survived longer than most of her fellows. She was purged in the late 1960s and spent the next decades exiled in the countryside. She resurfaced in the late 1980s, after two decades in the camps, but never regained her influence.

Apart from Kim Il Sung himself, only one 1949 Politburo member, Hǒ Hǒn, died of natural causes. In 1949 he was 63 years old, in bad health, and had only two years to live.

Thus, out of the ten people who ran the country in 1949, only two avoided persecution and died natural deaths. Of the others, two were killed by people whom they regarded as enemies. Of the remaining six, all were purged by their own comrades.

> Should we see them as sincere idealists and tragic victims, or should we notice that many of these supposed victims, while in power, had sent a striking number of people to the execution grounds? Maybe it would be best to leave these questions unanswered. . . .

liberalization and rallied around Kim. Having defeated the challengers, in 1957–1959 Kim launched a new, more thorough purge of party functionaries who had worked with the Soviets and Chinese by exposing their connections—whether real or alleged.[9]

The purges of the 1950s led to a nearly complete reshuffle of the North Korean leadership. From the late 1950s onward nearly all top positions in the North Korean party-state were controlled by the former Manchurian guerrillas and other Kim Il Sung appointees (including a small but growing number of his family members). They stayed in control, more or less unchallenged, until their own physical demise in the 1980s and 1990s.

Only a few of them had graduated from high school and an absolute majority of them had no formal schooling whatsoever—being children of poor subsistence farmers, they could not attend even a primary school.[10] Their earlier experience was also of little help in running a modern state. Nonetheless they were unconditionally loyal to Kim Il Sung and shared his vision of the country's future. And this was the thing that really mattered.

BETWEEN MOSCOW AND BEIJING: THE FOREIGN POLICY OF KIM IL SUNG'S NORTH KOREA

As we have mentioned above, until the late 1950s, North Korea was essentially just another "People's Democracy," a term the newly established pro-Soviet regimes chose as a self-description. In the late 1950s things began to change. What emerged as a result was a unique state that had almost no equivalents in 20th-century history—a truly fascinating topic for any cultural anthropologist, historian, or sociologist.

There were many reasons behind the emergence of Kim Il Sung's North Korea. For example, the personal changes in the leadership were important:

the Communist leaders of the first generation were largely university graduates who combined a measure of nationalism with a modern and relatively cosmopolitan worldview, but in the late 1950s they were replaced by the former guerrillas whose worldview largely reflected the dreams, values, and aspirations of the traditional East Asian peasantry. Like it or not, radical leaders like Mao or Pol Pot to a very large extent wanted to actualize the utopian dreams of premodern peasantry (which of course didn't stop them from killing and starving peasants in droves). Another contributing factor was the impact of the Korean War, which led to a militarization of North Korean society and helped to transform the entire country into a nearly perfect garrison state (or as the North Korean official propaganda prefers to put it, "made the entire country an impregnable fortress").

However, all these trends could develop only due to a massive geopolitical shift in the late 1950s—that is, the Sino-Soviet split. For nearly three decades the two major Communist states had fractious relations and sometimes came quite close to the brink of war. Each one was peddling its own version of Communism. The Soviet brand probably appeared more dull, and no longer attracted the starry-eyed radicals in Western university campuses, but it was also much more permissive and liberal, much less indifferent to the daily needs of the average citizen and marginally more efficient (or should we say "less inefficient"?) economically. The Chinese brand of Communism was all about the endless ideological mobilization, selfless dedication and sacrifice to the cause, and the omniscient leader.

The changes in the post-Stalin USSR were significant. In the decade that followed Stalin's death in 1953, the number of political prisoners in the Soviet Union decreased nearly a thousandfold, from some 1.2 million to between one and two thousand. Restrictions on the domestic movement of collective farm workers were lifted (contrary to the assumptions of many Westerners, the short-term domestic trips of the urban population were never seriously restricted in the USSR), large-scale housing construction programs were launched, and consumption goods became more affordable to the average Soviet citizen. In China, the same decade was marked by the collectivization of agriculture (i.e., the abolition of individual ownership of land) and the insane millennialism of the Great Leap Forward. These experiments might have looked attractive to the denizens of Paris cafés who (like Sartre) instantly switched their enthusiasm from Stalin's Russia to Mao's China. To the Chinese themselves, however, this "bold social experimentation" brought the worst famine in modern history, leaving between 20 and 30 million people dead.

Initially North Korea was much attracted to the Chinese austere and autocratic notion of Communism. The Maoist ideal resonated well with Kim Il Sung's own notion of the perfect Korea he hoped to build. In the vision of the North Korean leaders, their realm should become a country where all of the people would work hard on huge state-owned farms and factories, breaking the records of productivity while being motivated by unswerving ideological zeal and love for country. Everybody would be issued roughly the same ration of heavily subsidized food and basic consumption goods, and no selfish profiteering would be tolerated, so money would gradually be deemed useless. Such a society would be led by a small army of devout and selfless officials and presided over by the omniscient Great Leader, whose word would be the law. Obviously, at the time, many common North Koreans didn't find this ideal unattractive (it is not incidental that peasant rebels across the globe frequently dreamt of similar things).

When they talked of future prosperity, Kim Il Sung's promises were not too wild or too excessive. In the early 1960s he famously outlined his vision of coming affluence by saying that in the near future all North Koreans will "eat boiled rice and meat soup, dress in silk and live in houses with tile roofs." This promise—repeated by the Great Leader a number of times—does not sound too ambitious, but we should remember that for centuries the Korean farmers could not afford to eat rice every day (barley or corn was their staple), that a meat soup was a meal reserved for a special holiday occasion, and that only landlords could afford a tile roof rather than the thatched roof of the majority. Thus, Kim Il Sung promised his subjects that his regime would eventually deliver the standards of life that had been seen as reasonably luxurious by premodern villagers—but not much more.

Kim Il Sung's initial decision to side with China was only partially driven by ideological considerations. The pragmatic political calculations played a role, too: after the failed 1956 conspiracy, Kim Il Sung and his supporters began to see the Soviet Union as a source of dangerously liberal ideas. They soon grew frightened that the Soviet slogan of the "struggle against the personality cult" might be easily used against Kim Il Sung, whose own personality cult so obviously followed the Stalinist patterns.

After the 1956 crisis, the relations between North Korea and the Soviet Union began to deteriorate, reaching the point of almost open hostility between 1962 and 1963. References to the Soviet Union almost disappeared from the official media, and the Soviet advisers were sent home. The same was the fate of a few hundred Soviet and Eastern European wives of North Koreans who studied overseas and married women from other Communist countries. Their North Korean husbands were ordered to divorce foreign women, who were then summarily expelled from the country. By 1960, all North Korean students were recalled from the ideologically suspicious Soviet Union and Eastern Europe, and only two decades later were these student exchanges restarted—albeit on a significantly smaller scale.

Pravda and *Rodong Shinmun*, the major official newspapers of the USSR and North Korea, respectively, were engaged in open polemics: *Rodong Shinmun* accused the Soviets of being exploitative and ready to take advantage of Korea's weakness, while *Pravda* lamented the ingratitude of the North Korean leaders who suddenly became silent on the Soviets' significant aid efforts (indeed, since around 1960 and until after the collapse of the Soviet Union in 1991, North Korean media seldom admitted the very existence of continuing economic aid from the Soviet Union). A North Korean ambassador to Moscow wrote a highly critical letter to Kim Il Sung and then asked Moscow for asylum. His request was granted by the Soviet government—a nearly unprecedented situation in the history of the Communist bloc.

Pyongyang's relations with Moscow partially recovered after 1965. Changes in the Soviet leadership, specifically the replacement of impulsive and reform-minded Khrushchev with the more conservative Brezhnev, did play some part, but there were more important reasons. First, during the relations crisis, Soviet economic assistance declined, while China was proving to be neither willing nor able to compensate for this loss. Second, in 1966 China itself plunged into the bloody turmoil of the Cultural Revolution. For the North Korean elite, the Cultural Revolution was the embodiment of utter chaos; it might have been seen in Pyongyang as even more dangerous than Soviet liberalization (privately, when talking to Brezhnev in 1966, Kim Il Sung described the Great Proletarian Cultural Revolution as a "massive idiocy").[11]

Actually, the late 1960s were a period of grave crisis in the relations between North Korea and China. Ambassadors were recalled and tensions on the border mounted—much later, in May 1984, Kim Il Sung recalled in his confidential talk with East German leaders how much patience was necessary to deal with Chinese soldiers intruding into the North Korean territory.[12] In a telling sign, Kim Il Sung even asked Moscow to use Soviet air space for air travel by the North Korean official delegation, openly expressing fear that North Korean planes might be intercepted and forced to land by the Chinese.[13] The Chinese Red Guard groups openly criticized Kim Il Sung, describing him as a "neo-feudal ruler" living a life of luxury and self-indulgence.[14]

In the early 1970s North Korea finally switched to the "equidistance" policy, which continued until the early 1990s. It was essentially a diplomacy of balancing between two mutually hostile sponsors, China and the Soviet Union. North Korean politicians and diplomats discovered that the new situation of Sino-Soviet rivalry, in spite of ingrained instability, gave them remarkable political opportunities as well. With a measure of guile, they could extract aid from both sponsors without giving much in return.

The aid was increasingly important: in spite of the frenzy of ideological campaigns, from the late 1960s the North Korean economy, once the most advanced in continental East Asia, was sliding toward stagnation. Without a constant influx of foreign aid, North Korea would probably become economically unviable.

Neither Moscow nor Beijing had illusions about North Korea. They knew perfectly well that they were being manipulated, but still saw no viable alternative to providing Pyongyang with aid. Partially, their policy was driven by the need to keep North Korea as a stable buffer zone protecting both China's Northeast and Russia's Far East against the US military presence in Japan and South Korea. However, to a larger extent, the rival Communist giants were paying North Korea for remaining neutral in their own quarrel. Of course, both Moscow and Beijing preferred to see Pyongyang join their side unconditionally, but since that was not going to happen, they were at least determined not to let North Korea join the opposite camp. Thus, with remarkable skill North Korean diplomats squeezed aid from their two quarreling benefactors without making excessive concessions to them.

In the early 1970s, North Korea tried to rid its economy of dependency on Moscow and Beijing, and began to borrow heavily on the international market. At that time, immediately after the oil crisis of 1973, Communist regimes were considered to be exemplary debtors while the international market was awash with newly arrived petro-dollars. Therefore, securing loans was not that hard. Probably, North Korean leaders hoped to use this additional income to overcome the slowdown that was taking hold of their economy. The scheme did not work: the loans were wasted on a number of prestige-boosting and/or ill-conceived projects, with Pyongyang soon refusing to pay interest. Between the years of 1979 and 1980, North Korea became the first Communist state to default. This left them with significant debt—in 2007, $600 million in principal plus $1.2 billion in accrued interest.[15] Their foray into the world of high international finance ended in debacle and seriously damaged North Korea's credit ratings.

Around the same time, during the mid-1970s, more unseemly incidents began to occur. With increasing frequency, North Korean diplomats and officials were discovered traveling with large amounts of expensive contraband, illicit drugs, and counterfeit money.

In late October 1976, the Norwegian police caught North Korean diplomats selling 4,000 bottles of smuggled liquor and a large quantity of smuggled cigarettes. In those days, the Scandinavian governments imposed exorbitant taxes on alcohol, which made the importation of tax-free liquor an extremely profitable business. Pyongyang officials transported large quantities of tax-free liquor and cigarettes inside diplomatic luggage. It was estimated that the DPRK Embassy in Norway sold liquor and cigarettes with a black market value of some one million dollars (in 2011 prices, this would be at least three times that amount).

After the incident involving Norway and Denmark, the same network was discovered in two other Nordic countries—Finland and Sweden. The scale of operations in Sweden was probably the largest, and the affair was widely discussed in the local press. One night, mischievous Swedish students put a sign reading "Wine and Spirits Co-op" on the entrance of the DPRK Embassy—to the great annoyance of its inhabitants.

Soon afterward, the North Korean authorities began to deal with far more dangerous substances. In May 1976 the Egyptian customs officials discovered the presence of hashish in luggage belonging to a group of North Korean diplomats—the first in the long chain of incidents of this type. The North Korean operatives even drew knives, but were overpowered by the Egyptian officers. Their diplomatic passports ended up saving them from prosecution. A similar incident then occurred in, of all places, Norway. In October 1976 the North Korean diplomats were caught handing a large amount of hashish to local drug dealers. In the subsequent decades, North Korean officials and diplomats were again occasionally found smuggling drugs in various parts of the world.

Apart from narcotics, North Korea also seemingly began to produce and disseminate high-quality counterfeit US dollar bills (the so-called supernotes), albeit in this case the evidence is largely circumstantial.[16]

It is often speculated that these smuggling operations were related to the new attitude toward the North Korean missions overseas: once the economic slowdown made its mark in the mid-1970s, the missions had to follow the self-reliance principle. In effect, North Korean embassy officials now had to pay for their own expenses from the funds its staff somehow earned.

It seems, however, that contrary to a popular misperception, these illegal activities never developed into major hard currency earners. Even from the regime's point of view, smuggling and counterfeiting did more harm than good: these incidents made the North Korean government look odious without bringing in much income. In the early 2000s there were signs that these activities were finally downscaled, but one wonders why this did not happen earlier.

Another bizarre feature of North Korean foreign policy of the 1970s was their spy agencies' strange taste for abductions. These operations began earlier: in the late 1950s, North Korean intelligence attempted the abduction of a number of dissenters from the USSR. Not all operations were successful; Ho Chin (Lim Un), a young poet and dissenter, managed to escape from his kidnappers and was granted asylum in the USSR, where he eventually became a prominent journalist and historian. But not all were so lucky. A young North Korean musician was kidnapped by North Korean agents from downtown Moscow and was never seen again. This led to a major crisis in relations between Moscow and Pyongyang, with the Soviet Union expelling the North Korean ambassador—another event with few parallels, if any, in the entire diplomatic history of the Communist bloc.

In the late 1970s the major targets of these operations were Japan and South Korea. Unlike earlier incidents, these kidnappings did not target dissenters or defectors. Abductees were average men and women off the street. In many cases it seems that the abductions were opportunistic, with North Korean commandos taking any person who was unlucky enough to stroll along some Japanese beach where the commandos were lying in wait. Indeed, these abductions were so bizarre that many reputable journalists and scholars (overwhelmingly—but not exclusively—of leftist inclinations) in the 1980s and 1990s wasted tons of ink insisting that North Korea had nothing to do with the strange disappearance of Japanese citizens in the 1970s.

These people were made to look foolish by Kim Jong Il himself. In 2002 Kim Jong Il admitted responsibility for the abductions and ordered the return of a number of survivors back to Japan. This was obviously done to improve relations with Japan, but produced a completely opposite outcome. Accusations that had been often perceived as the fantasies of the Right were suddenly proven to be completely correct, and the Japanese public exploded. The Japanese government demanded the immediate return of all abductees. In response, the North Korean authorities stated that all survivors had been returned home, with any additional abductees having already died (this was in 2002). Few believed this statement, and as a result the trade and exchanges with Japan, once quite important for the regime, were completely frozen.[17]

Thus, the North Korean leaders were paradoxically punished for their rare attempt to be honest and admit past wrongdoings. No doubt they have learned their lesson and from now on will probably think twice before admitting to more of their past misdeeds.

Obviously, the Japanese were abducted to take advantage of their native language skills and their knowledge of Japanese daily life in order to train the North Korean agents. For example, Yaeko Taguchi, a former hostess kidnapped in 1978 (she was then aged 22), trained Kim Hyŏn-hŭi, a North Korean intelligence agent whose cover was to be a Japanese national. This decision to rely on the abductees was rather strange since the North Korean authorities could count on the enthusiastic support of a number of people who spoke Japanese as their first language and had firsthand knowledge of modern Japan. Those people were members of Chongryon (Chosen Soren), a powerful pro-Pyongyang group of Koreans in Japan.

Some 700,000 ethnic Koreans lived in Japan in the early 1950s. Most of them arrived there in the 1930s and early 1940s, either in search of a better livelihood or forcibly relocated by the colonial authorities as providers of cheap labor. In 1951 ethnic Koreans were formally deprived of Japanese citizenship. In Japan the ethnic Koreans were subjected to considerable discrimination and were kept in unskilled or semi-legal occupations. This ensured their affinity with the Japanese Left, but eventually it was pro-Pyongyang leftist nationalists who succeeded in organizing them.

In the late 1950s a majority of ethnic Koreans in Japan opted for North Korean citizenship, even though only a tiny minority of them had come from what became North Korea after 1945. Those "overseas citizens of the DPRK" created the aforementioned Chongryon.

During the late 1950s and early 1960s pro-Pyongyang activists successfully persuaded many ethnic Koreans to "return" to the North. These returnees numbered an impressive 93,000, an overwhelming majority of whom had never previously lived in the country to which they now moved. They wanted to escape discrimination and contribute toward the building of a perfect new society in their native land. North Korean propaganda had lured the returnees, but, as the recent research shows, Japanese right-wing groups also promoted the migration in the hope of reducing the number of people they saw as a "fifth column" within Japan.[18]

Most of the returnees were gravely disappointed by the destitution they saw upon arrival. They soon realized, however, that there was no way back. Stuck in a destitute police state, they (and their children) now found themselves in a strange position: they were simultaneously privileged and discriminated against. On the one hand, the returnees were seen as ideologically unreliable. On the other hand, most of them received money transfers from Japanese family members who were wise enough not to go to the Socialist Paradise. This allowed them to enjoy a life that was affluent by North Korean standards. It was permissible for the returnees to ask relatives back in Japan for money as long as the letters included an obligatory eulogy to the Leader and his system.

Remittances began to dry up in the 1990s, with predictably grave results for the second- and third-generation returnees. The main reason for this was the generational shift. The immediate relatives of the returnees began to die out, and the next generation had no inclination to send money to people they had never met. Around the same time, Chongryon membership began to dwindle, too, with the younger generations of ethnic Koreans either accepting Japanese citizenship or switching to a South Korean passport. Nonetheless, until the early 1990s money transfers from Japan were a major source of income for Pyongyang.

WOMEN'S WORK?

Soviet Communism, as well as its local variants, had a strictly male face. The top Communist bureaucrats of the 1960s and 1970s are remembered as aging males in badly tailored suits. Indeed, women were remarkably underrepresented at the apex of Communist power.

This was not always the case. In the early 1900s, revolutionary Marxism was arguably the most feminist of all major ideologies of the era. It did not limit itself to demands for legal gender equality, but went one step further by demanding full economic and social equality for men and women.

In the Soviet Union of the 1920s and 1930s, there was, for all intents and purposes, an affirmative action program. The exploits of female pilots, engineers, and military officers were much extolled by the media.

However, this was to change in the late 1930s, when the government of Stalin's Russia discovered the political usefulness of the traditional family and the values associated with it. From then on, while the importance of female labor in the workplace was not disputed (and, indeed, continued to be encouraged), the primary social function of women was to be wives and mothers.

When Soviet troops brought Communism to Korea in 1945, it was in its most nationalist and antifeminist stage. Some measures to bring about gender equality were enforced, however, including the 1946 Gender Equality Law, which abolished concubinage, eased restrictions (mainly social in nature) on divorce, and enshrined female property rights in law.

That said, North Korean female participation in higher-level politics remained low. Out of some 260 cabinet ministers between 1945 and 2000, a mere six were women. It was a common assumption in the Kim Il Sung—era North Korea that women should not aspire to have careers in politics or administration. The common wisdom was that a girl should look for a proper husband and, if possible, for a job that would leave her enough time to fulfill her primary duties as a mother, wife, and daughter-in-law.

Actually, work was not seen as a necessity. Unlike other Communist nations, the North Korean state was quite positive in its attitude toward women who wanted to become housewives. In the Soviet Union and Eastern Europe of the 1970s, a full-time housewife was a very rare creature, while in the North Korea of the same time, maybe up to one-third of all married urban women stayed at home (no exact statistics are available).

Unsurprisingly, there were few female faces among the top leadership. In the 1940s and 1950s, North Korea had a small number of female

(continued)

politicians who were essentially left over from the earlier period of heroic (and feminist) revolutionary Marxism. The most remarkable of them was Pak Chŏng-ae (born Vera Ch'oe), once a Soviet intelligence operative and later a Politburo member and ardent supporter of Kim Il Sung. The latter did not save her from being purged in the 1960s, however.

Another example was Ho Chŏng-suk, daughter of prominent leftist lawyer Hŏ Hŏn. She herself fought in the Chinese Civil War, even becoming a political military commissar of a regiment. In North Korea, she rose to the position of justice minister, and in this capacity oversaw the initial stages of North Korea's Great Purge. In the 1960s, however, Ho Chŏng-suk was pushed out of top-tier politics and relegated to ceremonial positions.

From around 1960, virtually all women in top political positions in the North got their power as a result of being members of the ruling Kim family. For instance, there is Kim Sŏng-ae, the second wife of Kim Il Sung. She obviously had some political aspirations in the 1970s, but her ambitions were cut short by the rise of her stepson Kim Jong Il, who had her sidelined. Another important woman of the Kim family is Kim Kyŏng-hŭi, Kim Jong Il's younger sister—one of the regents assisting Kim Jong Un in the first months of his rule.

In North Korean society at large, the relative power of women increased dramatically after the collapse of the state Socialist economy. In the 1990s males were expected to continue attending to their nonfunctioning plants, while women, who were—or could easily become—housewives, were free to engage in the manifold activities of the nonofficial economy. As a result, women became the major breadwinners in the majority of North Korean families.

The increase in income predictably produced a remarkable change in the gendered division of labor as well as in gender relations in general (hence, for example, a rise in the number of divorces initiated by women). In the countries of Eastern Europe, the collapse of state Socialism generally led to a massive decline in gender equality. Conversely, in North Korea, the years of crisis led to the empowerment of women—at least the ones who did not perish in the famine.

DEALING WITH THE SOUTH

The Korean War did not end in a peace treaty. Only an armistice—a ceasefire—was signed in 1953. Tellingly enough, the ROK government refused to become a signatory of the document. The actual reasons were complicated, but officially they reasoned that the ceasefire was tantamount to the semi-recognition of the North Korean state.

Until the late 1960s, any foreign government had to choose which Korean state it should maintain diplomatic relations with. If a foreign nation granted diplomatic recognition to Pyongyang, it meant the immediate and automatic severance of diplomatic ties with Seoul (and vice versa). This principle was quietly revoked in 1969, and since then it has become possible for a foreign government to maintain diplomatic relations with the two Korean states simultaneously.[19] However, the conflicts between these two states remained frozen and unresolved.

For the first few years after the armistice of 1953, North Korea's government did not show much interest in South Korean issues. Kim Il Sung was too busy rebuilding the economy and eliminating real and potential rivals within the top leadership. It was also assumed that no revolution was likely to break out in South Korea, where leftist forces were wiped out by police terror and self-imposed exile (the majority of prominent North Korean leftists fled to the North, just to be exterminated there in the purges of the 1950s). Apart from that, Kim Il Sung understood that the Soviet Union was not going to approve of any major attack on South Korea—and with a large US presence in the South, such an attack would be suicidal at any rate.

However, the events of the early 1960s made Pyongyang reconsider its passive approach to the unification issue. For one thing, the sudden outbreak of the April Revolution in 1960 led to a collapse of the Syngman Rhee regime in Seoul. The April Revolution produced an unstable democratic regime that was soon overthrown by the military. Kim Il Sung saw these events as proof that a revolution in South Korea was possible. Indeed, the 1960s and 1970s outbreaks of mass opposition movements occurred in South Korea frequently, and huge rallies on the streets of Seoul encouraged optimism in Pyongyang.

The decline of Soviet influence in Pyongyang also encouraged hopes of unification. In the new situation, Kim Il Sung could hope that he would be able to take advantage of a favorable turn of events in the South without worrying excessively about Moscow's position.

Another event that had significant impact on North Korean thinking was the steady escalation of the war in Vietnam. Indeed, Vietnam and Korea had a lot in common. Their histories and cultures have remarkable similarities and after the Second World War both countries were divided into a Communist North and capitalist South. Like their North Korean comrades, Vietnamese Communists once reluctantly accepted a ceasefire under pressure from Moscow and Beijing. However, unlike the North Koreans, the Vietnamese Communists did not keep the promises they made under duress, and began to increase their support for Communist guerrillas in the South Vietnamese countryside. Eventually this led to a full-scale US intervention, but by the late 1960s it became obvious that this intervention was failing. For Pyongyang leaders, Vietnam increasingly looked like an encouraging example.

With the wisdom of hindsight, it is clear that these expectations were unfounded, since South Korea was no South Vietnam. In the 1960s the South Korean government became remarkably efficient in promoting economic growth, while the South Vietnamese government was the embodiment of corruption, inefficiency, and factional strife. The brutal experiences of the North Korean occupation of 1950–1951 made the majority of South Koreans staunchly anti-Communist. Whatever they secretly thought about the then current government in Seoul, they saw Kim Il Sung as the greater evil. Last but not least, South Korean terrain made guerrilla operations difficult. At the time, before the successful reforestation program of the 1970s, most of South Korea's land was treeless and hilly, so guerrillas would be sitting ducks for choppers and light planes.

Nonetheless, all of this became clear only later. In the late 1960s the North Korean government made another bid for unification—so intense, actually, that it is sometimes described as the "Second Korean War."[20]

The North Korean plan for unification generally followed a well-established Communist pattern, known as the "United Front" strategy. At

first, North Korea hoped to create a broad left-leaning opposition movement that would be led and manipulated by clandestine organizations of
the South Korean Communists (or rather, Jucheists). It was assumed that
a broad coalition would first topple a pro-American military regime. After
this, the clandestine pro-Pyongyang core would discard and, if necessary,
destroy their temporary allies and eventually emerge as the driving force
of a truly Communist revolution.

Kim Il Sung and his people, being former guerrillas themselves, also
pinned great hope on the emergence of armed guerrilla resistance
within South Korea. Obviously in emulation of Vietnamese experience,
they expected that a small number of North Korean commandos, often
of South Korean extraction, would serve as a nucleus for a future South
Korean guerrilla army.

In the 1960s, encouraged by the signs of the leftward drift of some South
Korean intellectuals, Pyongyang undertook a few attempts to establish an
underground party in Seoul. The most successful of these attempts was the
"Revolutionary Party of Unification" established in 1964. The party, however, never managed to reach prominence and was finally destroyed by the
South Korean authorities. Some of its leaders were executed while others
were sent to jail for years.

There have been subsequent attempts to reestablish the pro-Pyongyang
underground and recruit some promising young leftists to its ranks. The
present author personally knows people who once used to commute to
Pyongyang via submarine (the usual way of ejecting and infiltrating agents
or full-time activists out of and into South Korea). In three cases that I am
personally aware of, these trips and a short exposure to Pyongyang life led
to an immediate disillusionment with North Korea.

The South Korean Left was revived around 1980, as we'll see later.
Indeed, it is hard to deny that the Korean leftists, self-proclaimed "de-
fenders of the human rights and enemies of authoritarianism," have demonstrated a surprisingly high level of sympathy—or, at least, toleration—for
a hereditary Stalinist dictatorship in Pyongyang. It is not impossible that
some of the prominent leftist activists have been occasionally sponsored
by Pyongyang and in one instance the existence of such subsidies was

eventually proven (I am referring to the case of Professor Song Du-yul, a prominent leftist/nationalist ideologue who admitted that he received such subsidies). However, one should not believe in the conspiracy theories that are so popular within the South Korean Right. Both the revival of the South Korean Left and the remarkable popularity of Generalissimo Kim among its followers have few if any relation to the efforts of Pyongyang's spies, but rather reflect the peculiarities of South Korean capitalism and the South Korean political structure. On balance, North Korea's United Front strategy has been unsuccessful.

Military operations have also ended in failure. On January 21, 1968, 31 North Korean commandos infiltrated Seoul. Their goal was to storm the presidential palace and slaughter everybody inside. Obviously, Kim Il Sung believed that this bold attack, to be attributed to the local guerrillas, would be good for revolution and perhaps would spark a mass armed resistance. The raiding party was intercepted at the last minute, so an intense firefight took place in downtown Seoul. One commando escaped North, where he received a hero's welcome and eventually became a general; another was captured alive to become a Protestant pastor in South Korea; and all others were killed in action.

In late 1968 some 120 North Korean commandos landed on the East Coast, where they hoped to establish a Vietnamese-style guerrilla base. They took over a few villages and herded villagers into ideological indoctrination sessions where the farmers were harangued about the greatness of the Great Leader, the happiness of their northern brethren, and the assorted wonders of the soon-to-come Communist paradise. But inflexible, doctrinaire North Korean propagandists were no match for their North Vietnamese comrades, and failed to impress the villagers. Thus, the expected uprising didn't happen, and the commandos were hunted down by the South Korean military.

At the same time, the North Koreans began to escalate tensions on the DMZ, often attacking South Korean and American border patrols. In January 1968, almost immediately after the Blue House Raid, the North Korean Navy captured the US naval intelligence ship *Pueblo* and kept the ship and its crew in captivity for more than a year. After it occurred, the episode was seen as part of a grand Communist strategy. Actually, though, the oral tradition of the Soviet diplomatic service holds that on the night after the seizure, Soviet experts spent sleepless hours looking for an excuse that would allow the Soviet Union to avoid entering a potential war between the United States and North Korea. Finally, they found one: the 1961 treaty between the USSR and the DPRK stated that the Soviet Union had a duty to defend its ally against acts of military aggression, but because the *Pueblo* seizure was an act of aggression by North Korea, the Soviet Union had no duty to intervene.

However, between 1971 and 1972 it became clear that all these adventurous and sometimes bloody efforts had come to naught. South Korean "toiling masses" were not going to take up arms and go to the mountains. The average South Korean remained anti-Communist or, at least, deeply suspicious of North Korea.

In this situation, the North Korean leaders made a U-turn and began secret negotiations with the South, on assumption that some kind of provisional coexistence (until the forthcoming revolution) would be necessary. In July 1972 the South and North issued a North-South Joint Communiqué that theoretically committed them to the goal of eventual peaceful unification of the country. It was rhetoric pure and simple, but it created a framework within which the two Korean states began to talk and interact when they considered it necessary. The policy of mutual nonrecognition continues to this day (and is likely to endure into the foreseeable future), but since 1972 Pyongyang and Seoul have always maintained direct contacts of various kinds.

There were, however, some occasional relapses into revolutionary adventurism. In 1983 North Korean intelligence operatives planted a powerful bomb in Rangoon, Burma, where the South Korean president was on a state visit at the time. The device was detonated too early, so the president survived the explosion, but a number of dignitaries were killed. The three North Korean operatives, none of whom spoke Burmese, could not escape. Two were taken alive after an unsuccessful suicide attempt, and another was killed after a firefight with the Burmese soldiers. Not only the Burmese (never staunch opponents of Pyongyang) but even the Chinese were annoyed by this adventurism.

Another act of open violence was the bombing of a South Korean passenger jet in November 1987 by two North Korean intelligence officers. Obviously this was done in order to create the impression that Seoul would be an unsafe place for the coming Olympic Games of 1988. The bombing killed 115 crew members and passengers (many of whom were construction workers on their way back from the Middle East). One of the two agents was captured, another committed suicide, but the overall political impact of the operation was close to zero.

There might have been other undisclosed or aborted operations of a similar kind, but on balance from the mid-1970s the North Korean leadership came to the conclusion that a South Korean revolution was unlikely to happen any time soon. The support for the South Korean "revolutionary forces" was never completely dropped from the Pyongyang agenda, but as time went on its significance steadily diminished. From the early 1990s, when the economy began to fall apart, Pyongyang's agenda was dominated by the necessity of defense, not offense.

ICONS

The personality cult of the Kim family has long been a peculiar and often bizarre feature of North Korean society—and like any cult, it has iconography. Normally, four members of the Kim family are considered worthy of depiction—Generalissimo Kim Il Sung, Marshal (from 2012, posthumously, also Generalissimo) Kim Jong Il, General Kim Jong Un, and General Kim Jong Suk (the latter being Kim Il Sung's first official wife and Kim Jong Il's mother). Some other members of the family are occasionally depicted as well, but the images of those four are virtually omnipresent and come in many forms.

North Korea is a country of portraits. From the 1940s, depictions of Kim Il Sung were common, but from the 1970s, it was decreed that every house should have a portrait of the Great Leader. The state bestowed people with portraits and directed them to put them in their living rooms. They were to be placed on a wall devoid of any other adornments and cleaned regularly.

From 1972, Kim Il Sung's portrait was also placed at the entrances of all factories, railway stations, and airports. A portrait of Kim Il Sung (from the mid-1980s) was to be present in all railway and subway carriages, but for some unknown reason not in buses or trams. In the late 1970s, North Koreans were directed to place standardized portraits of Kim Jong Il alongside those of his father.

A further layer of complexity was added in the 1990s. From then on, every single Korean house was to have three portraits: one of Kim Il Sung, one of Kim Jong Il, and yet another of the two great men talking about some highly important matters of statecraft. Privileged officials, however, were lucky enough to be issued with a different third picture, the visage of Kim Jong Suk. Due to reasons unknown, many offices still have portraits of the Dear Leader and Great Leader only.

Another important icon of the personality cult is the badge that all adult North Koreans have been required to wear permanently since the early 1970s. This badge usually depicts Kim Il Sung. (In some rare cases badges feature a portrait of Kim Jong Il alongside the visage of Kim Il Sung.) There are a great number of badges, and an experienced observer can learn a lot from the type of badge a North Korean wears. Officials of some important government agencies are issued their own particular type of badges.

Of course, we should not forget statues. The first statues of Kim Il Sung appeared in the late 1940s, but the vast majority of them were constructed in the 1970s and 1980s. Most counties and cities have their own statue of Kim Il Sung, located in the central part of the area. If such a statue is absent, the symbolic center will house a large mural depicting one of the Kims. Similar murals can be found on major crossroads in the cities and occasionally in the countryside.

During every major official holiday, all North Koreans are expected to pay a visit to a local statue and, after a respectful bow, to leave flowers honoring the Generalissimo (usually Kim Il Sung, but in some cities other members of the Kim family can be commemorated as well). The largest and most important statue(s) is located on Mansu Hill in downtown Pyongyang. Initially the

(continued)

22-meter-high statue was gilded, but in 1977, for some reason, the gold was removed and replaced with gold paint. Recently, in April 2012, the statue got company. The likeness of Marshal (now Generalissimo) Kim Jong II was placed next to his father. The original statue of his father had a face-lift: a broad smile and pair of glasses were added to his face, which had been up until then very austere and stern looking. Interestingly, in Kim Jong II's lifetime, very few statues of Kim Jong II were constructed.

In an emergency, statues and portraits are to be protected whatever the cost, as any sacred object should be—and North Koreans are reminded that they must safeguard the images. For example, in 2007 the official media widely reported an incident that allegedly occurred in August of that year.

During a severe flooding, Kang Hyong-kwon, a factory worker from the city of Ich'on, was trying to make his way to safety through a dangerous stream. While leaving his flooded house, he took the two most precious things in his life—his five-year-old daughter and portraits of Leaders Generalissimo Kim Il Sung and Marshal Kim Jong II. Suddenly overwhelmed by the current, he lost grip of his daughter, who fell into the swollen waters, but still managed to keep hold of the sacred images. The media extolled North Koreans to emulate Kang Hyong-kwon, a real-life hero.

THE COMMAND SOCIETY

In the decades during Kim Il Sung's rule, North Korea became a society where the level of state control over the average citizen's public and private life reached heights that would be almost unthinkable in any other country, including Stalin's Russia, which in many cases served as a prototype for Kim Il Sung's social experiments. In a sense, Kim Il Sung and his supporters managed to out-Stalin Stalin himself.

Private initiative was almost completely eliminated from North Korea's economic life, and the role of money diminished greatly. Few items could be freely bought and sold in Kim Il Sung's North Korea. In 1957 the private trade in rice and other grains was banned, so that grains (by far the most important source of calories in the diet of the average North Korean) could be distributed by the state alone. From that time and until around 1990 grains could be acquired almost exclusively through the public distribution system (PDS). Every North Korean was made eligible for a fixed daily grain ration, which was provided for a token price.

The exact size of the ration depended on one's job; the average working adult received a grain ration of 700 grams a day, a housewife would be given merely 300 grams, while a person doing heavy physical work (a miner or, say, a jet fighter pilot) was eligible for the highest daily ration of 900 grams. The ratio of rice to other (less nutritious) grains in a ration depended largely on one's place of residence. During the affluent 1970s, the privileged inhabitants of Pyongyang received more than half of their grain rations in rice, while in the countryside nearly the entire ration came as corn and wheat flour, with rice being a luxury food reserved for special occasions.

In 1973, when the economic situation began to deteriorate, rations were cut for the first time. For example, a typical adult's ration of 700g was reduced to 607g. The next cut came in 1987, when the same standard daily ration went down to 547g. Officially, these cuts were considered to be "voluntary donations," but nobody asked the North Koreans whether they were willing to "donate" their food to the state.

Rationing was not about the grain alone. Other foodstuffs were rationed as well: people were issued rations of soy sauce, eggs, cabbage, and other basic ingredients of the traditional Korean diet. Meat was distributed irregularly, a few times a year, usually before major official holidays, but fish and other types of seafood were more readily available. In autumn there might have been occasional distribution of apples, melons, and other fruits.[21]

Basic consumer goods were also rationed, even though the mechanism of their distribution could be different. Items like wrist watches and black-and-white TV sets—the major symbols of consumerism during the 1960s and 1970s—were usually distributed through people's work units. In some cases, especially valuable items were given to distinguished individuals as "presents of the Great Leader." This particular form of distribution clearly was good also for the ideological health of the nation, since it reminded the North Koreans whose wisdom and hard work kept them fed and well-provided with daily necessities.

Contrary to what has often been claimed, private markets were never banned in North Korea. They operated under manifold restrictions and were small in scale, but they existed nonetheless. However, the average North Korean of Kim Il Sung's era seldom shopped at the market. Items on sale at the marketplace were overpriced and usually seen as unnecessary luxuries. The average North Korean was seldom prepared to pay above half of his/her monthly wage for a chicken, and this was a normal market price for a chicken in the early 1980s. In most cases, the North Korean consumers were quite content with what they got through the PDS.

Every able-bodied North Korean male was required to work for the state, and this requirement was enforced with great efficiency. Between 1956 and 1958 small private workshops were nationalized, while all farmers were pressed to join agricultural cooperatives. These "cooperatives" were essentially state-run, state-owned farms in all but name. Farmers worked for the same standard 700g daily ration, the only difference being that in their case rations were distributed not twice a month, as was the case in the cities, but rather once a year, soon after harvesting.

The forced switch to state farms was a common feature of nearly all Communist states, but the North Korean state farms had some peculiarities. Most significantly, farmers were allowed only tiny private kitchen gardens. In Stalin's Soviet Union, a farmer usually had a private plot whose size might exceed 1,000 m², but in Kim Il Sung's North Korea private plots could not exceed 100 m², and not all farmers were allowed to have plots even of such a small size. The assumption was that farmers, being deprived of any additional source of income and calories, would have no choice but to devote all their time and energy to toiling in the fields of the state.

This is very different from the Soviet prototype. Soon after the forced collectivization of agriculture in the 1930s, Soviet farmers' individual plots still provided more than half the country's total production of potatoes (a major source of calories in Russia in those days) and a significant share of other vegetables. Nor did this situation change much in subsequent decades: in the early 1970s Soviet consumers obtained more than 60 percent of their potatoes and eggs from the private agricultural sector, which also produced 40 percent of their fruit, vegetables, meat, and dairy products.[22] A similar situation could be observed in Communist Vietnam, where farmers were allocated merely 5 percent of the total land to be used as their private plots. Throughout the 1960s and 1970s, farmers in North Vietnam earned between 60 and 75 percent of their income from the private cultivation of these "5-percent plots," even though the plots were not officially allocated fertilizer or other state-supplied resources.[23] Farmers of North Korea were deprived of this option from the very beginning: obviously, the policy planners believed that the farmers would be more productive on the state fields if they were not distracted by the temptations of working their own land.

Unlike the USSR where people were usually expected to look for jobs themselves, the North Korean system didn't tolerate such dangerously liberal behavior. After graduation from high school, all North Koreans were assigned to their jobs. Those who were seen as both academically smart and politically reliable would be allowed to sit for college entrance exams. Changing one's job was possible, but had to be approved beforehand by the authorities and required much paperwork (the only exception being women, who often became full-time housewives after marriage).

One of the most striking peculiarities of Kim Il Sung's North Korea was the extent to which the daily lives of its citizens were monitored by the authorities. Even Stalin's Russia appears to be a relatively liberal place if compared to the North Korea of the 1960–1990 period. The government strove to control every facet of an individual's life, and these efforts were remarkably successful.

The place of residence could be changed only with the approval of authorities, normally in cases when real or alleged needs of the national economy would require somebody to be allocated to a new job in a different place. Women were an exception since they were allowed and indeed were expected to move to the husband's abode after marriage.

Not merely longtime residence but also short-term travel had to be approved by the authorities beforehand. A North Korean was not allowed to travel outside his or her native county or city without a special travel permit, to be issued by local authorities. The only exception was that a North Korean could visit counties/cities that had a common border with the county/city where he or she had official household registration. If found outside his or her native county without a proper travel permit, a North Korean was arrested and then "extradited" back home for an investigation and appropriate punishment.

There had to be valid reasons for issuing a travel permit, unless the person went on official business. Usually, the application was first authorized by the party secretary in one's work unit and then by the so-called second department of a local government (these departments were staffed with police officers). A travel permit clearly specified the intended destination and period of travel, and it had to be produced when purchasing a ticket or when one stayed overnight either in an inn or with friends. A trip to some special areas, like the city of Pyongyang or districts near the DMZ, required a distinct type of travel permit that had to be confirmed by the Ministry for the Interior—and such "confirmed number permits" were exceedingly difficult to get.

Incidentally, the "travel permit" system set North Korea apart from other Communist countries. Being a native of the Soviet Union, the present author was surprised to discover the average Westerner's belief that the Soviet citizen once needed official permits to travel domestically. This was not the case in the post-Stalinist Soviet Union (and for the vast majority of the urban people, it was not the case even under Stalin). There *were* areas within the Soviet Union that were closed to the average traveling person, but these areas were few and far between. The right to reside in a city of one's choice was restricted indeed, but short-term domestic travel was essentially free in the former USSR.

In the enforcement of the domestic travel control, as well as in the general surveillance, a special role was played by a peculiar North Korean institution known as an *inminban* or "people's group." These groups still exist, even though their efficiency as surveillance institutions has declined since the early 1990s.

A typical inminban includes 20 to 40 families. In neighborhoods consisting of detached houses, that is, in the majority of North Korean neighborhoods, one inminban includes all inhabitants of a block, while in apartment buildings an inminban includes all families sharing a common staircase (or two to three adjacent staircases if the building is not so large). Inminban membership is, essentially, inescapable: every North Korean of any age or sex belongs to an inminban.

Each inminban is headed by an official, always a woman, usually middle-aged. Her duties are numerous. Some of these duties involve the neighborhood maintenance routine (garbage removal, for example) while many others are related to surveillance. The inminban heads are required to learn about the incomes, assets, and spending habits of all of their charges in their respective inminbans. The present author once interviewed a number of former inminban heads for a research project and was surprised to hear most of them cite a statement they probably heard often during their training sessions: "An *inminban* head should know how many chopsticks and how many spoons are in every household!"

The police supervise the inminban's activites. Every inminban is assigned to a "resident police officer" who regularly meets its head (actually, her appointment must be confirmed by this officer). During such meetings an inminban head must report suspicious activities that have come to her attention.

The inminban also plays a major role in enforcing control over people's movement. Every evening the inminban head is required to fill in a special register where she records all outside visitors who intend to spend the night in her inminban. If a relative or friend stays overnight, the household must report this to the inminban head, who then checks the person's ID (if the overnight visitor comes from outside the city or county, his/her travel permit is checked as well). A few times a year, specially assigned police patrols, accompanied by an inminban head, conduct a midnight random check of households, just to make sure that all people spending the night there have registered themselves properly. Additionally, they check the seals on the radio sets, making sure the tuning system remains disabled, so that the set cannot be used for listening to foreign broadcasts.

Alongside the inminban system, there was (and still technically exists) another ubiquitous system of surveillance and ideological indoctrination—the "organizational life." The underlying assumption of the "organizational life" is that every North Korean has to belong to some "organization" that both controls and directs his/her social activities. To simplify the picture, virtually all North Koreans are expected to join the Party Youth organization at the age of 14; a minority of them might then join the ruling Korean Workers' Party. Contrary to rather widespread belief, party membership in itself is not a privilege: actually, the KWP rank and file is often subjected to even stricter demands than the general populace. However, during Kim Il Sung's era, party membership was much coveted by the upwardly mobile and ambitious, since it was a necessary prerequisite for *any* social advancement (only KWP members were eligible for promotion in nearly all cases).

Those who were not lucky enough to join the KWP remained in the Party Youth organization until they turned 30 and then became members of the Trade Union organization at their workplace (farmers entered the Agricultural Union instead of the Trade Union). Even housewives are not left outside this ubiquitous web of surveillance and indoctrination: if a woman quits her job after marriage, she automatically becomes a member of the Women's Union, where she would conduct her "organizational life."

It was important that every single North Korean was a member of one of the above-mentioned five "organizations" at his/her workplace, and also a member of the inminban in his/her neighborhood. Technically, this is still the case, even though the significance of the system declined in the 1990s.

The "organizational life" usually consisted of frequent and soporifically long meetings. Typically there were three meetings every week, each lasting one or two hours. Two meetings would be dedicated to ideological indoctrination: their participants were lectured on the greatness of their Great Leader Kim Il Sung and his family, the glorious achievements of the Korean Workers' Party, and the incomparable triumphs of the North Korean economy. The diabolical nature of US imperialism and sufferings of the destitute and oppressed South Korean population were also discussed frequently (as we'll see below, however, in the recent decade the sufferings of South Koreans are being presented in a slightly different light).

One of the three weekly meetings is, however, quite different from the other two. It is known as a "Weekly Life Review Session" but better recognized under the descriptive translation as a "Self-Criticism and Mutual-Criticism Session." Such a session usually meant that every participant (that is, every North Korean above the age of 14) was supposed to give a brief report about the misdeeds and unsound actions of him/herself in the week under review. Concurrently, another member of the same "organization" is expected to criticize the particular person for the same or different misdeeds. Of course, in real life these sessions are somewhat akin to theatrical performances, since people are street-smart enough to not admit anything that might lead to serious consequences. Typically, individuals would admit to being late for their shift or not being diligent enough in taking care of portraits of the Great Leader (surprisingly, the latter is seen as a minor deviation). Nonetheless, these self-criticism and mutual-criticism sessions help to keep the population in line and in some rare cases even lead to the exposure of significant ideological deviations.

One of the truly unique features of Kim Il Sung's North Korea was a reemergence of hereditary groups, each one having a clearly defined set of privileges and restrictions. In this regard, Kim Il Sung's North Korea was surprisingly reminiscent of a premodern society, with its order of fixed and hereditary castes (or "estates" as they were sometimes known in premodern Europe). Starting from 1957 the authorities began to conduct painstaking checks of the family background of every North Korean. This massive project was largely completed by the mid-1960s and led to the emergence of what is essentially a caste system.

This system is known to the North Koreans as *sŏngbun*. According to the sŏngbun system, every North Korean belongs to one of three strata: "loyal," "wavering," or "hostile." In most cases people are classified in accordance to what the person or his/her direct male ancestors did in the 1940s and early 1950s.

Children and grandchildren of former landlords, Christian and Buddhist priests, private entrepreneurs, and clerks in the Japanese colonial administration, as well as descendants of other "suspicious elements" (like, say, courtesans or female shamans) are classified as part of the "hostile" strata. This involves a great deal of discrimination. For example, people born in the hostile caste cannot be accepted to prestigious colleges or reside in major cities—even if they are culprits' great-grandchildren.

Conversely, people whose direct male ancestors greatly contributed to the establishment or defense of the Kim family regime are considered members of the "loyal" stratum. This privileged caste includes prominent officials, descendants of fallen heroes of the Korean War, and others whose deeds are lauded by the regime. As a rule, only members of this stratum are eligible for the most prestigious jobs.

Another rule is that one cannot change not only one's own place in this hierarchical system but also the place of one's children. Only in exceptional cases can a humble "bad sŏngbuner" be reclassified and promoted— for example, it would help if she or he saves a portrait of Kim Il Sung from a flooded house or does something equally heroic.

Sŏngbun is inherited through the male line; the present author knows one family whose wife is a descendant of revolutionary guerrillas and hence has an exceptionally good sŏngbun. Nonetheless, her husband is the progeny of a minor landlord, and hence children of the couple (incidentally, one of the most perfect, long-married couples I've seen in my life) were not eligible for admission to good colleges. Such unequal marriages were unusual: like any other stratified society, in Kim Il Sung's North Korea, the young and, especially, their parents were not enthusiastic about "marrying down." Marriages, therefore, were usually concluded between the families of roughly equal social standing—and, indeed, countless times my North Korean interlocutors cited sŏngbun as an important, even decisive, factor in the choice of a marriage partner.

The sŏngbun system might appear blatantly unjust to somebody with modern (or postmodern) sensibilities, but it is surely an efficient way to keep people in line. In Kim Il Sung's North Korea, every aspiring dissenter knew that it is not only he or she who would pay dearly for an attempt at resistance. Potential challengers were aware that their immediate family would remain the target of discrimination for generations. Needless to say, this made people even less willing to change the system.

All Communist regimes believed (and with good reason, one must admit) that their populace should be kept isolated from unauthorized knowledge of the outside world, but few if any of these regimes could rival North Korea in maintaining a self-imposed information blockade. This exceptional reclusiveness was a result of North Korea's peculiar and vulnerable position as a divided state.

When the severe self-isolation policies were first introduced around 1960, the regime probably did this to make sure that the North Korean people would not be influenced by the dangerously liberal ideas emanating from the "revisionist" Soviet Union. However, it was the fabled "economic miracle" in the South that became the major source of political anxiety for North Korea's leaders from around 1970. The ruling elite understood that the average North Korean should be kept unaware of the affluence enjoyed by his/her brethren under an alternative social and political system. As time went by, the gap between the two Koreas grew, as did the political importance of maintaining the strictest self-isolation regime.

North Korea was the only country that banned the use of tunable radios in peacetime. From around 1960 onward, all radios officially sold in North Korea had fixed tuning, so that only a small number of official North Korean channels could be listened to. If one bought a radio in a hard-currency shop or brought it from overseas (which was legal), the owner had to immediately submit the radio to police, where a technician would permanently disable its tuning mechanism. Since a technically savvy person can easily repair a radio that has been set to one station, all privately owned radio sets had to be sealed. During the above-mentioned random household checks, the inminban heads and police were required to make sure that these seals remained unbroken.

This presents a remarkable contrast with the Soviet Union, where, after Stalin's death, listening to foreign broadcasts—even those deemed to be "subversive" in nature—became a perfectly legal activity. In the Soviet Union, the foreign stations were frequently jammed, but this jamming was ineffectual outside major cities, while high-quality shortwave radios could be freely purchased in the Soviet shops. A 1984 research project stated that in an average week some 14 to 18 percent of adult Soviet citizens listened to the Voice of America, 7 to 10 percent to the BBC, and 8 to 12 percent to Radio Liberty.[24] Incidentally, such decadent permissiveness surprised North Koreans. I remember the shock of a minor North Korean official who learned from me (in the mid-1980s) that it was perfectly legal to listen to foreign broadcasts in the USSR. Stunned by such outrageous liberalism, he asked: "And what if the programming is not ideologically healthy?"

In the late 1960s, the authorities undertook a massive campaign aimed at the physical destruction of the foreign books (largely Soviet and Japanese) that were then privately owned by the North Koreans. In libraries, all foreign publications of a nontechnical nature were (and still are) to be kept in a special section, with only people possessing a proper security clearance allowed to peruse them. Remarkably, no exception was made for publications of the "fraternal" Communist countries: Moscow's *Pravda* and Peking's *People's Daily* were deemed to be potentially as subversive as the *Washington Post* or Seoul's *Chosun Ilbo*.

The North Korean authorities were aware that dangerous information could penetrate the country not only via media like radio or print but also through unsupervised personal interactions between the North Koreans and foreigners. They therefore took care to reduce such interaction to a bare minimum. North Koreans have always been aware that close contacts with foreigners outside one's clearly defined official duties would be seen as dangerous.

When the present author lived in Pyongyang in the mid-1980s, we Soviet exchange students had to deal with an impressive array of restrictions placed on our daily lives. Sometimes these restrictions (like, say, a ban on visiting movie theaters) were hard to explain, but the overall underlying tendency was clear: authorities strove to eliminate possibilities for uncontrolled interactions between ideologically contaminated Soviet students and North Koreans. We were not allowed to attend classes together with North Korean students. We could not visit private homes, nor could we go to certain museums. In an interesting twist, foreigners were not allowed to enter into the catalog rooms of major libraries. Needless to say, most adult North Koreans would avoid personal contact with us.

Finally, in a truly Orwellian twist, the North Korean authorities took care to isolate the populace not only from the foreign media but also from the official publications of earlier years. All North Korean periodicals and a significant number of publications on social and political topics were regularly removed from common access libraries and could only be perused by people with special permissions. With periodicals the removal was done automatically, with all newspapers published more than 10 to 15 years ago being made inaccessible for the laity. This rule was obviously introduced to ensure that the changes in the policy line of the regime would remain unnoticeable to the populace. For example, during the 1970s and 1980s, the government did not want the average North Korean exposed to the paeans Kim Il Sung used to deliver to the great Soviet Army and Comrade Stalin during the 1940s. Nor did they want them aware of the harangues against "Soviet revisionism" that were common in the Korean press of the early 1960s.

A COUNTRY OF CAMPS

Kim Il Sung's regime was brutal, but one of its most peculiar features was emphasis on the prevention of ideological deviation rather than open state terror. People who expressed ideologically unwholesome ideas were first dealt with through the institutions of "organizational life" and/or the inminban system. A majority of the people were fully aware that they could be the object of surveillance at any moment, so they knew better than to break the rules or express the slightest doubts about official ideology. Nonetheless, political persecution was still very much a part of life in Kim Il Sung's North Korea. After all, with all the advantages of unceasing surveillance and control, arbitrary arrest and the institutionalized use of violence were also important for maintaining internal stability.

As a result, North Korea had an extensive system of prison camps whose number of inmates was estimated to be some 150,000 in the early 1980s. Actually, the figure remained stable through a few decades: in 2011 the number was thought to be 154,000, though larger estimates have been suggested as well.[25] The above-mentioned figures are estimates based on analysis of aerial photos and testimony from prison camp survivors and former guards, since the government of North Korea has—predictably— never admitted the existence of the prison camp system, let alone published official statistics about its scale.[26]

The above-mentioned figures indicate that during the late Kim Il Sung era, some 0.6 to 0.7 percent of the country's population were political prisoners. To put things in the proper perspective, this is slightly higher than the ratio of political prisoners to the general population of the Soviet Union in the last years of Stalin's rule. Indeed, the North Korean system of persecution owed much to Stalin's model, but it also had some peculiarities that likely developed under the influence of Mao's China.

To start with, the system is unusually secretive. The macabre tradition of show trials, so typical of Stalin's Soviet Union, was discarded by North Korea's policy makers long ago. The last show trial in North Korean history took place in December 1955, when Pak Hon-yŏng, founder of the Korean Communist Party and most prominent first-generation Communist, was sentenced to death as a spy of Japan and the United States. From then, Kim Il Sung's victims began to disappear without a trace; the government simply did not bother informing the public that some prominent dignitary was found to be a lifelong South Korean saboteur or American spy (if such reports were issued at all, they were classified and targeted only lower reaches of the elite, not the population at large). In some cases, the disappearance did not mean death—years later, the person would make a sudden comeback, without any explanation of his/her long absence.

There are some indications that as a rule, a political criminal in North Korea is not even present at his/her own trial and does not know the term he/she is supposed to serve. The person is normally intercepted by the security agents at work or on a street, taken to an interrogation facility (they are not allowed to notify anybody at the time of arrest), and then shipped to the camp. This is a major difference with the USSR, where even in the worst times of Stalin-era purges, a mock trial—lasting 10 minutes or less—was deemed necessary to keep up appearances.

When the condemned met an overworked execution team, the victim at least became aware of which political crime he or she had allegedly committed. David Hawk remarked that "forced disappearance" might be a more suitable way to describe what is normally referred to as "arrest" in North Korea, and he might be right.[27] In North Korea only common criminals have the luxury of a formal trial, however biased and unfair.

Unlike the former USSR and most other countries, in North Korea there is a clear separation of the camps that handle the common criminals and the camps reserved exclusively for political prisoners. The latter are known as *kwanliso*, and currently there are six such camps in operation (in the past, there were about a dozen of them, but in the course of time some were closed while those remaining grew larger).

Another remarkable feature is the North Korean repressive system of family responsibility, created in Kim Il Sung's era but much relaxed in the late 1990s when Kim Jong Il ascended to power. According to the system, if someone was arrested for a political crime, his entire family— technically speaking, all people who shared his household registration address and were his relatives—would be placed in a prison camp, but not with the criminal himself. This is another difference with Stalin's justice: under Stalin, only family members of the most significant victims of the purge were sent to the camps, while under Kim Il Sung this was a standard procedure, routinely applied even to families of relatively minor political criminals.

Actually, the family responsibility principle might be counted among factors that contributed toward the regime's stability. While the repressive system in North Korea remains very secretive, it has always been public knowledge that if somebody says or does something politically improper, not only the culprit but his entire family disappears. People who might risk their own life are understandably deterred by the realization that their entire family will pay a terrible price as well—including, perhaps, yet-to-be-born descendants.

A typical example of the family responsibility principle is the fate of Kang Ch'öl-hwan, arguably the best-known of all former inmates of the

North Korean system. Kang was sent to Camp 15 together with his family in 1977, when he was only seven years old, and remained there for 10 years. The reason for his imprisonment was an old conflict between his grandmother, a former activist of Chongryon, and Han Tŏk-su, the notorious leader of ethnic Koreans in Japan, who enjoyed significant political clout in Pyongyang. The Kang family joined those Koreans who chose to return to the "Socialist Motherland," and his grandfather, a successful businessman, contributed significant amounts of money to the construction of the Kim Il Sung mammoth statue on Mansudae Hill. However, as soon as the family entered North Korea, Han decided to settle old scores, and they were all sent to a camp—only Kang Ch'ŏl-hwan's mother, being a daughter of a successful North Korean spy, was spared. Children are common in these camps, so schools are operated for them, with political police personnel acting as teachers (Kang Ch'ŏl-hwan, for instance, himself graduated from such a school).[28]

This story is interesting in another regard, too: while it was Kang's grandmother whose nationalist-cum-revolutionary zeal placed the family in trouble, the major punishment was inflicted on Kang's grandfather, a rather apolitical businessman. This is a remarkable, albeit paradoxical, reflection of the deeply patriarchal nature of North Korean society, where men might be held responsible for the serious misdeeds of "their" women— on the assumption that the man, being the natural boss of the household, must keep an eye on everything that happens there and stop any improper activities.

Inside the camps, there are zones with differing regimes: the softer "zones of revolutionization" and the stricter "zones of absolute control." In the latter, prisoners are deprived of the right to live with their families and are subjected to prisonlike conditions. It is assumed they are never released.

On the other hand, "zones of revolutionization" are relatively mild by the standards of Gulag-style prison camps. Such zones are believed to exist only in two camps—Camp 18 and Camp 15. Inside these zones inmates are usually allowed to stay with their families and live in individual houses or family quarters. They go to work and then are free to move within the assigned zones, somewhat spared the regimented existence usually associated with a prison. Model prisoners might even be allowed to have children—of course, those children still remain with their parents inside prison fences. In exceptional cases prisoners might even be allowed to write letters home, but this is very rare (such leniency reportedly existed only in Camp 18). In most cases, however, the inmates are completely cut off from the outside world, so their friends and relations do not know what has happened to them—and, being conditioned by the experience of life in North Korea, they know better than to ask too many questions. The most important difference between the two zones of the North Korean prison camps is that people can be occasionally released from "zones of revolutionization"—and this is the reason why we know so much more about these zones than about the "zones of absolute control."

It seems that as a rule, family members of a political criminal are released when the main culprit dies—but nobody knows this for sure. Normally, the main culprit is sent to a different place, ostensibly the "zone of absolute control" from which he has almost no chance of emerging alive.

The camp routine consists of 10 to 12 hours of backbreaking labor, followed by boring indoctrination sessions. There is one day of rest per month, and inability to meet quotas is punished by beatings as well as the reduction of food rations. Even full rations are barely sufficient for physical survival, however, and consist almost exclusively of poor-quality corn.

To make sure that no deviation, let alone dissent, will remain undetected, the North Korean political police, known as the Ministry for Protection of State Security (MPSS), have an extensive network of informers. Defecting officers of the MPSS, some of whom I know personally, claim that under normal circumstances there is supposed to be one informer for every 50 adults in the entire population. If this instruction is followed, it means that some 250 to 300,000 North Koreans are now paid police informers—and many more have had such experience at some point in their lives.

THE WORLD ACCORDING TO KIM IL SUNG

So what was the worldview that common North Koreans were expected to hold? What were the ideas and assumptions that had to be protected from the corrosive influence of uncontrolled and uncensored information from the outside? A look at the North Korean ideology of Kim Il Sung's era would reveal a peculiar mix of Leninism and Maoism, heavily spiced with rather extreme forms of nationalism and Confucian traditionalism.

Perhaps the most striking part of the North Korean "ideological land-scape" from the late 1960s was a personality cult of Marshal (eventually Generalissimo) Great Leader Kim Il Sung, the Sun of the Nation, the Ever-Victorious General. Initially, his cult was patterned on the cults of Mao and Stalin, but by the early 1970s it took on dimensions that were unprec-edented in the modern world.

Apart from its intensity, Kim's cult had one peculiar feature that made it somewhat different from the cults of other Communist leaders. Mao and Stalin were presented officially as the successors of Marx, Engels, and Lenin, as the best disciples of the dead Communist sages. In other words, they were just the most recent among the incarnations of Marxist wisdom and omniscience. The visual representation of, say, Stalin's standing were oft-reproduced group portraits where Stalin's profile was superimposed next to those of Marx, Engels, and Lenin—obviously, in order to demon-strate their equality in ideological terms. In China, another version of the same group portrait was also popular, with Chairman Mao superimposed on Stalin so that the image simultaneously depicted the five alleged found-ing fathers of Chinese-style Communism.

Kim Il Sung was never presented in such a way. North Korean propa-ganda of the early 1950s sometimes referred to Kim Il Sung as "Stalin's loyal disciple," but this was done in the times when the alleged primacy of the Soviet Union still remained a core element of the regime's ideological discourse. Such references disappeared by the late 1950s.

In later eras, some ideological indebtedness to Marx and Lenin was begrudgingly admitted, so their portraits could sometimes be seen in North Korea as well (it seems that the last publicly displayed portrait of

Marx was removed in April 2012, when the country celebrated the dynastic succession of Kim Jong Un). But these references were to a large extent intended for overseas consumption—devices used to placate visiting dignitaries from other Communist countries or to forge better ties with politically useful Western progressives. For domestic audiences, Kim Il Sung was not presented as an heir to, a disciple of, or the recipient of the guidance of any foreign leader, philosopher, or thinker. He was the founding father in his own right, the creator of the "Immortal Juche Idea" and the Greatest Man in the Five Thousand Years of Korean History. "National solipsism" (to borrow the words of Bruce Cumings), the tendency to see Korea as the decisive element of the entire world system, has always been an important feature of the North Korean worldview, so this later statement essentially implied that Kim Il Sung was the greatest human being to ever live.

Since 1972, all North Koreans above 16 years of age were required to sport a badge with Kim Il Sung's visage when they left their homes. Kim Il Sung portraits needed to be placed at every office and every house; from around 1980 portraits of his son and successor Kim Jong Il were displayed alongside the father (in the 1990s, the portrait of Kim Chŏng-suk, Kim Il Sung's wife and Kim Jong Il's mother, was added). There were (and still are) complex regulations that prescribe how the pristine condition of the sacred images should be maintained. If the portraits were damaged, such an incident would be carefully investigated and the people responsible for the maintenance of the portraits would be punished if found guilty of neglect. The North Korean media was (and still is) full of stories about the heroic deeds of North Korean citizens who willingly sacrificed their lives to save portraits of the Great Leader and his son.

Kim Il Sung's statues were erected across the country, with the largest statue being built on Mansu Hill in Pyongyang in 1972 (it is 22 meters high and initially was gilded with gold leaf). The statues were made centers of elaborate rituals. For example, on the Great Leader's birthday and some other major official holidays, every North Korean was supposed to go to the nearest statue and after a deep bow lay flowers at the feet of the great man's visage.

Names of Kim Il Sung and, eventually, Kim Jong Il are to be typed in bold script in North Korean publications (Kim Jong Un's name began to be typed in bold in late December 2011, a few days after his father's death). Every major article needs to start with a proper quote from either Kim Il Sung or Kim Jong Il. No exception is made for purely academic publications, including, say, works of liquid state physics or molecular biology. Fortunately for scientists, in his long life Kim Il Sung delivered many speeches and signed many articles, so a proper quote can always be found.

The list of titles of Kim Il Sung and his immediate family members was formalized in the 1970s. Thus, every North Korean knows how to distinguish between the "Great Leader" (Kim Il Sung) and "Dear Leader" (Kim Jong Il) and is also aware that "three Great Generals of the Paekdu Mountain" are Kim Il Sung, his wife Kim Jong Suk, and their son Kim Jong Il. After Kim Jong Il's death and the ascendency of his son, Kim Jong Un, the latter was given the title of "Supreme Leader."

Official propaganda established that the Kim family had played a major role in the last 150 years of Korean history. For example, in the 1970s schools began to teach North Korean students that the March 1st Uprising of 1919, the largest outbreak of anti-Japanese, pro-independence sentiment, started in Pyongyang (not in Seoul, as actually was the case) and that its major leader, of course, Kim Il Sung's father Kim Hyŏng-jik. They also claim that Kim Il Sung, then merely seven years old, took part in the March First rally. In real life Kim Hyŏng-jik, like a majority of the educated Koreans of the era, was indeed sympathetic toward the independence movement and was even briefly detained for participation in anti-Japanese activities. Nonetheless, he was by no means a prominent activist, let alone a leader, of the nationalist movement.

The official North Korean historiography didn't admit the role played by the Korean Communist Party in spreading Marxism in Korea in the 1920s. This is not surprising since nearly all of the founders of this party were eventually purged by Kim Il Sung. According to the North Korean official narrative, the history of Korean Communism began when Kim Il Sung in 1926 founded the Anti-Imperialist Union. This means that Kim Il Sung single-handedly launched the Korean Communist movement at the age of 14—but nobody in Korea would dare not suspend one's disbelief when it comes to claims of the superhuman qualities of Kim's family.

One of the recurring features of this official narrative is an attempt to play down or conceal the foreign influences and connections of Kim Il Sung and his family.

As part of this systemic manipulation, the official narrative does not admit that Kim Jong Il was born in the Soviet Union on a military base in the vicinity of Khabarovsk. After all, the successor to the Juche Revolutionary Cause and future head of the ultra-nationalist state could not possibly have been born on foreign soil! North Korean propagandists therefore invented a secret guerrilla camp that allegedly existed on the slopes of Mount Paekdu in the early 1940s, claiming Kim Jong Il was born there.

In an interesting twist, in the 1990s, when the Soviet Union was safely dead and Soviet influence was no longer seen as a danger, North Korean official media finally admitted that Kim Il Sung did spend the early 1940s in the Soviet Union. However, this admission did not lead to disavowal of the Paekdu Camp story, which by that time had become a cornerstone of the official propaganda. Nowadays, a North Korean is supposed to believe that in the early 1940s, Kim Il Sung lived in Soviet exile but still personally led daring guerrilla raids into North Korea (Soviet documents indicate that this was not the case). Allegedly, he did so in the company of his pregnant wife and she thus gave birth to their first child on the sacral—and purely Korean—slopes of Mount Paekdu. To support these improbable claims the North Korean authorities built a "replica" of the Paekdu Secret Camp complete with a log cabin where Kim Jong Il was allegedly born, and made it a site of obligatory pilgrimage.

The complete control over information flows within society, combined with isolation from the outside world, gave North Korea's propagandists opportunities their worldwide peers could not dream of. They could successfully hide from the populace even things that would be considered common knowledge in many other societies. At the same time, they could exaggerate or create nonevents with impunity.

In the media of Kim Il Sung's era, North Korea was presented as a People's Paradise, a place where the entire population continually lived in the

THEIR MAJESTIES AND THEIR WOMEN

As is the case in any dynastic state, the personal and sexual lives of the rulers are by definition political. All candidates for the top job are chosen by their predecessors, and this means that family affairs are difficult to distinguish from the affairs of state.

The personal lives of Kim Il Sung and Kim Jong Il are quite convoluted and full of unexpected drama. TV producers should be happy about this since stories of passion and jealousy in Kim-era Pyongyang will likely achieve high ratings for the foreseeable future.

Kim Il Sung was married three times. Not much is known about his very first wife—even her existence is sometimes questioned. She is believed to have been another guerrilla, and most think that the first marriage was childless.

By the late 1930s, Kim Il Sung had entered his second union, with a girl named Kim Jong Suk. She was also a guerrilla, and she crossed the Soviet frontier in late 1940 together with Kim Il Sung. Barely literate, but kind to and popular with her comrades, she gave birth to three children. Their first son was Kim Jong Il, who would eventually become the North Korean leader.

Kim Jong Suk died in childbirth in 1949. Soon afterward, Kim Il Sung married Kim Song-ae, who worked at his office at the time. Kim Song-ae remained invisible in North Korean politics until the late 1960s, when she briefly made an attempt to position herself in public politics. She was soon eclipsed by the rise of her stepson, Kim Jong Il. Kim Song-ae bore three children. When Kim Jong Il was finally chosen as successor, they were sent to prestigious diplomatic jobs far away from Pyongyang—a move that provided them with an agreeable lifestyle while rendering them politically harmless (Kim Song-ae's eldest son serves as North Korea's ambassador to Poland).

In his youth, Kim Jong Il had the reputation of a playboy. Indeed, he was popular with girls—not only because he was a crown prince but also because he seems to have been charming (at least if available sources are to be believed). He had a good sense of humor, knew much about cinema and popular culture, and, in spite of being slightly overweight, loved riding motorbikes.

It seems that Kim Jong Il never formally registered a marriage, so the line between a proper wife and a live-in girlfriend was blurry. However, of all of Kim Jong Il's women, only two have significance as far as dynastic policy is concerned.

Kim Jong Il's first known partner was Song Hye-rim, a stunning movie star who had to divorce in order to move in with Kim Jong Il. In 1971 she gave birth to Kim Jong Nam, the Dear Leader's first son. However, Song Hye-rim never managed to win the approval of Kim Il Sung, Kim Jong Il's mighty father—obviously because she was a daughter of South Korean Communists, whom Kim Il Sung never trusted. At any rate, Song Hye-rim's relationship with Kim Jong Il collapsed in the early 1970s. Song Hye-rim was sent to a comfortable exile in Moscow, where she died in 2002.

Her son, Kim Jong Nam, also developed uneasy relations with the rest of the family. Since the early 2000s he has been living in Macao, and occasionally did not act to his father's liking (including granting remarkably frank interviews to foreign journalists).

Meanwhile, Kim Jong Il would fall in love with another beauty, Ko Yŏng–hŭi, a dancer from a family of ethnic Koreans in Japan. She had two sons, Kim Jong Chol and Kim Jong Un. For a while in the late 1990s Ko acquired minor political clout, but like her predecessor she died at a relatively young age in 2004.

After Ko Yŏng–hŭi death, Kim Jong Il reputedly developed relations with the strong-minded and ambitious Kim Ok, his former secretary. Her somewhat special standing was confirmed when Kim Ok appeared at some funeral ceremonies after Kim Jong Il's death in December 2011.

It was against such a backdrop that in late 2008, Kim Jong Il finally chose his third son, Kim Jong Un, as his successor. At the time of writing it appears that Kim Kyong Hee, Kim Jong Il's younger sister, and her husband are expected to act as regents if the Dear Leader dies too soon. But such arrangements are always a murky business and the same can be said about dynastic politics in general.

(continued)

Finally, Kim Jong Un broke with all conventions when in July 2012 he began to appear in public with his young and stunningly beautiful wife Ri Sol Ju, of whose background not much is known (it is, however, known that she loves expensive Dior handbags).

state of unimaginable happiness. The North Korean cultural products of the period—unlike, for instance, the works of Soviet art of Stalin period—seldom if ever mentioned the existence of internal enemies. Rather, all North Koreans were presented as happy children living under the fatherly care of the omniscient Great Leader. In a remarkable gesture, North Korean banknotes bore the motto "We have nothing to envy," thus reminding the North Koreans that they were, after all, the happiest nation under heaven.

Much in line with this old approach, in 2011 the North Korean media published a worldwide rating of happiness. It stated that the happiest people live in China, with North Koreans coming in second (obviously, they were so moderate in their claims because by that time North Koreans became aware that China had much higher standards of living). Needless to say, the two lowest places in this curious rating were taken by the United States and South Korea.

Indeed, there was a striking contrast between Korea and the outside world. Predictably, the Communist nations were assumed to be relatively prosperous. Even so, the propaganda of Kim Il Sung's era did not spend much time eulogizing the achievements of Soviet cosmonauts or Hungarian milkmaids. In this regard it was remarkably different from other nations of the Communist bloc: as we remember, Kim Il Sung's leadership saw other Communist countries as dangerously liberal, a source of ideological corruption, and hence did not want to encourage excessive attention to their real or alleged achievements.

Propagandists also presented the countries of the Third World, especially those who styled themselves as Socialist, in a favorable light. When it covered the developing world, the North Korean media loved to dwell on the great popularity of the Juche Idea across Asia, Africa, and Latin

America. If *Nodong sinmun* of the 1970s was to be believed, perusing works of Kim Il Sung was a favorite pastime of many an African villager.

For a brief while, attempts to create a worldwide Jucheist movement were an important part of North Korea's internal and external propaganda. Nearly all of these propaganda operations took place in the Third World. In the developed West such an ideological offering would have few takers, while maintaining such a movement there would be costly. In the Communist bloc, Juche propaganda had an even lower chance of success than in London or Geneva. After all, the surveillance apparatus in these Communist countries was powerful enough to ensure obedience to the most correct brand of Communist ideology—that is, the brand currently accepted by the local leaders. Ordinary people in Communist countries also tended to be unsympathetic toward Juche, which they typically saw as a rude caricature of their own official ideologies.

Thus, North Korean diplomats and spies concentrated their efforts in the developing world. In the 1970s they created a network of study groups and research institutes there, dedicated to the propagation of Kim Il Sung's ideology and heavily subsidized by Pyongyang. It soon became clear, however, that the scheme did not work as intended: many entrepreneurial activists were happy to receive cash, but their commitment to the Great Leader was doubtful, as was their ability to influence the politics of their home countries. Nonetheless, the subsidies for the worldwide Juche movement, while reduced around 1980, were never completely stopped since the movement was all too useful for domestic purposes. The North Korean leadership understood that it would be good to expose the North Koreans to the sight of exotic foreigners who allegedly come to Korea to lay flowers at the statues of the Dear Leader and confess their unwavering admiration for the Greatest Man on Earth. The government of North Korea had to pay for return air tickets and accommodation, but in domestic policy terms it might have been a good investment.

During the Kim Il Sung era, the media would report that inhabitants of the Communist bloc and Third World were doing relatively well, but remained inferior to the North Koreans. Things were different in the countries of the West—above all in the United States, the embodiment of all things evil. The United States was a country of aggressors who made a living by robbing the world of its resources, a nation of blood-thirsty war-mongers and sadists. Since kindergarten, the North Koreans were exposed to endless tales about acts of sadistic brutality perpetrated by the disgusting Yankees during the Korean War. They were also reminded that the same acts were still committed in South Korea by these evil monsters (one of the most common sobriquets used for Americans in the North Korean media was "the American imperialists, the two-legged wolves").

Indeed, the worst place on earth to live was South Korea, "a land without light, a land without air." Until the late 1990s, South Korea was presented as a destitute American colony, whose population lived in abject poverty. In movies and paintings of that period, the South Korean cityscape looked positively hellish. People dressed in rags, lived in shacks, and looked for edible garbage at the dumping grounds near US military bases. Those disgusting "Yankees" were often present in the picture as well—fat American soldiers, with hugely protruding noses and ugly, caricatured features, riding in jeeps (if such a jeep hit a Korean girl, they would be laughing approvingly) or standing on the major crossroads with automatic rifles, always ready to kill innocent Koreans.

The Year One textbook presents North Korea's children with an enlightening picture: "A school principal in South Korea beats and drives from school a child who cannot pay his monthly fee on time."[29] In high school they learn that "Nowadays, South Korea is swamped with seven million unemployed. Countless people stand in queues in front of employment centers, but not even a small number of jobs is forthcoming. The factories are closing one after another, and in such a situation even people who have work do not know when they will be ousted from their position."[30] Needless to say, these horror stories are pure fabrications—primary education is free in South Korea and even in the worst times of economic crisis there were never "seven million unemployed."

Of course, there was resistance. Heroic South Koreans were secretly publishing works of Kim Il Sung and Kim Jong Il, holding revolutionary meetings in basement rooms adorned with portraits of the Great and Dear Leaders and, while imprisoned, professing their loyalties to the

Juche Idea in spite of the unspeakable tortures inflicted upon them by the pro-American puppet police.

The explicit assumption was that an overwhelming majority of South Koreans envied their prosperous and happy brethren in the North and dreamt about a day when they too would enjoy life at the bosom of the Great Leader. Only a large US military presence and an iron-fist rule by a handful of shameless collaborators prevented this great dream from coming true.

To what extent did the average North Koreans of Kim Il Sung's days believe these propaganda messages? By the late 1980s, a majority of the North Korean population had no personal memory of times when things were seriously different and had no access to alternative sources of information. There must have been some skeptics, especially among better-educated people or among those who had some exposure to overseas life. But, these people were wise enough to remain silent. In North Korea, the unusual intensity of propaganda was combined with the self-imposed information blockade and decades-long consistency of the ideological message. This ensured that the official worldview remained unquestioned by a majority. After all, the people had their own lives to live and were not that much concerned about how sincere in their statements Juche worshippers from Venezuela or Zimbabwe really were.

BE READY FOR BODY COUNT

Considering the North Korean regime's habit of politicizing everything, one should not expect North Korean math textbooks to be free from politics.

Let's have a brief look through the Year Two math textbook for North Korean primary schools, published in 2003 (or officially Year 91 of the Juche Era). This textbook is a masterpiece of politicized math and I would like to introduce some representative gems of this treasure chest.

Admittedly, the majority of the questions in the textbook are not political—indeed they have no backstory at all. Kids are required to

(continued)

deal with abstract numbers and areas. However, some 20 percent of all questions are different—they include a story, to make the math appear more interesting and relevant. Some of the stories are quite innocent—about a train's timetable or kids' games. But some are not.

For instance, take an engaging quiz from page 17: "During the Fatherland Liberation War [North Korea's official name for the Korean War] the brave uncles of Korean People's Army killed 265 American Imperial bastards in the first battle. In the second battle they killed 70 more bastards than they had in the first battle. How many bastards did they kill in the second battle? How many bastards did they kill all together?"

On page 24, the "American imperialist bastards" fared better and were lucky to survive the pious slaughter: "During the Fatherland Liberation War the brave uncles of the Korean People's Army in one battle killed 374 American imperial bastards, who are brutal robbers. The number of prisoners taken was 133 more than the number of American imperial bastards killed. How many bastards were taken prisoner?"

The use of math for body counts is quite popular—there are four or five more questions like this in the textbook. As every North Korean child is supposed to believe, his South Korean peers also spend days and nights fighting the American imperialist bastards. Thus, this also creates a good opportunity to apply simple math.

On page 138 one can find the following question: "South Korean boys, who are fighting against the American imperialist wolves and their henchmen, handed out 45 bundles of leaflets with 150 leaflets in each bundle. They also stuck 50 bundles with 50 leaflets in each bundle. How many leaflets were used?"

Page 131 also provides kids with a revision question about leaflet dissemination: "Chadori lives in South Korea which is being suppressed by the American Imperial Wolves. In one day he handed out 5 bundles of leaflets, each bundle containing 185 leaflets. How many leaflets were handed out by boy Chadori?"

That said, North Korean children are not supposed to be too optimistic. Life in South Korea is not just composed of heroic struggle but also great suffering. On page 47 they can find the following question: "In one South Korean village which is suffering under the heel of the American imperialist wolf bastards, a flood destroyed 78 houses. The number of houses damaged was 15 more than the number destroyed. How many houses were damaged or destroyed in this South Korean village all together?"

These sufferings are nicely contrasted with the prosperity enjoyed by the happy North Koreans. On the same page, the question about destroyed South Korean houses is immediately followed by this question: "In the village where Yong-shik lives, they are building many new houses. 120 of these houses have 2 floors. The number of houses with 3 floors is 60 more than the number of houses with two floors. How many houses have been built in Yong-shik's village?"

Indeed, feats of productive labor often become topics of North Korean questions, with robots, tractors, TV sets, and houses being mentioned most frequently. Interestingly, in some cases questions might produce results that were clearly not intended by the compilers. For example, on page 116 one can find the following question: "In one factory workers produced 27 washing machines in 3 days. Assuming that they produce the same number of washing machines every day, how many machines do they produce in one day?" One has to struggle hard to imagine a factory that manages to produce merely nine washing machines a day, but the irony clearly escapes the textbook's authors (after all, a washing machine is a very rare luxury item in North Korea).

Activists love to say that everything is political. Whether this is true in general, I know not, but primary school math textbooks in North Korea clearly are.

THE SILVER LINING IN A SOCIAL DISASTER

This description of Kim Il Sung's North Korea might appear extremely unappealing to an inhabitant of a developed liberal democracy, or even an aspiring liberal democracy; indeed it is fair to say that in the 1960s Kim Il Sung managed to create a society that was arguably the closest approximation to an Orwellian nightmare in world history—and then maintained this society for nearly 30 years.

Most people whose lifelong experiences are very different probably imagine that the average North Korean would constantly feel restive and dissatisfied when living under such a regime. However, this was not the case. When living in North Korea myself, I could not help but find it remarkable how "normal" the daily lives usually were. North Koreans of the Kim Il Sung era were not brainwashed automatons whose favorite pastime was goose-stepping and memorizing the lengthy speeches of their Leaders (although both these activities had to be a part of their lives). Nor were they closet dissenters who waited for the first opportunity to launch a pro-democracy struggle or studied subversive samizdat texts (and not only because samizdat simply could not possibly exist in such a thoroughly controlled system). Neither were they docile slaves who sheepishly followed any order from above.

Of course, there were zealots as well as dissenters and people broken by the system but, on balance, the vast majority of North Koreans did not belong to any of these categories. Like most people of all ages and all cultures, they did not normally pay too much attention to politics, even though the state-imposed rituals were performed and obligatory statements were delivered when necessary. People in Kim Il Sung's North Korea were mainly concerned about much the same things people in other societies focused on. They thought about their families, they hoped to get a promotion, they wanted to educate their children, they were afraid of getting sick, they fell in love. They enjoyed romance, good food, and good books, and didn't mind a glass of liquor. The political and ideological was more prominent in their lives than in the lives of the average person elsewhere, but it still did not color most of their experiences.

On top of this, in the 1950s and 1960s the promises of Kim Il Sung's national Stalinism did look attractive to many North Koreans. Had they possessed the benefit of hindsight they would have probably had second thoughts about their initial enthusiasm for—or, at least, acceptance of—the system. The grave consequences, however, did not become apparent until it was too late.

Indeed, for the average North Korean living in the 1950s Kim Il Sung's system did not look uninviting. It assured modernity and economic growth (first in industrial output and then in living standards). It vowed to maintain material equality while opening avenues of social advancement to people of humble origins. It promised to deliver justice to pro-Japanese collaborators whom the average Korean of the colonial period hated. This system was not democratic, to be sure, but its nondemocratic nature was probably seen only as a minor impediment by the majority.

We should not forget that Kim Il Sung was imposing his system on a country whose population overwhelmingly consisted of the sons and daughters of premodern subsistence farmers. These people had never been exposed to democracy even in theoretical terms, and Kim Il Sung's system seemed to be better than what they had experienced before—being at the mercy of a feudal absolute monarchy and then a remarkably brutal colonial regime.

Information from the outside world did not hint at the existence of attractive alternatives elsewhere. The developed West had unsavory associations with colonialism and at any rate was too far removed and little known to be a viable object of emulation. South Korea until the late 1960s did not constitute a particularly attractive alternative, either. Contrary to what many ideologically biased historians claim nowadays, even at its lowest ebb the South Korean regime of Syngman Rhee was remarkably more permissive than its North Korean counterpart. Nonetheless, it was brutal—from available statistics, between the years 1945 and 1955 the number of people massacred for political reasons was actually larger in the South than in the North (a result of brutal anti-guerrilla campaigns). The South Korean regime also had a less equal distribution of wealth and to a large extent was dominated by former pro-Japanese collaborators. So until the late 1960s even a well-informed and unbiased observer would not have many reasons to see the South Korean system as vastly preferable to Kim Il Sung's version of nationalist Stalinism.

At the time, even the material situation did not look so bad to the average North Korean. In the early 1960s tens of thousands of ethnic Koreans from China fled to North Korea to escape famine and chaos resulting from the Great Leap Forward and the other insane experiments of Chairman Mao. Those refugees were granted housing and assigned work by the North Korean authorities. A man who was part of this exodus recently recalled his surprise at walking into a North Korean shop for the first time and discovering plastic buckets of various shapes and sizes for sale. Everybody could buy these wonderful items without coupons, and there was not even a need to queue!

If compared with other countries of similar income levels, Kim Il Sung's North Korea demonstrated a measure of success in such areas as secondary education and health care. Propaganda exaggerated these successes, but they were real nonetheless.

Just before the famine of the 1990s, life expectancy in the North peaked at 72, only marginally lower than the then life expectancy in the much more prosperous South. According to the 2008 census results, which are largely seen as plausible by the foreign experts, life expectancy at birth seems to be 69 years nowadays.[31] This is some ten years shorter than in the South, but still impressive for such a poor country.

In 2008 child mortality in North Korea was estimated by the World Health Organization at 45 per 1,000 live births. This is a bit higher than China, but remarkably lower than in many developing countries of a comparable economic level. For example, in Chad the child mortality was 120 per 1,000, and, if the CIA estimates are to be believed, Chad and North Korea have roughly similar levels of per capita GDP (actually, there are good reasons to suspect that the CIA estimates of the North Korean GDP are inflated, so the actual contrast might be even more dramatic).

These achievements appear to be even more of a paradox if we take into account the serious and systematic underfunding of North Korean health-care facilities, even at the best of times. Most hospitals occupy derelict buildings with small crowded rooms, and their equipment is roughly the same as that used by Western doctors in the 1950s, if not the 1930s. Access to good drugs was also very limited. Doctors definitely did not constitute a privileged or well-paid group in North Korean society: medical professionals in the North were no different from average white-collar clerical staff in their social standing and income.

Surprisingly, the primary reason for these remarkable achievements might have been the very ability of the government to control everyone with little or no concern for privacy. These are the essentials for a police state, but they can be very conducive to maintaining public health through the use of preventative medicine.

The entire population of Kim Il Sung's North Korea were subjected to regular health checks. The checks were simple and cheap—like, say, chest X-rays, but they helped to locate medical problems at the early stages. The checks were obligatory, and no North Korean could avoid an inspection, since the entire state machine saw to it. The same was the case with immunization. A Western doctor who frequently goes to North Korea with aid missions put it nicely in a private talk with the author: "For a health care professional, a police state is a paradise. I came with my medical van to a North Korean village, the local official blew a whistle, and in 10 minutes everyone in the village was waiting in front of our van. Every single person! No excuse was tolerated, and nobody dared to evade us. In other developing countries it was so different!"

Even the low salaries of doctors were not necessarily a bad thing. This allowed the rather poor state to support a large number of medical doctors—32.9 physicians per 10,000 persons, roughly the same rate as in France (35.0) and significantly above the US level (26.7).[32] A relative shortage of nurses should be taken into account—North Korean doctors often have to perform tasks that in other countries are usually done by nurses. Nonetheless, the number of doctors is impressive.

This emphasis on cheap prophylactics and easy availability of basic— not to say primitive—health care is what made the North Korean achievements possible. After all, people of younger ages seldom die because of some chronic conditions that require expensive treatment: untreated appendicitis is much more likely to kill somebody in his or her 40s and 50s. Complicated diseases usually develop at an advanced age, while at earlier stages the majority of the threats to life come from seemingly minor ailments that can be easily treated if identified early enough, and if there is a doctor nearby.

Of course, even in the best of times there were serious problems with high-end medicine. The North Korean health-care system worked well when it dealt with fractured bones of tractor drivers or pneumonia among infantry soldiers, but it was poorly equipped to treat more complicated conditions. More sophisticated surgery was available only in the exclusive hospitals for the regime's top brass (like Ponghwa clinic in Pyongyang). The lesser orders were (and still are) left to their sorry fate if they were unlucky to catch something serious, with the status of the physically and mentally handicapped being especially low.

Education—above all, primary and secondary education—was another area where a North Korean–style police state scored a remarkable success. Like basic medical care, primary education doesn't cost that much—especially if one can afford large class sizes and doesn't care about sophisticated equipment. After all, for running a village primary school one needs a building, a blackboard, and a reasonably qualified teacher; one also needs to make sure that more or less all children of school age will attend school. The North Korean state has managed to sort out these issues.

Not to a small extent the emphasis on education is driven by ideological concerns since intense ideological indoctrination is an integral part of schooling. Significantly, the most important school subjects of the North Korean curriculum are "the revolutionary history of the Great Leader" and "the revolutionary history of the Dear Leader." However, one should not reduce the entire contents of North Korean education to the level of indoctrination and brainwashing: the average North Korean child acquires good skills in basic literacy and numeracy as well.

In regard to college-level education, the results are far more mixed. North Korean college students might be motivated, but the shortage of funds and excessive ideological controls are adversely influencing their performance (with a handful of military-related fields being an important exception). Some of the problems were structural, but many others were related to the persistent shortage of funds and resources. These shortages became progressively acute as time passed.

Indeed, the major problem of the North Korean state and North Korean society was a gradual economic slowdown. This became obvious around 1970. The official media kept insisting that the economy was growing by leaps and bounds, but the North Korean people could easily see from their own experiences that this was not the case. The system looked so attractive in theory and briefly seemed to work well, but in the early 1970s began its slow downhill slide.

THE BIRTH OF JUCHE, THE RISE OF THE SON, AND THE SLOW-MOTION DEMISE OF A HYPER-STALINIST ECONOMY

To solidify its newly acquired autonomy in regard to both China and Soviet Russia, the North Korean regime felt compelled to invent an ideology of its own. This ideology came to be known as Juche. The usual explanatory translation of the term is "self-reliance" but this is misleading. A better translation would be "self-importance" or "self-significance," that is, the need to give primacy to one's own national interests and peculiarities.

The Juche Idea was first mentioned by Kim Il Sung in a 1955 speech but remained marginal until the mid-1960s, when it was remodeled into the official ideology of the North Korean state. As a doctrine, it remained imprecise and vague, so one cannot help but agree with Brian Myers's remark: "a farrago of Marxist and humanist banalities that is claimed to have been conceived by Kim himself, Juche Thought exists only to be praised."[33]

The North Korean ideologues failed when in the 1970s they attempted to market the Juche Idea across the globe, but domestically it worked fine. The Juche Idea was presented as the highest and most up-to-date brand of progressive ideology worldwide. It justified the superiority of the North Korean leadership, who now could confront the Soviet and Chinese ideological pressures by stating (or, at least, hinting) that the Juche Idea was inherently superior to both Maoist and post-Stalinist versions of orthodox Marxism-Leninism. Actually, it was superior to Marxism itself. Kim Jong Il made things clear in an article first written in 1976:

> Both in content and in composition, Kimilsungism is an original idea that cannot be explained within the framework of Marxism-Leninism. The Juche idea which constitutes the quintessence of Kimilsungism, is

an idea newly discovered in the history of human thought. However, at
present there is a tendency to interpret the Juche idea on the basis of the
materialistic dialectic of Marxism. [. . .] This shows that the originality
of the Juche idea is not correctly understood.[34]

These statements might have massaged Kim Il Sung's ego—he was
surely pleased to fancy himself a great theoretician of the world significance, a person in the same league as Marx, Confucius, and Aristotle.
However, these boastful claims served pragmatic functions as well. When
North Korean propagandists marketed Juche as a philosophy superior to
good old Leninism, they created a doctrinaire justification for Pyongyang's political independence from Moscow and other self-proclaimed
guardians of Marxism-Leninism.

In domestic politics, the most remarkable peculiarity of the period
between 1965 and 1980 was the rise of Kim Jong Il, son of Kim Il Sung by
his first wife, Kim Chŏng-suk. Kim Il Sung's unprecedented decision to
designate his son as a successor made North Korea the world's first Communist monarchy. This was understandable: Kim Il Sung could see what
happened in the Soviet Union, where immediately after Stalin's death the
late strongman came to be bitterly criticized by the people who were once
seen as his most trusted lieutenants. Kim Il Sung also obviously took note
of Chinese experience, where Chairman Mao's designated successor, Lin
Biao, could not even wait until the Chairman's natural death and tried to
hasten the process by staging a coup. Kim Il Sung, who in the early 1970s
was rumored to be seriously ill, therefore needed to find a successor whose
legitimacy would be dependent on that of Kim Il Sung himself and who
hence would be unlikely to use his newly acquired power to destroy Kim
Il Sung's legacy. The choice came naturally: like countless powerful men in
human history, Kim Il Sung decided that his son Kim Jong Il would
become the perfect candidate for such an important job.

The rise of Kim Jong Il began in the late 1960s, when he was put in
charge of the cultural sphere. Later, in 1974, he became a Politburo member and finally, in 1980, at the 6th Congress of the Korean Workers' Party,
he was officially pronounced successor of his father.

Young Kim Jong Il had a reputation as a playboy (not entirely unde-served) and initially was not taken seriously by foreign analysts, who often predicted that Kim Jong Il would not outlive his father for too long, at least politically. However, neither a string of stunning girlfriends (often dancers or movie stars) nor a well-known predisposition for vintage French wines and expensive Swiss cheese (not to mention first-rate sushi) prevented Kim Jong Il from becoming a charismatic politician and shrewd manipu-lator who eventually proved to be a match for his ruthless and street-smart father. He needed these skills, to be sure, since the time of the power trans-fer (which began in the mid-1970s) was also the time when the North Korean economy began its slow-motion decline.[35]

At the time of the Korean peninsula's partition, the North effectively got a massive endowment. From approximately 1930 the Japanese Empire began to invest in Korea on a grand scale. At the time, Korea was seen as a natural rear base for the future advance of the Empire into China, and nobody in Tokyo dreamed that Korea could become an independent na-tion again. As a net result, by 1945 North Korea became the most indus-trially advanced region in East Asia outside of Japan. Meanwhile, the southern half of the Korean peninsula remained an underdeveloped agri-cultural region.

By 1940 what would soon become Kim Il Sung's "People's Paradise" produced 85 percent of metals, 88 percent of chemicals, and 85 percent of all electricity in Korea at that time.[36] The Hamhŭng chemical plant was the world's second largest and the power generators of the Yalu River hydro-power stations so impressed the Soviet experts in 1946 that they disas-sembled the machines for the purposes of reverse engineering. Needless to say, the massive US air raids during the Korean War destroyed a signif-icant part of this sophisticated infrastructure. Nonetheless, many indus-trial facilities survived the war or were quickly repaired and put back into operation in the 1950s.

Making comparisons between a market economy and a centrally planned one is a notoriously tricky and imprecise business. In the partic-ular case of the two Koreas the case is made even more complicated by the secretive nature of the Pyongyang regime: beginning around 1960, virtually all economic statistics were classified, and this remains the case at the time of writing. The only exception is population statistics and some data about food production that, since the 1990s, were occasionally provided to major international agencies. Everything else about the state of the North Korean economy is guesswork. Regardless, nobody doubts that until the mid-1960s (at the very least) in terms of basic macroeconomic indicators the Socialist North was ahead of the Capitalist South. Some scholars have argued that this superiority persisted well into the 1970s even though to the present author this statement seems to exaggerate the economic power of the North.

However, by the late 1960s the North Korean economy began to slow down. This fact could not be hidden from the population; they could see it at their shops. The number of items sold freely without rationing coupons was steadily diminishing, and in the early 1970s retail trade essentially ceased to exist. A state distribution system replaced it almost completely.

Nowadays a majority of elder North Koreans express their nostalgia for the late 1960s, which are still seen as a bygone era of great prosperity. This era was by no means a paradise of unlimited consumption, but in retrospect this nostalgic attitude is easy to understand: from the early 1970s on, the quality of life began to go downhill and never recovered again. This was especially unnerving for the North Korean leadership, who—unlike the common populace—knew perfectly well what was then happening in South Korea, which was experiencing one of the greatest economic success stories of the 20th century. From 1960 to 1985, South Korea enjoyed one of the world's highest growth rates. Throughout this period, South Korea's per capita GDP, measured in constant 1990 dollars, increased almost fivefold, from $1,200 to $5,700.[37]

As a result of the "Miracle on the Han River" (as this remarkable economic transformation is popularly known) by 1980 South Korea became the most advanced nation of all continental Asia. The speed of this transformation was incredible. Nowadays, South Korea has the world's second largest number of high-rise residential buildings. It is rather difficult to believe that in 1963, when the first Korean apartment block was constructed, it was impossible to sell the flats since no one was willing to live above the second floor. South Korean television began to broadcast in color only in 1980, and the South Korean automobile industry, now the world's fifth largest, virtually did not exist until 1974 (ditto the ship-building industry).

The tremendous economic success of the capitalist South coincided with the growing stagnation of the North. This was to have extremely important political consequences. In a sense this yawning gap in economic efficiency might be the single most important factor in determining the political situation in and around the Korean peninsula nowadays.

The reasons for the failure of the Leninist economic model have been studied thoroughly and in the case of North Korea they were essentially the same as elsewhere: distorted price information, lack of incentives for innovation and quality improvement, and an ingrained inability to handle data efficiently. Nonetheless, it is worth noting that many features of Leninist state Socialism were especially pronounced in North Korea, and hence one should not be surprised that the failure of this model was also especially spectacular there. North Korea first accepted an inherently inefficient system of economic management and then modified it in ways that further amplified its already remarkable inefficiencies.

To start, North Korea had an unusually high level of military spending. In the 1990s, this small country had a standing army of some 1.1 to 1.2 million people—the world's highest ratio of military personnel to the general population (to put things in comparison, it was roughly the same ratio as in the United States of 1943). The military spending was also exceptionally high.[38]

Admittedly, there was some strategic logic behind this level of militarization. Until at least the early 1970s, if not longer, the North Korean government saw the forceful unification of Korea as a realistic political task, and even as its major long-term strategic aim. In order to outgun the army of South Korea, which had twice as many people, the state had to invest heavily in military hardware and also require an unusually long period of obligatory military service (North Korean males spend between seven and ten years of their lives under arms). Once South Korea began to pull ahead

between 1965 and 1970, North Korea still strove to maintain its equality
with the South by further increasing the already high share of the military
spending. Burdened by this additional spending, the North Korean
economy slowed down even further, and this slowdown in turn prompted
North Korea's leaders to increase military budget allocations. This was a
classic example of a vicious circle and the sorry results were only too
predictable.

Another specific factor that exacerbated North Korea's economic woes
was the policy of economic autarky. The slogan of "Self-Reliance" was bor-
rowed verbatim from Mao's China around 1960, even though few North
Koreans were aware of its foreign origin. Indeed, the slogan was repeated
ad nauseam in Kim Il Sung's times and—unlike many other slogans—
seems to have been taken seriously. Kim Il Sung and his guerrilla comrades were devoted nationalists, but their understanding of economics
was remarkably patchy. They believed that Korea should make the economy
as self-sustaining as possible in order to minimize the political leverage
that foreign states could use over it.

It was officially assumed that North Korea can and should produce
everything of economic significance within its own borders. The leadership thought that only imports of raw materials were ideologically permissible, but even they should be kept at a bare minimum. It was also
believed that provinces, cities, and even individual factories should take
care of their own logistical requirements whenever possible, expecting
little from the central government.

Sometimes this insistence on self-reliance might have appeared comical to an outside observer. For example, while reading through a North
Korean newspaper, I once came across an admiring report about workers
at a Pyongyang granary who found a patriotic and politically correct solution for one of their logistics problems. They needed a diesel locomotive
to move railway carriages filled with grain. Instead of ordering it from the
state, they used the granary's small workshop to manufacture the locomotive. Their "revolutionary spirit of self-reliance" was lauded by the report,
but it said nothing about the quality and reliability of this curious hand-
made contraption. This story reminds one of the notorious wooden trucks

the Chinese villagers were ordered to make during the Great Leap Forward (and under virtually the same slogan of "self-reliance"). The North Korean media of Kim Il Sung's era unceasingly published eulogies to such dubious triumphs.

Taking into consideration the small size of the North Korean economy, such deliberate rejection of economic specialization was a dangerous misjudgment. Among other things, this policy was aimed at reducing North Korea's dependence on foreign powers and—above all—on its major sponsors, the USSR and China. However, it probably yielded the opposite result: by making the cumbersome North Korean economy even less efficient, this policy actually might have *increased* North Korea's dependency on Soviet and Chinese assistance.

Indeed, Soviet and, to a lesser extent, Chinese aid was vital for the survival of the North Korean system. The scale of this support can never be estimated with real precision, since much of this aid was provided indirectly, through subsidized trade. For example, Soviet foreign trade organizations were frequently ordered by the Kremlin to accept substandard North Korean goods in lieu of payment for Soviet merchandise, which would have been much more expensive had the market mechanism been in operation. Most of the trade between North Korea and its sponsors was nonreciprocal—essentially it was aid, thinly disguised as trade. The Soviet Union was sending to North Korea spare parts for MiG jet fighters, crude oil, and Lada cars whilst being paid with canned pickles and bad tobacco that nobody wanted to smoke. The relations with other countries of the Communist bloc were not much different. It would be just a minor exaggeration to say that if we define "trade" as reciprocal exchange in goods, Kim Il Sung's North Korea *never* conducted much trade as commonly understood, but rather swapped geopolitical concessions for economic subsidies.

As long as the Soviet Union and China, driven by their own geopolitical considerations, were willing to pump this aid in, the North Korean economy remained afloat, even though its growth rate was decelerating. Nonetheless, since the early 1960s the very existence of Soviet and Chinese aid was seldom if ever admitted openly. Perhaps not only the average

North Korean but even the decision makers in Pyongyang did not fully appreciate how great their dependency on Soviet giveaways had become. The sudden termination of this aid in the early 1990s therefore delivered a mortal and sudden blow to Kim Il Sung's North Korea. A new society grew out of the ruins of Kim Il Sung's "national Stalinism" and—in spite of some superficial continuity from the previous era—this new North Korea was in fact very different.

Two Decades of Crisis

The system built by Kim Il Sung in North Korea was fatally flawed—it was unsustainable economically. It could function only as long as Moscow and Beijing were willing to provide Pyongyang with systematic aid. Kim Il Sung's "Stalinism with national characteristics" consequently did not outlive the abrupt end of the Cold War, which plunged North Korea into an acute crisis. Many observers initially expected that North Korea would share the fate of other Communist regimes and either collapse (like the Communist countries of Eastern Europe) or initiate market-oriented reforms (like Vietnam and China). These expectations did not materialize: North Korea neither collapsed nor reformed itself. But a lack of government-initiated reform did not mean that North Korea remained unchanged. Post-1994 North Korea is very different from the country established and run by Kim Il Sung. It might be run by the same people (or their children and nephews) and the state might sound the same, but its society is very, very different.

AND THEN THE WORLD CHANGED

In 1985 Mikhail Gorbachev became the general secretary of the Communist Party of the Soviet Union. He immediately embarked on a program of radical social, economic, and political reforms that triggered the collapse of the Soviet Union in 1991. Around that time, China's leaders learned how Communist sloganeering can be seamlessly combined with a rather Dickensian—but very efficient—version of capitalism. In turn, by the late

1980s, relations between the USSR and the PRC, which had been charac-terized by rivalry and discord since the 1950s, became cooperative. The rivalry between the USSR and the United States also lost its sharpness. In the early 1990s both the Soviet elite and the Soviet public saw the United States not as an enemy to contain and undermine, but rather as a shining example to be admired and emulated (such a rosy view did not survive for long in Moscow, but this is irrelevant to our story).

Considerations that conditioned Soviet (and Chinese) policy toward North Korea for decades suddenly disappeared. Moscow and Beijing policy makers saw no more need to maintain North Korea as a buffer zone against the United States or to buy its neutrality in the Sino-Soviet schism. Concurrently, the economic transformation of the USSR meant that newly independent Russian enterprises, formerly state operations, were no longer willing to ship their wares to North Korea for nothing. Russian businesses would be (and still are) quite happy to sell spare parts for MiG fighters or crude oil, but they expected to be paid for their shipments in hard cur-rency. North Korea has no hard currency. Sponsoring Pyongyang there-fore became both politically unnecessary and economically unsustainable.

Within the first perestroika years bilateral trade between North Korea and the Soviet Union decreased roughly tenfold: from $2.56 billion in 1990 to a mere $0.14 billion in 1994. Incidentally, it has remained at roughly this level ever since ($0.11 billion in 2011)—further proof that without state subsidies and political pressure, Russian companies are not terribly interested in doing business with North Korea.[1] Since North Korea's trade with Communist countries was essentially aid in disguise, the dramatic drop in trade meant a comparable decline in the availability of free or subsidized products.

The start of the new era in the North is usually linked to Kim Il Sung's death in July 1994. However, the social transformation of the 1990s had almost nothing to do with this political change at the top. Some of the measures undertaken by Kim Il Sung in the last years of his long rule were strikingly similar to what would become the norm under his son. None-theless, for the sake of convenience we will describe this new era in North Korean history as the "era of Kim Jong Il."

The sudden disruption of foreign aid led to the collapse of the state economy. Being deprived of free spare parts and subsidized oil, many industries stopped functioning. Since all vital economic statistics in North Korea are a state secret, the exact scale of this economic collapse is disputable. Nonetheless, it seems that by the year 2000, industrial output in the state economy was approximately half of what it was in 1990. Officially, most factories were not closed and employees were still required to attend their place of work daily. Most workers remained idle at work, however, with nothing to do.

From the early 1990s, when official corruption started to grow exponentially, the most savvy and entrepreneurial among the managers of state enterprises began to make money by selling their nonoperating equipment to China as scrap metal. In more extreme cases, old factories, often built in the colonial times, became empty shells, devoid of any equipment.

In many regards, North Korean infrastructure has not changed much from late colonial times. With the exception of a few highways (off-limits to local traffic), paved roads are very rare outside major cities and the railways continue to make occasional use of steam locomotives of 1930s vintage. However, in the mid-1990s infrastructure suffered much more than it had up until that point. Frequent electricity outages meant trains that mainly relied on electric locomotives could be late by days—a remarkable circumstance for a country as large as Pennsylvania.

But the worst blow was felt by the agricultural sector. Like nearly all Soviet-style agricultural systems, that of North Korea was inherently and hopelessly inefficient. Modern farmers usually work well if they toil upon their own land and have some control over the harvest. This was not the case in North Korea, where the state owned the land and directly managed it in ways that even Joseph Stalin himself would see as excessive.

Structural inefficiencies were exacerbated by a multitude of technical and political errors. To start with, North Korean agriculture had become heavily reliant on the use of chemical fertilizer. Initially this policy decision made some sense because North Korea inherited highly developed fertilizer production facilities from the colonial period. But while this was the case, production itself was dependent on the supply of Soviet aid and was highly energy-intensive.

Another mistake was the heavy reliance on artificial irrigation that was made possible by the existence of large pumping stations. In some cases water had to be first pumped up a few hundred meters above the level of its natural source and only then directed toward the rice paddy fields. This worked well as long as electricity was in plentiful, cheap supply. The decline of electricity production, however, made this system unsustainable.

Last but not least, the ill-conceived idea of terraced fields contributed to the natural disasters of the years 1995 through 1996. This idea was once loudly lauded as a great invention of Kim Il Sung's personal genius. Terraced fields might be perfectly suitable for the farming conditions of southern China, but not in North Korea—as North Korean agricultural managers learned in due time and to their peril. Terracing increased soil erosion and made areas under cultivation more vulnerable to torrential rains. Such rains hit North Korea in the summer of 1995, and then again in 1996.

Official propaganda always blames subsequent events on these rains, which are described as "a once a century natural calamity." The rainfall was indeed heavier than usual, but it is worth noting that the same rains produced almost no impact on the agriculture of South Korea, where the only notable result of the alleged "unprecedented natural calamity" was a marginal increase in the price of cabbage and onions. For the North, the floods of 1995–1996 were the proverbial straw that broke the camel's back.

In order to feed its population, North Korea needs 5.0–5.5 million metric tons of grain (the exact figure is a subject of some debate between experts). Until the early 1990s the North Korean farmers managed to produce that much. Then the situation began to deteriorate. Deprived of fuel, electricity, and fertilizer, and manned by workers who had little incentive to care about the future harvest, the system collapsed. The 1996 harvest was a mere 2.5–2.8 million metric tons—half of what would have been enough to keep the population fed.

For the average North Korean this collapse of agriculture meant a sudden termination of the PDS (public distribution system), which had been the major or even the only source of food for the North Koreans since 1957. From 1993 to 1994, rations were increasingly delayed and/or delivered only partially. The delays began in more remote areas of the countryside, but soon spread to major cities. After the floods, the PDS rations almost completely stopped. Even the privileged population of Pyongyang was issued partial rations, and there were periods (for example, in 1998) when distribution completely failed. Outside of Pyongyang only party cadres, police personnel, military officials, and the workers at military factories continued to receive their rations, and even those privileged groups did not necessarily receive full allowances in the years between 1996 and 2000.

For the average North Korean, this was a disaster. A twice-monthly trip to the grain distribution center was as normal as a weekend drive to a supermarket for an American family. Famine would ensue, and soon took on disastrous dimensions.

The number of people who perished in the Great North Korean Famine of 1996–1999 will probably never be known with absolute certainty. Some NGOs put the number as high as three million whilst the North Korean government in confidential communications with certain foreign guests put the figure as low as 250,000. The first estimate is clearly a serious exaggeration whilst the second is a face-saving underestimate. At the time of writing, there have been two serious attempts to estimate the scale of this disaster impartially. In 2001 Daniel Goodkind and Loraine West concluded that excessive deaths most likely numbered between 600,000 and one million in the period from 1995 to 2000.[2] In 2010, analyzing officially published results of the most recent 2008 North Korean population census, Pak Keong-Suk estimated that excessive deaths reached 880,000 in the 1993–2008 period, with the loss of about 490,000 being attributable to mortality increase, about 290,000 to fertility decline, and about 100,000 to outbound migration and its effect on fertility.[3] In 2011 Goodkind and West (together with Peter Johnson) revised their earlier estimates of excess deaths downward to 490,000.[4]

Even if we accept the lowest estimate of 450,000–500,000, it still means that some 2.5 percent of the entire population perished in the disaster. This is roughly equal to the ratio of Chinese farmers who perished from starvation during the Great Leap Forward of the early 1960s. In other words, it was the largest humanitarian disaster East Asia had seen for decades. Nevertheless, the majority of North Koreans survived the famine. They did so by creating new ways of life, socially and economically. In essence, the North Korean people rediscovered capitalism while the North Korean state had little choice but to relax its iron grip over the populace.

THE SORRY FATE OF KATYA SINTSOVA

Have you ever heard of Katya Sintsova? The beautiful Russian girl whose naïve admiration for capitalism and its debased "democracy" brought ruin to her and her entire family? A girl whose sorry and lamentable fate is so reminiscent of the tragic fate of her country, which deviated from the true path of Socialism?

Katya Sintsova is a fictional (and highly improbable) character who appears in a North Korean short story, "The Fifth Photo." This short story was produced by a North Korean writer named Rim Hwawon and is quite representative of the current North Korean writings about the collapse of Soviet and Eastern European Communism.

As Tatiana Gabroussenko remarked in her soon-to-be published study of this peculiar kind of North Korean fiction, in the 1940s and 1950s the Russians were portrayed in North Korean literature as the leaders and guides helping their Korean comrades. In the 2000s, however, it is the Koreans who are the shining example, the embodiment of Socialist virtues, who are looked upon as advisers and as leaders. Russians are nowadays conversely presented as weak and naïve but still basically decent, noble human beings who flourish under the wise guidance of their North Korean friends.

For instance, in one of these stories the CIA plants a bomb on a US passenger airliner. The reason for this operation (and as every North Korean knows this is the type of operation the CIA does frequently) is to kill a Russian scientist who refused to cooperate with the US military-industrial complex. In the story the Russian and his fellow passengers were lucky to have a North Korean on the same plane. The North Korean takes control of the situation and saves his fellow travelers from another vicious American plot.

Of these stories, Rim Hwawon's "The Fifth Photo" is quite typical. Katya Sintsova, its main character, is a beautiful Russian girl who comes from a family with impeccable Communist credentials. Her great-grandfather died a heroic death in 1919 during the Russian Civil War, her grandfather sacrificed his life fighting the Nazis, and her father was a selfless and hardworking party bureaucrat of the Brezhnev era. Her brother also became a top bureaucrat in the Moscow Party Youth Committee and was also equally selfless and hardworking.

Katya was accepted to a top university due to her exceptional gifts in the arts. But at the university she fell under the spell of the wrong ideas.

She began to interact with people whose ideological bent was less than healthy, and she even interacted with foreigners (the latter behavior is seen by Rim Hwawon as especially outrageous). She is upset about the contents of party meetings being so boring and she is overcome by materialism and a lust for change.

An American seduces and impregnates her, after which she has an abortion. Meanwhile, her father dies, his last words being "Long live the Communist Party!" Katya loves him and feels sorry about his death, but still considers him an old fool. This is when she meets the book's North Korean narrator, to whom she tries to sell photos from her precious family archive.

The narrator is an example of flawless revolutionary virtue, and his own daughter is free from all the frivolous but dangerous ideas that have ruined Katya's life—the exemplary North Korean girl dreams only of serving the Party and Leader better. The narrator's sons are brave officers of the Korean People's Army, always ready to fight the US imperialists. They are even treated to the highest honor imaginable, being granted an audience with the Dear Leader Marshal Kim Jong Il.

Katya, meanwhile, travels overseas in search of her American lover. An awful discovery awaits her: he was not really an American, but the

(continued)

descendant of an anti-Communist Russian landlord family. Almost a century before their lands were nationalized, the vicious landlords' family has spent all their time dreaming of revenge. Katya's seduction was actually a part of a plot aimed at taking the lands back from the farmers and giving it to greedy and cruel landlords.

Katya Sintsova's sufferings don't end with this awful discovery. While alone and helpless in the brutal West, she suffers a car accident and loses a leg. In order to survive she becomes a prostitute serving perverts in the city of Munich.

The message of this story is simple and easy to understand: Katya is Russia herself. She was lured into a trap by the Western propaganda and scheming descendants of landlords, she was fooled into selling her great heritage, and she ended up a pitiful prostitute at the bottom of the merciless capitalist heap. The story is written to serve as a clear warning to North Koreans, who should not listen to the seductive voices from abroad and should remain on guard against their enemy.

CAPITALISM REBORN

In postfamine North Korea the old state-run and state-owned economy was replaced by a great multitude of private economic activities usually associated with what is described as a "black market"—somewhat misleadingly, as we shall see below. It was recently estimated that between 1998 and 2008, the share of income from informal economic activities reached 78 percent of the total income of North Korean households.[5]

However, as said above, North Korea's social transformation is rather different from near-contemporaneous developments in China and the former Soviet Union in that it was neither initiated nor endorsed by the authorities. For political reasons to be discussed later, Kim Il Sung's socioeconomic system still remains an ideal for the North Korean elite. Nonetheless, this commitment does not go beyond words most of the time: the elite lack the resources and resolve that would make a revival of Kim Il Sung's "national Stalinism" possible.

When rations suddenly stopped coming, people began to learn ways to cope with the new situation—the only alternative being death by starvation. For farmers the most natural reaction was to start growing their own food. This was not that easy because, unlike their Chinese counterparts, North Korean bureaucrats showed no inclination to disband the notoriously inefficient state farms. The state farms' fields were therefore usually guarded, preventing farmers from using the best arable land for their production. A majority of farmers had to look for alternative places to farm for themselves.

North Korea is a mountainous country and thus it is not too difficult to find a steep slope that is not used for regular agriculture. A quick look at satellite pictures shows the presence of numerous small fields of irregular shapes and sizes located in the mountains. These are *so'to'ji* (literally "small fields"), the private plots of North Korea's farmers and inhabitants of smaller towns. Generally, the further away one lives from major administrative and political centers, the easier it is to develop such a field. In more remote parts of the country, so'to'ji now produce more than half of the harvest but the nationwide average seems to be close to 20 percent.

While farmers were working on their illicit plots, the urban population reacted to the new situation by discovering private commerce. Most urban families began by bartering household items for food, but soon switched to trade and household production. Beginning in 1995, huge markets began to grow in North Korea's cities. They became the focal point of economic life in the country. Millions of North Koreans, women in particular, began to earn the family's income through trade and household handicraft production.

Women make up the majority of North Korea's market operators. Market vendors in North Korea are by no means the kind of street toughs one might encounter in the black markets of other countries. Instead, they are largely housewives and mothers who make and sell to keep the family alive.

This is partly due to North Korean society itself. For decades, the North Korean state required every able-bodied male to be employed by a state enterprise. Married women of working age, however, were allowed to stay at home as full-time housewives.

When Kim Il Sung's system began to fall apart in the early 1990s, men continued to go to work. People expected that sooner or later things would return to what they thought of as "normal"—that is, to the old Stalinist system. They knew from their experience that people who have at one time shown disloyalty to the state—for instance, those who collaborated with the South Korean authorities during the Korean War—were assigned a bad sŏngbun. Thus, not only those people, but also their children and grandchildren, faced many official restrictions. Men believed that it would be wise to keep their "official" jobs for the sake of the family's future. On top of these class anxieties, men also faced massive pressure from the state's lower officials. An absentee worker ran real chances of being sent to a prison for a few months of "labor reeducation."

The situation for women was markedly different. They had spare time, and their involvement with private trade was seen as politically less dangerous—precisely because of the patriarchal nature of a society where only men really mattered. In some cases women began by selling household items they could do without. Eventually, these activities developed into larger businesses, and today some three-quarters of North Korean market vendors are women.

As one would expect, soon thereafter, in the late 1990s, more successful businessmen (or rather businesswomen) moved from retail trade to whole-sale trade. In many cases they were the members of once discriminated-against groups who benefited most from the new situation. For example, until the 1990s, it was a major handicap for any career-minded North Korean to have relatives overseas. In the 1990s the opposite suddenly became the case. Relatives overseas, especially in China, could often provide small amounts of capital (quite large by then North Korean standards), give sound business advice, or even create a formal or informal joint venture.

A typical story is of my acquaintance, a young school teacher who, in the early 1990s, was asked by visiting Chinese relatives to buy them a large quantity of dried fish. She discovered that in merely a few days she earned well over her official *annual* salary, and decided to become a professional trader. Being a woman, she could leave her job without repercussions.

By the early 2000s some wholesalers had large sums at their disposal; they sometimes invested in new types of enterprise—eateries, storage facilities, semi-legal transportation companies. Indeed, the growth of the market that was initially centered around small-scale retail activities soon produced many kinds of associated private ventures.

The restaurant industry is illustrative in this regard. Between 1996 and 1997 the state-run restaurant industry collapsed everywhere except for a few major cities. Private capital, however, almost immediately revived it, and most North Korean restaurants are now run by private entrepreneurs. Officially, they are not supposed to exist, and such eateries are technically state-owned. According to official papers, an eatery is owned by the state and managed by the relevant department of the municipal government. However, this is a legal fiction. A private investor makes an informal deal with municipal officials, promising them a kickback, and he/she then hires workers and buys equipment. It is assumed that a certain amount of the earnings will be transferred to the state budget. In return the private owner runs a business at his/her discretion, investing or pocketing profits. A 2009 study came to the conclusion that some 58.5 percent of all restaurants in North Korea are de facto privately owned.[6]

Similar trends exist in the retail industry. While the fiction of state ownership is maintained, many shops are, essentially, private. The manager-cum-owner buys merchandise from wholesalers as well as (technically) state-owned suppliers, and then sells it at a profit. The earnings are partially transferred to the state, but largely pocketed by the owner himself (or rather, herself). The above-mentioned study estimated that in 2009 some 51.3 percent of shops were actually private retail operations.[7]

Transportation underwent similar changes. A large number of trucks and buses that traverse the dangerous dirty roads of North Korea are owned privately. Private investors discovered that grossly inadequate transportation facilities were a major bottleneck the emerging North Korean merchant class had to deal with. Investors began to buy used trucks and buses in China and bring these vehicles to the North. In the North, the vehicle would be registered as the property of a government company or agency. The actual owner would pay the manager of this agency an agreed amount of money, usually on a monthly basis. Interestingly, the amount of money is contingent on the agency/company type. The registration of one's truck with a military unit or a secret police department is most expensive, while some humble civilian agency (like, say, a tractor repair workshop) would charge the least. Owners sometimes prefer to pay more, however, because military registration plates might sometimes come in handy with the police.

Large transportation companies have developed: I met a person who owned seven trucks in North Korea. He used these trucks to move salt from salt farms on the coast to wholesale markets (incidentally, salt farms are private as well). This man also augmented his income by moving large sacks of cement that were stolen by workers from the few cement plants continuing to function in post-1994 North Korea. It was a nice income but he expressed his surprise at the ingenuity of workers who managed to somehow steal such a large amount of cement.

Indeed, one of the major problems for the state has been the growth of criminal and semi-criminal activities. Workers and managers steal from their factories everything that can be sold on the private market. The large-scale looting of archeological sites from the Koryo (10th–14th century AD) and Choson (14th–19th century AD) periods became a problem in spite of all efforts to stop it. People responsible for antique smuggling or equipment sale often faced severe penalties; there were even rumors about public executions of such people. Nonetheless, the temptation was far too large.

Drug production started to boom around 2005. In earlier days, drugs were produced for clandestine export by government agencies, but private business also discovered the great money-making potential of addictive substances—and officials are not too eager to enforce the bans and regulations (they usually get a slice of the profits). Private production usually concentrated on what is known as "ice," that is, methamphetamines. Drugs were marketed domestically and also exported to China, where authorities had to step up border control. "Ice" became surprisingly popular among younger North Koreans, so much so that in 2010, foreign visitors spotted antidrug posters in Pyongyang colleges. Incidentally, around the same time, the old state-sponsored drug production program was scaled down. Frankly, the entire project obviously did the regime more harm than good, damaging its international reputation while bringing only small payoffs.[8]

China features prominently in the unofficial North Korean economy (and in the official economy as well, as we will see below). Nearly all trade links either begin or end in China. Part of this trade is completely unofficial, while other transactions are entirely legal. North Korean merchants mainly import consumption goods from China—garments, shoes, TV sets, and so on. Food also constitutes a significant part of North Korean imports from China.

Paradoxically, thanks to this, the years of crisis became a time when the average North Korean began to dress well—or, at least, better than in earlier times. In Kim Il Sung's days most people were clad in badly tailored Mao suits or military uniforms; now, even in the countryside, people you see on the street are dressed colorfully, usually in cheap Chinese imported clothes.

To balance the trade account, North Korean merchants export to China that which can be sold there. Apart from minerals, which are still usually handled by the state, they sell seafood, traditional delicacies, and Chinese medical herbs as well as quite exotic items—like, for instance, "frog oil," a fatty substance extracted from live frogs of certain species that have to be harvested under special conditions.

China's ubiquity in the Northern economy has resulted in the "Yuanization" of the market: large-scale payments in postfamine North Korea are normally made in foreign currency. Dollars, yen, and euros are not unknown, but it is the Chinese yuan that reigns supreme. This situation has led to the emergence of money dealers who trade in foreign currencies, and are also sometimes known as "loan sharks," providing loans at the annual interest rate of 100 percent or more.

A special role in the new economy is played by a particular form of entrepreneurial activity that is neither private nor state—the so-called foreign currency earning enterprise (FCEE). Such enterprises have existed since Kim Il Sung's era but greatly increased in number, size, and reach from the late 1990s.

Unlike the Soviet Union, in North Korea, foreign trade was never under the exclusive control of a single state agency. In accordance with the "spirit of self-reliance," large North Korean companies and influential state agencies were allowed to sell anything that could be sold on the international market. They would then use the earned foreign currency to import what couldn't be produced domestically. This practice was greatly expanded in the late 1990s when provinces, ministries, and even the military and police began to set up their own FCEEs. These enterprises did not usually limit themselves to what was produced in-house, but looked for anything that could be sold for a profit.

Technically, the FCEEs are owned by the state, but they hire adventurous and entrepreneurial people whose job is to use the company's official clout and connections to earn as much money as possible. It is implicitly understood that these people pocket a large share of their earnings, but as long as they know their limit and provide their supervisors with sufficient kickbacks, profiteering is tolerated.

THE STATE WITHERS AWAY

The collapse of the state-run economy had far-reaching political and social consequences. In order to function properly, Kim Il Sung's system required a small army of enforcers and indoctrinators. A considerable workforce was necessary to ensure that every North Korean slept in a home where he or she was registered, did not travel to another city without a proper permit, and did not skip a self-criticism session. In the early 1990s the government discovered that it did not have the resources to reward the zeal of these overseers and indoctrinators. Of course, the regime did what it could to keep police officers and party officials on the payroll and issued them rations even in the middle of famine. Nonetheless, there were too many such people to be taken care of properly. Thus, in the mid-1990s, a police sergeant, a clerk in the local government office, or a low-level indoctrinator faced a real threat of starvation. Like the average factory worker or schoolteacher, these small cogs of the bureaucratic machine depended on

PDS rations for their food. When the PDS shrank dramatically, they were not considered important enough to remain on a new, much shorter, list of distribution targets.

A number of my North Korean interlocutors state that in the famine years between 1996 and 1999, people who had the highest chances of dying were honest officials and clerks: those who did not take bribes, did not abuse their official position, and took the regime's promises seriously. However, most petty bureaucrats made a rational choice and adjusted their behavior to the new situation. They began to turn a blind eye to illegal activities. In many cases they had to be bribed to adopt such an attitude, but in other instances they did so out of sympathy for the common people or because they saw no use in enforcing obviously pointless regulations.

One of the best examples is the near complete loss of control over domestic travel. Theoretically, up to the time of writing, North Koreans are expected to apply for a travel permit if they plan an overnight trip outside the borders of their county or city. Starting from around 1996 to 1997, however, these controls became easy to circumvent. Nowadays one can bribe a police official and obtain a permit for a relatively small fee, the equivalent of $2–3. Alternatively, one can choose a cheaper but more troublesome option, and depart without any travel permit. For that, one must be ready to bribe policemen at checkpoints and in trains. Only the city of Pyongyang has not been touched by this relaxation, remaining off-limits to people from the countryside who do not have proper papers—and such papers are still difficult to get.

Sometimes, North Koreans could and can get away with what used to be seen as political crimes. For example, possession of a tunable radio set has been a political crime for decades. This still technically remains the case, but nowadays a bribe of roughly $100 can buy a way out of punishment for someone unlucky enough to have been caught while listening to such a radio (police would probably even give the offending radio set back to the culprit). Of course, $100 is by no means a trivial amount of money for the average North Korean, since the average monthly salary in 1995–2010 fluctuated around the $2–3 mark (the actual monthly pay, however, was and is significantly higher—some $15–20 a month—since a majority of the North Koreans make most of their income in the unofficial economy).

Another result of the new situation was the near collapse of control over the Sino—North Korean border. Smugglers have taken advantage of the situation, paying bribes to ensure that border guards always look the other way when necessary. For a large-scale smuggler, a bribe might be as high as a few hundred dollars, but for this amount he or she would be able to move sacks of valuable merchandise across the border (even being helped by the border guards themselves). Apart from smuggling, the government has relaxed its attitude toward official cross-border trips, which are usually justified by the need to visit relatives in China but often are of a commercial nature. From 2003, for the first time in North Korean history, the authorities began to issue passports to North Koreans who went overseas as private citizens—provided they have the right connections, good family backgrounds, and the resources to pay the necessary bribe.

Some regulations (often truly absurd) are safely ignored by the very people who are supposed to enforce them. For example, theoretically, North Korean women in cities are not allowed to wear slacks because such attire is considered to not befit a woman and "goes against the good habits and beautiful traditions of Korea." Women are also theoretically forbidden to ride bicycles in the city. There are even bans of some "subversive" types of haircuts. Police have occasionally enforced these nonsensical bans in the past, but from around the mid-1990s, became increasingly uninterested. From time to time, ideological authorities will remind people of the moral harm that might be caused by a woman clad shamelessly in slacks, prompting police to levy fines on violators of the ban for a few weeks. These kinds of campaigns never last long, however, and seldom bear fruit.

Most of the above-mentioned changes are spontaneous in nature, being driven primarily by greed/need as well as by a loss of ideological fervor on the part of those who upheld the status quo. In some cases, however, the relaxation has been initiated by the authorities. For example, around 1996, an illegal border crossing into China, hitherto a serious crime, was reclassified as a relatively minor offense. Around the same time, the Kim Il Sung—era family responsibility principle was relaxed. In the past, if a North Korean was arrested for political crimes, his or her entire family would have to be shipped to a prison camp. Now, such measures are used selectively, only in cases of crimes considered especially dangerous.

The general relaxation is quite palpable for somebody who has been dealing with North Korea for decades. Nowadays, North Koreans are less afraid of foreigners and more willing to discuss potentially dangerous matters. It doesn't usually mean that they will deviate from the official line too openly, but the limits of what is permissible have clearly widened in the last 15 to 20 years. North Korean refugees also admit that in Kim Jong Il's North Korea, one often could do or say with impunity something that would get you imprisoned or killed in Kim Il Sung's era.

Take the story of Yi Yŏng-guk, the former bodyguard of the Dear Leader himself. Disappointed in the North Korean system, he fled to China and attempted to defect to South Korea. He was caught by North Korean agents in China and sent back home. In the not-so-distant times of Kim Il Sung, the fate of such a high-profile defector would have been sadly predictable: torture and death awaited any person who betrayed the *personal* trust of the Great Leader. But in the liberal 1990s, Yi was treated with surprising leniency: he was sent to a prison camp and then released (yes, released!) following the intercession of Kim Jong Il himself. He used the opportunity to repeat his escape attempt and reached Seoul.[9]

THE NEW RICH

North Korea is a poor place, no doubt. Nonetheless, 2012 Pyongyang has a booming restaurant scene and the traffic on its broad streets— once notoriously empty—is steadily increasing in volume. Well-fed North Koreans are frequenting newly opened sushi bars and beer houses as well as a local hamburger joint. On the streets of the North Korean capital, one can see a lot of visibly undernourished people, but also a number of women clad in designer clothes.

(continued)

These sights can be encountered not only in Pyongyang but also in a number of other major North Korean cities. The growth of "grassroots capitalism" predictably brought in a remarkable income inequality.

Who are they—the North Korean new rich? How did they make money—and do they spend this money nowadays?

Take, for example, Mr. Kim, who is in his early 40s. Mr. Kim is a private owner of a gold mine. The gold mine is officially registered as a state enterprise. Technically, a foreign trade company owns it, and in turn it was managed by the financial department of the Party Central Committee. However, this is a legal fiction, pure and simple: Mr. Kim, once a mid-level police official, made some initial capital through bribes and smuggling, while his cousin had made a minor fortune through selling counterfeit Western tobacco.

They then used their money to grease the palms of bureaucrats, and they took over an old gold mine that had ceased operation in the 1980s. They hired workers, bought equipment, and restarted operations. The gold dust was sold (strictly speaking, illegally) to Chinese traders. The cousins agreed with the bureaucrats from the foreign trade company on how much money they should pay them—roughly between 30 to 40 percent. They then used the rest to run the business and enjoy life.

One step below this, we can see even humbler people like Ms. Young, once an engineer at a state factory. In the mid-1990s she began trading in Chinese second-hand dresses. By 2005 she was running a number of workshops that employed a few dozen women who made copies of Chinese garments using Chinese cloth, zippers, and buttons. Some of the materials were smuggled across the border, while another part was purchased quite legally, largely from a large market in the city of Rason (a special economic zone that can be visited by Chinese merchants almost freely).

Ms. Young technically remained an employee of a nonfunctioning state factory, which she was absent from for months on end. She had to pay for the privilege of missing work and indoctrination sessions, deducting some $40 as her monthly "donation." This is an impressive sum when compared with her official salary of merely $2.

The North Korean new rich might occasionally feel insecure. They might be afraid of the state, because pretty much everything they do is in breach of some article of the North Korean criminal code. It is a serious breach indeed—technically any of the above-described persons can be sent to face an execution squad the moment the authorities change their mind. They provide officials with generous kickbacks, and in recent years massive crackdowns have been infrequent. Yet the fear lingers nonetheless.

It is, however, difficult to say that they try to keep a low profile. On the contrary, nowadays one can see a lot of conspicuous consumption in North Korea.

It is no surprise that the new rich enjoy consumption. Some kinds of consumption activities are impossible—for example, overseas trips are out of the question, and domestic tourism seems to be unfashionable: North Koreans, rich or poor, usually travel out of necessity, not for pleasure.

However, there are many outlets that cater to the needs of the "masters of money" (*tonju*), as North Korean entrepreneurs are known. The new rich frequent restaurants where a good meal would cost roughly as much as the average North Korean family makes in a couple of weeks. They buy and renovate houses—technically the sale of real estate is illegal in North Korea, but in the last two decades North Koreans have developed many techniques that allow the circumvention of these restrictions. The new rich buy all kinds of household appliances, flat screen TVs, computers, large fridges, and motorbikes. Even private cars—an ultimate status symbol, a North Korean equivalent to a private jet—have begun to appear, and since around 2009 one can see traffic jams on the streets of Pyongyang, once famously empty.

In good old Confucian spirit, the new rich invest in the education of their children. A good teacher of a popular subject—like, say, English or Chinese—might earn a decent income nowadays. Less practical subjects are also in demand, although piano and dance lessons are deemed suitable for girls only.

TAKING THE EXIT OPTION: NOT AN EXODUS YET, BUT . . .

From the mid-1990s, North Koreans began to move to China in large numbers. It was not that difficult because most of the length of both the Yalu and the Tumen is shallow, narrow, and frozen in winter.

This being the case, between 1998 and 1999, when the famine was at its height, it was estimated that anywhere from 150,000 to 195,000 North Koreans were hiding in China.[10] After 2005 the numbers shrank dramatically, but it is estimated that at any given moment, there are still between 20,000 and 40,000 North Korean refugees hiding in China.[11] Most of these people hide in villages and towns along the border, where ethnic Koreans constitute a majority of the population. Refugees do all kinds of odd jobs that were avoided by the locals: they wait tables at cheap eateries, work at construction sites, and labor in the timber industry. Since women constitute a majority of refugees, many of them cohabit with Chinese men— sometimes being abducted but more frequently through personal choice.

Many of these unions result in disaster, while others work just fine. Indeed, it might benefit both sides: a Chinese-Korean man of advanced age and moderate income gets a wife, while a North Korean woman gets a sense of security and a standard of living unthinkable back home. The local Chinese authorities usually turn a blind eye to such unions, especially if the couple has children. Nonetheless, a North Korean common-law wife (such unions cannot be registered officially) is still not free from the worst fear of any North Korean refugee in China: arrest and deportation.

Until the mid-1990s, every North Korean who had crossed over into China and was unfortunate enough to be extradited back would face a few years of imprisonment and, upon release, lifelong discrimination. This is not the case anymore because border crossing itself is seen as a minor offense. When people are extradited from China, they are usually investigated for a week or two (this investigation usually involves some beating). Investigators want to make certain that the suspects have had no contacts with South Koreans and non-Chinese foreigners during their stay in China, and that they were not involved with any Christian missionary group. If no such suspicious connections are discovered, the extradited refugee spends a few months in a milder type of labor camp and is then released. Upon release, many of them flee again. After all, they often have families and jobs back in China.

Some refugees decide to move further, to South Korea, though this is not as simple as it sounds. Long gone are the times when every North Korean who decided to defect and was lucky to get overseas could just walk into the nearest South Korean consulate or embassy and inform the cheerful staff that he had just "chosen freedom," as the Cold War cliché went. Nowadays, while a two-star general of the North Korean air force or a district party secretary can still count on an enthusiastic welcome, the same does not hold for a middle-aged housewife from a rural area—and such a housewife is the typical defector of the past decade. As a rule (there are exceptions), South Korean missions in China prefer not to deal with the average refugee. This is explained in terms of a fear of diplomatic complications with China, but the South Korean government also is not all that enthusiastic about the increasing number of refugees in the South. At the same time, the fiction of "one Korea," still maintained by both Seoul and Pyongyang, means that every single North Korean is automatically eligible for South Korean citizenship and consular protection. For a majority of the refugees the only way to reach South Korea is to get to a third country (usually Thailand or Mongolia) where South Korean diplomatic missions, sometimes reluctantly, process refugees and issue them with travel documents and air tickets to Seoul.

This, however, means that a refugee has to traverse all of China first, then illegally cross the Chinese border into Mongolia or Laos. Such a trip is almost impossible for the average refugee who speaks poor if any Chinese and has little money and no local knowledge. The only way, therefore, is to make a deal with a professional escape specialist known as a "broker." Such a broker assembles a group of 5 to 15 aspiring refugees, arranges transportation and safe accommodation, and then escorts them to China's southern border (if the final destination is Bangkok) or to Mongolia. There, he or she arranges a border crossing and then accompanies the refugees on their perilous trip across the Gobi Desert or the jungles of Laos.

Brokers usually do not work for the actualization of some lofty ideal. Some of them might have ideological convictions, but in the main, defection has long become a commercial operation, pure and simple. For a "no thrills defection," one must pay between $2,000 and $3,000, while a VIP version of the service would cost between $10,000 and $15,000. This expensive option would involve a fake South Korean or Chinese passport, North Korean border guards escorting the defector across the border, and a comfortable air trip from a major Chinese airport straight to South Korea.[12] The cost of even the cheapest defection is exorbitant for the average North Korean refugee in China whose wages are between $50 and $100 a month. Usually the sum is provided by relatives in South Korea or elsewhere overseas, most frequently by a family member who has managed to defect to the South first and probably now waits tables in Seoul restaurants (as we will see, most defectors are not exactly successful in South Korea).

As of early 2012, there were some 23,000 North Korean refugees living in South Korea. It doesn't sound like a large figure, especially if we consider that between 1961 and 1989—during the years of the Berlin Wall—an average of 23,000 East Germans crossed into West Germany *every single year*. However, it sounds far more impressive if we remember that as recently as 2000 there were merely 1,100 refugees residing in the South. This is by no means an exodus, but, for the first time since the end of the Korean War, there emerged a significant group of North Koreans who managed to get away from "the loving care of the fatherly leader."

These people are very different from the Communist bloc refugees who arrived in the West during the Cold War. Cold War refugees from the Eastern bloc tended to be well educated and were usually motivated by political convictions—at least partially. Conversely, most North Korean refugees are women from impoverished areas along the border who were looking for a better income and security rather than for the realization of some lofty political ideals. Elite refugees exist, but they are well below 10 percent of the total. With a touch of somewhat frivolous generalization, a typical refugee of the Soviet Union in the 1970s might be described as a young, brilliant, Jewish chess player. In contrast, the average refugee from North Korea is a rural housewife in her 50s.

It is important to mention, however, that refugees remain in touch with their families back home. It helps that most refugees come from borderland areas whose population can cross the border more easily. People frequently call their families using Chinese cell phones, which work perfectly well on the North Korean side of the border. From around 2003, a number of relay stations were built just on the border and this greatly increased mobile phone coverage (signals can be received miles away). This being the case, Chinese cell phones have become common among more affluent North Koreans in the borderland, most of whom earn an income through legal and not-so-legal trade with China. Monetary remittances from South to North Korea constitute a blatant violation of both South Korean and North Korean laws, but nonetheless seem to be fairly frequent: a majority of refugees in the South use brokers to send money back to their impoverished native villages and towns. Brokers charge 25 to 30 percent per transaction, but the system is remarkably reliable and fast. The total annual amount of such transfers has been recently estimated at some $10 million—by no means an insignificant sum for the tiny North Korean economy.[13]

ARRIVAL IN PARADISE, AKA CAPITALIST HELL

The fate of refugees in South Korea does not bode too well for the post-unification population of North Korea (assuming that unification will happen one day). Most of them will find themselves in a low-income bracket, often the object of discrimination by their newly found brethren.

North Korean refugees are eligible for aid that is quite generous by the standards of South Korea, a country where the social welfare system remains underdeveloped as compared with Europe and the United States. For the first few years, refugees are paid a small stipend—not enough to live on but still of help. They are also provided with subsidized rental housing and scholarships for vocational training. Those who are young enough can apply for university admission. They do not compete with South Korean high school pupils. Rather, they sit for their own, easier, exams.

That said, the statistics are discouraging. In December 2010 research confirmed that the average income of a North Korean refugee in the South is merely 1.27 million won ($1,170), that is, roughly 50 percent of the average South Korean salary. Unemployment is high—depending on which of a few different studies you believe and how you define "unemployment," it is estimated to be between 10 and 40 percent. Even the most optimistic estimates are depressing at best if one takes into account that South Korea has one of the lowest unemployment rates among countries in the developed world. Only 439 defectors (merely 4 percent of all employed defectors) were working in skilled jobs, while 77 percent were employed in unskilled jobs.[14]

Furthermore, North Koreans discover that mainstream South Korean society looks upon them with a measure of suspicion. A sad story was recently told to me by a North Korean acquaintance. In 2011 a South Korean television company wanted to make a TV show about North-South couples (i.e., North Korean refugee women married to South Korean men). Participants were promised significant monetary rewards and thus many female refugees initially agreed to the proposal. A few days later, however, most of the candidates called back the program's producers to say that they would not participate in the program regardless of how much money was offered. It was their husbands who decisively opposed the idea. They did not want their neighbors, coworkers, and social contacts to know they had married a North Korean woman. My North Korean female interlocutor said: "You know, here in the South it is sort of assumed that only down-and-outs, people who can't get a proper South Korean woman, marry mail-order brides from South-East Asia or North Korean refugees."

Surprisingly, even refugees with elite educations can face big challenges in the South. Unless their job directly relates to dealing with the North (and the supply of such jobs is limited), they have great trouble finding any prestigious job. This is partially a result of suspicions that most employers have about their skills and partially because of their inability to use the extended personal networks that are so central to success in South Korean society. These networks usually unite people from the same region, members of the same clan, or graduates of the same university. North Korean refugees usually do not belong to any of these groups.

Last but not least, the graduation rate for refugee university students is low: a majority of those who enter university drop out. Even though the dropout rate in South Korean universities tends to be very low, North Korean students often discover that they lack what is considered to be basic knowledge and social skills—advantages their South Korean peers possess. Added to that, many of them have to work to make a living, unlike their South Korean classmates who usually work merely for pocket money. To make up for the gaps in their background knowledge they have to study harder than their South Korean peers, but economic pressure makes this difficult.

Despite these issues, it would be wrong to assume that North Koreans feel regret about their move to the South. There have indeed been a few cases of refugees fleeing the South in order to head back North. But for every such case, there are hundreds of instances where individuals and entire families work hard to pay a broker in order to bring their relations to the South.

Nonetheless, the problems are real. And they are likely to increase in magnitude in the case of unification. After all, refugees, as a self-selecting group, have an above-average ability to adjust to the differences between North and South. It follows that a group of people who have consciously chosen a different life will face fewer problems adjusting to massive change than a group of people who have had a different life forced upon them. Therefore, when and if unification comes, the above-mentioned problems are merely a sample of the social and economic issues that will face the South Korean state and the North Korean people above all.

A NORMAL DAY . . .

It is not that difficult to find the most representative North Korean newspaper. Everyone knows that this role has been reserved for *Rodong Shinmun*, the ruling Korean Workers' Party mouthpiece. This is not just a humble newspaper, but the voice of the Party and State itself.

One day last year, while dropping by the National Library, I decided to have a look through the latest issue of this venerable newspaper. The

(continued)

latest available issue happened to be published on July 11, 2011, and the choice was completely random.

The entire front page was taken up by one large, unsigned article that informed the reader of the greatest event of late. The Dear Leader, Marshal Kim Jong Il, inspected the largest department store in the city of Pyongyang and provided its personnel with a wealth of managerial guidance on the best way to run this retail outlet. The article was accompanied by two pictures: one depicts the Marshal taking an escalator with some of his entourage, and another shows the Leader standing with the top management of the department store.

The upper part of the second page was occupied by a report of another great event: Marshal Kim had inspected the Pyongyang Zoo and taught its personnel a thing or two about animal rearing and zoo management.

The second page also included official telegrams sent to and received from China on a diplomatic event—the 50th anniversary of the treaty of friendship and alliance between China and North Korea. The page also had a small report about an event to commemorate the 117th birthday of a humble rural school teacher, Christian missionary, and nationalist named Kim Hyŏng-jik. He happens to also be the grandfather of Marshal Kim Jong Il and the father of Kim Il Sung.

The third page contained a half-dozen reports about labor enthusiasm and production achievements. Somewhat uncharacteristically, these reports almost exclusively focus on the light industry—obviously resulting from the recent emphasis on the production of consumption goods.

An article in the bottom right corner attracts some attention—it tells of how housewives of a particular county created a model reconstruction brigade to work on irrigation projects in the area. A small picture depicts the construction site: women are neatly dressed but there is not a machine to be seen, so they use only shovels and their bare hands to line the walls of the irrigation canals with block-like rocks.

The fourth page was filled with reports of foreign visitors who had come to North Korea to express their admiration for the country's great achievements. Most delegations are Chinese, but it is reported that a group of Russian police officials have also come to join the chorus and have expressed their admiration for "the great successes of North Korea, achieved under the wise leadership of Comrade Kim Jong Il."

The fifth page dealt with South Korea and foreign policy. The largest article was titled "The Hatred of Treacherous Regime," and told North Koreans how much their South Korean compatriots hate the current South Korean administration of President Lee. There are reports of strikes, police abuse, and an unfolding scandal in the South involving US military use of defoliants at a military base.

A small photo depicted a student's rally in Seoul, whose participants were demanding a 50 percent cut in tuition fees. The accompanying article did not even hint at the fact that such a cut was actually suggested by "the treacherous regime of Lee Myung Bak." Instead, it deliberately created the impression that South Korean students have begun this revolutionary fight spontaneously, because they could not bear the prohibitively high burden of tuition fees.

The final page again dealt with foreign policy. It began with a large and boring (even by *Rodong Shinmun*'s notorious standards) article about the eternal friendship between China and North Korea. It also included reports from other parts of the world that talk about how much the people of the world admire Generalissimo Kim Il Sung, the founder of the North Korean dynasty. According to the newspaper, commemorative events to honor the memory of the late Generalissimo Kim had been held in Romania, Nigeria, Congo, and Thailand.

The sixth page also contained an article commemorating UN World Population Day. The article concentrated on gender inequality in the capitalist world and contained some statistics about the sorry fate of Western European women (clearly the world's greatest victims of gender discrimination).

Another article on the sixth page dealt with the complex situation of the world food market. Obviously, it was published in order to tell the readers that North Korea is not unique in having grave food shortages. Nonetheless, this article stood out because it was almost free from demagogy and indeed contained an interesting analysis of current

(*continued*)

international trends (perhaps the only piece in the entire newspaper that deserves to be called an article).

Such is the daily fare of news and views provided to North Koreans by their media—day by day, for decades, without much change.

CHANGING WORLDVIEWS

Approximately a half-million North Koreans have visited China over the last 15-odd years, and most of them have eventually returned home, voluntarily or otherwise. They have to be cautious, but nonetheless manage to tell stories about China's prosperity—descriptions that are indeed shocking to any first-time North Korean visitor.

Once, while in Northeast China, I had a conversation with a member of an NGO who occasionally brings junior North Korean officials to a sleepy, dirty Chinese town in Manchuria. I asked him about the typical reaction of these North Koreans, to which he responded, "They cannot sleep for the first couple of nights, they are so shocked and overwhelmed by the prosperity of the place, by the bright lights and nightlife of the town." (To the present writer, this particular Chinese town during the night looked more like an abandoned steel mill.)

Chinese prosperity might be overwhelming at first, but soon North Korean refugees discover that these Chinese—whom they regard as filthy rich—actually consider their own country poor in comparison to South Korea. Indeed, it's not difficult to learn a lot about South Korea when in Northeast China. South Korean satellite TV is widely watched by ethnic Korean families and South Korean soap operas with Chinese subtitles are a staple of local TV networks. At any given moment, roughly one out of seven ethnic Koreans of the Yanbian area resides in South Korea, usually being employed there on some unskilled, badly paid job. It does not take long for a North Korean refugee to learn that more or less everything that he or she used to read in the official media about the South is a blatant and grotesque lie.

This discovery does not necessarily make him or her dream about going to Seoul—after all, such a step requires considerable resources, is inherently risky, and might be simply not to everybody's liking. Nonetheless, stories of the fairy-tale land south of the DMZ are shared with trusted friends and family members back home.

From around 2000, VCRs and, soon afterward, DVD players began to spread in North Korea in large numbers. These machines are cheap and perfectly legal. It was assumed that North Koreans would use them to watch officially approved and ideologically wholesome fare, like, say, biopics of the Dear Leader and his extended family. However, North Koreans usually prefer to watch something different and rather ideologically suspicious: smuggled foreign movies and TV dramas, often those produced in South Korea.

As always is the case with North Korea, statistics are highly unreliable. According to Chinese customs, 350,000 DVD players were brought to North Korea in 2006 alone—a large number for a country with a population of some 24 million.[15] It seems that in border areas and major cities, one out of every three or four families has a DVD player nowadays. A study by the InterMedia research group concluded that in 2009 the penetration rate was 21 percent and 5 percent for VCD and DVD players, respectively.[16] From my own research, it seems that in the borderland areas of the country, some 70 to 80 percent of all households were in possession of DVD players by early 2012. We can be sure that more or less all of these families have watched South Korean programs. These shows (unlike the DVD players themselves) are illegal, but small entrepreneurs in China make good money by recording them and then smuggling the copies across the border.

Even computers are becoming increasingly common among the more affluent part of the population. Estimates vary, but one can surmise that the number of privately owned computers, or computers that can be accessed with relative ease, now definitely exceeds 100,000 and is likely to reach a few hundred thousand. A Western diplomat recently related to the present author that USB memory sticks have become a popular fashion accessory among the privileged Pyongyang youth. The message is unmistakable: by sporting a USB, an individual demonstrates that he/she has access to a computer, one of the important status symbols in present-day

Pyongyang. Nowadays, possession of a computer in North Korea is some-what akin to ownership of a sports car in more affluent societies.[17] North Korean computers are not connected to the Internet, and only some of them have a dial-up connection with the national intranet, known as the Kwangmyŏng network. However, even without an Internet connection, a computer remains a powerful information dissemination device—largely thanks to USB and CD-R drives. The authorities are aware of these threats, and therefore all computers are registered and their hard drives subject to random checks by the authorities (recently, the security bureaucracy cre-ated a special division—the so-called Bureau 27—to monitor and control privately owned computers). Frankly, however, one should be skeptical about the effectiveness of such checks: a teenage computer enthusiast will always outsmart an aging policeman, especially if the latter does not see a good reason to be excessively vigilant.

As to South Korean movies and TV dramas, North Koreans do not nec-essarily always believe everything they see. Their own movies have always presented a grossly embellished picture of life in North Korea and they expect this to be the case everywhere in the world. For example, as my own talks with North Korean refugees confirm, few of them believed that the average South Korean family had a car when they saw their first South Korean TV dramas (in actual fact, more or less every South Korean family does own a car—as of 2010, the country with a population of 50 million had 13.6 million passenger cars). The interior of a normal South Korean apartment, frequently shown in movies, did not look plausible to them, either—they believed it to be a set, and that such a lifestyle (with that un-believably large fridge in the kitchen!) would be available only to a select few. Nonetheless, they also know some things are difficult or impossible to fake—like, say, the Seoul cityscape with all its high-rise buildings and giant bridges—and they use these trustworthy images as visual clues, sur-mising that South Korea must be very rich indeed.

North Korean people are now increasingly aware about South Korea's prosperity. As one defector, a woman in her late 50s, remarked to the pre-sent author, "Well, perhaps children in primary school still believe that South Koreans are poor. But everybody else knows that the South is rich."

But there are two important caveats. First, it is not quite clear how far this new consciousness has spread outside of the borderlands and a few major cities. Second, while the average North Korean has begun to suspect that the South is ahead of the North economically, he or she seldom comprehends how huge this gap really is. After all, for the North Korean farmer or skilled worker, being wealthy means feasting on rich gruel every day.

Since around 2000, even North Korean propaganda began to take into account this slow change of mind—after all, Pyongyang's agitprop shock brigades are not as inflexible as they appear to many foreign observers (those who are seriously interested in the changes in North Korea's propaganda should read the informative works of Brian Myers and Tatiana Gabroussenko).

In the post-2000 propaganda, the alleged poverty of South Korea has ceased to be a topic worthy of mention. It is even grudgingly admitted that South Korea might be relatively affluent (of course, this affluence was described as a bubble economy, being propped up by the scheming US imperialists for their selfish interests, and hence inherently unstable). However, with all its wealth, South Korea is represented as basically a very unhappy place. The reason for this unhappiness is that South Koreans' national identity, their precious "Koreanness," has been spoilt and compromised by the domination of American imperialists who propagate their degrading and corrosive "culture." In the post-2000 propaganda narrative, South Koreans are suffering not from hunger, but rather from national humiliation as well as cultural and environmental degradation. South Koreans allegedly dream of liberation and envy happy Northerners, who might experience some temporary economic difficulties but nonetheless have managed to keep their pure national essence intact and have not sold out to those big-nosed servants of Mammon (the North Korean stereotype of Americans is remarkably similar to anti-Semitic stereotypes).

Another recurrent topic of this new propaganda is the inequalities and assorted social ills that permeate South Korean society. As a matter of fact, by international standards, South Korea is a society of remarkable income equality (the "Scandinavia of East Asia," as sociologist Aidan Foster-Carter once remarked), but the South Korean Left strongly believes otherwise.

North Korean newspapers therefore happily reprint articles from the South Korean leftist media painting a grim picture of a country where the pampered few suck the blood of a destitute majority. Alleged environmental pollution has become another large topic nowadays. Interestingly, in the past, North Korea loved to present itself as a country of enormous steel mills and smoky factories, but nowadays, after the industrial collapse of the 1990s, the propagandists love to wax rhapsodic about the allegedly pristine environment of the country—and contrast it with the industrial pollution and environmental degradation of the South.

To what extent does this propaganda work? This, of course, remains to be seen. Most likely a significant number of North Koreans buy this new propaganda line about "relatively-affluent-but-unhappy-and-debased" South Korea. But the "yellow winds of capitalism" and an understanding of South Korean prosperity is spreading as well.

This growing awareness of the outside world is merely one of many changes that have occurred in the era of "capitalism from below." North Koreans' attitude toward domestic issues is changing as well. People below the age of 30 simply have no experience of life under the old regime of comprehensive rationing and are therefore not inclined to see the state as a natural provider of all life's necessities. Many above the age of 30 have learned that they can do without the state and some of them came to enjoy this new situation.

Once again, these trends should not be exaggerated. From regular interaction with North Koreans, I have come to suspect that the average North Korean would much prefer a regimented life under Kim Il Sung to the uncertainties of the subsequent era. After all, in Kim Il Sung's era, everybody who was not unlucky to find themselves in a prison camp was certain that his or her subsistence-level rations would be forthcoming regularly. Sometimes people were malnourished, but they never starved. Soon after Kim Il Sung's death in 1994, this old stability had gone. It is likely that the less successful majority would prefer to go back to the comfort of regularly delivered rations, even if this means more boring indoctrination sessions and greater risks of being sent to prison for a misinterpreted joke.

At any rate, North Koreans do not have much choice. They have had to adjust, thereby modifying their career aspirations as well. For example, in spite of a significant increase in the intensity of militaristic propaganda after 1994, many North Koreans try to skip obligatory military service. In the past, the 7 to 10 years spent in the military were seen as attractive because soldiers could easily join the Korean Workers' Party, thus acquiring the most essential prerequisite for social advancement. But party membership is not as highly prized as it used to be: after all, for an upwardly mobile and adventurous individual, the marketplace provides a faster way to earthly success.

People have begun to ignore the institutions of state that were once created to keep them under constant surveillance. The notorious weekly mutual-criticism sessions as well as indoctrination meetings of various kinds still continue, but they have become somewhat less frequent and have lost much of their earlier intensity. One can even skip boring official functions in order not to miss a profitable day at the market, even though this might require a bit of bribery.

Although completely unthinkable in Kim Il Sung's North Korea, even riots began to occur occasionally. In March 2005, for example, Pyongyang experienced what was probably the first riot in the city in 60 years. The riot itself began at Kim Il Sung Stadium during a World Cup qualifying match between North Koreans and the Iranian team. In the middle of the game, an argument erupted between a North Korean player and a Syrian referee. The North Korean player shoved the referee, was sent off, and then violence erupted. Fans began to throw bottles, stones, chairs, and everything they could find at the Iranian players and referees. It took a few minutes before order was restored, while the stadium loudspeakers demanded that fans stay calm. The North Korean team eventually lost 2–0 and the violence resumed, continuing for almost two hours after the match. There were clashes between police and fans, and for a while Iranian players could not leave the stadium because of the unruly and outraged crowds outside. All of these events unfolded in front of foreign media, who did not miss an opportunity to take rare shots of North Koreans fighting with police. This was a patriotic riot, no doubt, driven by lofty and officially sanctioned emotions, but it nonetheless demonstrated that the foundations of social control were eroding.

Around the same time, market riots in the countryside—admittedly, less patriotic in their intentions—began to occur as well. The outbreak of public discontent usually happens at the markets when vendors believe that their right to make money is being unfairly infringed by some decision of the authorities. For example, between 2006 and 2007, when the government unsuccessfully tried to restart the PDS, some markets were closed, and a considerable part of the local population was deprived of the major source of their livelihoods. This resulted in numerous protests, usually by middle-aged women. Reportedly, their cry was "give us rations or let us trade!"—not exactly a pro-democracy demonstration, but still a challenge to the established authority.

The North Korean authorities have been remarkably—and unusually— lenient when dealing with these market riots. Taking into consideration the secretiveness of the North Korean legal system, one cannot rule out that some of the ringleaders in such incidents might have been secretly punished. But many of those who participated in the disturbances received only light punishment or escaped punishment completely.

These signs of social relaxation should not be overestimated. The North Korean state still remains one of the most repressive regimes in the world. In spite of some cracks, its surveillance system is still second to none in efficiency and brutality. Nonetheless, changes are palpable. North Korea is drifting away from Kim Il Sung's "nationalist Stalinism." The drift is slow and might take years or even decades before it results in dramatic consequences. But it seems clear: the society Kim Il Sung built is slowly but inexorably crumbling and being replaced. As this happens, contradictions between the existing old political order and the emerging social order will lead to more rapid change, and—just as importantly—to the demand for more rapid change. Where these demands will end, we cannot as yet be sure.

CHAPTER 3

The Logic of Survival (Domestically)

To an outside observer, the behavior of the North Korean leadership often appears irrational. It seems that there is a tested and easy way out of their predicament—but for some reason they refuse to see this way, let alone follow it. This allegedly "sure and tested" way is the path of Chinese-style reforms that, as many people believe, North Korean leaders will eventually follow as well. However, a closer look makes us skeptical about the alleged advantages of the "Chinese solution." It might be good for the country, but it is too dangerous for the elite—and hence unlikely to be implemented any time soon.

REFORM AS COLLECTIVE POLITICAL SUICIDE

The history of East Asia after the Second World War was, above all, the history of spectacular economic growth. The world has not seen anything like this since probably the dramatic rise of Europe after the Industrial Revolution in the late 18th century. During the period between 1960 and 2000, the average per capita GDP growth in East Asia reached 4.6 percent, while the same indicator for the world was 2.8 percent.[1] It is difficult to believe now that in 1960, in terms of per capita GDP, South Korea was slightly below Somalia, while Taiwan was lagging behind Senegal.[2]

This remarkable economic growth was presided over (or even brought in) by regimes that were decisively illiberal and undemocratic. These regimes are often described as "developmental dictatorships"—largely because they combined authoritarian politics with an obsession for economic growth.

The "developmental dictatorship" strategy was pioneered by the military regime in South Korea and by Taiwan (the latter between 1945 and 1988 was a one-party hereditary dictatorship, a bit like North Korea). These regimes combined anti-Communist rhetoric and some lip-service to the principles of the "free world" with a market-driven but government-controlled developmental strategy. Lacking natural resources, they emphasized cheap labor and economic efficiency, and they were successful beyond anybody's wildest expectations.

From the mid-1980s this "first generation" of the "developmental dictatorships" was emulated by the Communist regimes in mainland China and Vietnam. In both countries, the Communist Party elite kept the old slogans and quasi-Leninist decorum for the sake of domestic stability, but for all practical purposes switched to the developmental model pioneered by Taiwan and South Korea. If anything, their version of capitalism was even more unabashed and brutal—the quasi-Communist regimes treated labor with greater harshness and demonstrated a remarkable indifference to the yawning gap between the rich and poor. The model worked again, and the "second generation" of the "developmental dictatorships" also achieved spectacular results. Suffice it to say that Vietnam, which experienced a famine in the mid-1980s, by the mid-1990s became the world's third-largest exporter of rice.[3]

Thus, in China and Vietnam, the (technically) Communist oligarchy presided over an unprecedented economic growth while successfully maintaining domestic stability and enormously enriching themselves in the process. They can see themselves—with good reason—as benefactors and even saviors of their countries and also enjoy the power and comfort that was beyond the dreams of their mentors, who began their careers in the brutal and austere times of Mao and Ho Chi Minh.

This option seems to be irresistibly attractive, but it has failed to inspire the North Korean elite. Over the last two decades, at every sign of changes in the North, a number of newspaper columnists and academic commentators alike assured their readers (and, perhaps, themselves) that the unavoidable has finally happened, and that the long-overdue reforms have started at last. Such enthusiastic commentaries greeted the Joint Enterprise Law of 1984, the launch of the Rajin-Sonbong Special Economic Zone in the early 1990s, and the so-called 7.1 measures of 2002. I recall an article from 2003, written by a professor of marketing from Indiana, entitled "North Korea Moving from Isolation to an Open Market Economy: Is It Time to Invest or to Continue Observing?" Predictably, the suggestion was to invest before it was too late (to give the author his due, however, he did include some cautious warnings).[4]

Terence Roehrig, from the US Naval War College, expressing fairly typical sentiments of optimistic outsiders, said recently:

> To avoid the potential dangers of a sudden collapse in the DPRK, it may be a better route to promote a long-term, gradual transition that seeks to encourage the forces within North Korea and the ruling regime for change. Whether that regime is another member of the Kim family or a military/party collective of some sort, to further a process of economic opening and reform could lead to a subsequent path of political moderation and reform.[5]

Roehrig might be right when he is saying this—cynically speaking, it makes sense to persuade the Pyongyang leaders that they would have a bright future in a reformed North Korea. However, they have not shown much inclination to be persuaded by this siren song, and some suspect that the reforms would become their shortcut to ruin and self-destruction. Regrettably, they are very likely correct in this assumption.

Unfortunately for the common North Koreans, the Pyongyang leaders' unwillingness to emulate China has very rational explanations. North Korean leaders stubbornly resist reform not because they are ideological zealots who blindly believe in the prescriptions of the Juche Idea (they do not, and the idea itself is too nebulous to be a guide to a practical policy anyway) nor because they are ignorant of the outside world. They are neither irrational nor ideological—on the contrary, they are rational to the extreme, being, perhaps, the most perfect bunch of Machiavellians currently in operation. The North Korean leaders do not want reforms because they realize that in the specific conditions produced by the division of their country, such reforms are potentially destabilizing and, if judged from the ruling elite's point of view, constitute the surest way of political (and, perhaps, physical) suicide.

The existence of rich and free South Korea is what makes North Korea's situation so different from that of China or Vietnam. The regime lives next to a country whose people speak the same language and are officially described as "members of our nation," but who enjoy a per capita income at least 15 times (some claim even 40 times) higher than that of the North Koreans.[6] Even if the lowest estimate is believed, it is still by far the world's largest per capita income difference between two countries that share a land border. To put things in perspective, the income ratio in divided Germany was merely 1:3, and even this was enough to prompt the East Germans to overthrow the regime as soon as they had an opportunity to do so without fear of Soviet retribution. If ordinary North Koreans become fully aware of the prosperity their brethren enjoy only a mere hundred miles or so away, the regime's legitimacy would suffer a major blow and, quite likely, become untenable.

One can only imagine the mind-blowing effect that might be produced by the sight of the average Seoul street, a typical South Korean department store, or, for that matter, the flat of a humble, semiskilled manual worker. Perhaps 15 years of flourishing market activities somehow have made North Koreans immune to the sights of consumerist abundance at shops (after all, one can buy a lot in North Korea now if/when money is available). But one can easily imagine what will happen to a North Korean's mind when he or she discovers that a South Korean worker—supposedly a slave of American neocolonialism—enjoys the amenities and lifestyle that in North Korea are available only for a tiny minority, to people like successful drug smugglers or Central Committee officials.

Reforms worked in Vietnam and China because their situation is different—simply put, Chinese reform succeeded because there is not a prosperous "South China" whose size would be comparable with that of the China of the Communist Party. The prosperity of, for example, Japan or the United States is well known in China, to be sure, but is not seen by the common Chinese as politically relevant—after all, those are different nations, with different histories, so their remarkable prosperity does not necessarily demonstrate the inefficiency of the Communist Party rule.

And, of course, China is not going to join the United States, becoming its 51st state. Neither Vietnam nor China has a rich "other" with which to seek unification: Taiwan is too small to have a palpable impact on the average Chinese income in the event of unification, and South Vietnam ceased to exist in 1975. Thus, for the time being the common Chinese seemingly accept the same bargain accepted by the South Koreans or Taiwanese of the 1960s: they put up with authoritarian rule as long as they enjoy stability and economic growth. In North Korea, due to the allure of the rich and free South, such a bargain has very thin chances of success, and the Pyongyang leaders of Kim Jong Il's generation were well aware of this.

Reform is impossible without a considerable relaxation of the information blockade and daily surveillance. Foreign investment and technology are necessary preconditions for growth. Consequently, if Chinese-style reform were to be instigated, a large number of North Koreans would soon be exposed to dangerous knowledge of the outside world, and above all of South Korea. A considerable relaxation of surveillance would be unavoidable as well: efficient market reforms cannot occur in a country where a business trip to the capital city requires a weeks-long wait for travel permits and where promotion is determined not so much by labor efficiency but by demonstrated political loyalty (including the ability to memorize the lengthy speeches of the Dear Leader). Relaxation would entail information flowing within the country, and thus the dissemination of this information, as well as dangerous conclusions drawn from it, would become much easier. The situation is further aggravated by the recent dramatic improvement of the IT technologies, which make censorship even more difficult and therefore constitute a major political threat to the regime.

It is doubtful whether the North Korean population would acquiesce to enduring a further decade of destitution followed by a couple of decades of relative poverty and backbreaking work if they were to learn about another Korea—affluent, free, glamorous, and attractive. Would they agree to tolerate a reforming but still authoritarian and repressive regime on the assumption that this regime will on some distant day deliver a prosperity comparable to that of present-day South Korea? The North Koreans, unfortunately for their leaders, are much more likely to react to the new knowledge and new freedom in a different way: by removing the current regime and unifying with South Korea in order to partake in the fabulous prosperity of the wildly rich South.

One can easily imagine how discontent with the North Korean system, as well as information about the astonishing South Korean prosperity, will spread: first through the relatively well-heeled North Korean groups who are suddenly allowed to interact with South Koreans and foreigners, or who have better access to the foreign media and entertainment, and then down to the wider social strata. Once North Koreans come to the conclusion that they have no reason to be afraid of the usual crackdown, they are very likely to do what East Germans did in 1989.

There is another important difference between North Korea and China—and, once again, this difference is created by the existence of the successful South. It is an open secret that the Chinese party officials used the reforms to enrich themselves: the new Chinese entrepreneurial class to a significant extent consists of former officials as well as their relations and buddies. The situation in the post-Communist countries of the USSR and Eastern Europe is no different. With few exceptions, the political and economic life of those countries is dominated by the former second-tier party apparatchiks who once used their connections, experience, education, and, above all, their de facto control over the state assets to appropriate the government property and remake themselves into successful capitalists and/or politicians. It might be just a minor exaggeration to describe the collapse of Communism as a "management buyout," as Richard Vinen recently did.[7] On balance, in the 1990s the younger generations of Eastern European and Soviet *nomenklatura* jettisoned the system they never actually believed in, while enormously increasing their wealth, if not power, in the process.[8]

However, the situation of the North Korean elites is different. They stand little chance of becoming successful capitalists if the system is overthrown. In all probability, the regime collapse will be followed by the unification of the peninsula—after all, this is what the common people will likely want, on the (mistaken) assumption that unification will instantly deliver them the same level of consumption as enjoyed by their southern brethren. In such a case, all the important positions in the new economy will undoubtedly be taken by people from South Korea—people with capital, education, experience, and perhaps political support. The capitalism in the post-unification North is to be built not by born-again apparatchiks (as was the case in the former USSR), but rather by the resident managers of LG and Samsung, as well as assorted carpetbaggers from Seoul.

This fact is understood by at least some North Korean bureaucrats, but it seems that the majority has another, greater, fear. They know how brutal their rule has been. They also know how they would treat the South Korean elite (and their descendants) had the North won the intra-Korean feud, and do not see reasons why they would be treated differently by actual winners. This makes them very afraid of retribution. They are not merely afraid to lose power and access to material privileges (these privileges are quite modest, incidentally, by the standards of the rich in most other countries). They are afraid of being slaughtered or sent to prisons, of suffering the same fate they have bestowed on their enemies for decades. A few years ago, a high-level North Korean bureaucrat with an unusual frankness told a high-level Western diplomat: "The human rights and the like might be a great idea, but if we start explaining it to our people, we will be killed in no time." This seems to be a common assumption. It is also not coincidental that many visitors to Pyongyang, including the present author, had to answer the same question quietly asked by their minders: "What has happened to the former East German party and police officials?"

Perhaps one of the reasons behind the remarkable resilience of the North Korean regime is this universal assumption of its bureaucrats (including those who are quite low in the pecking order) that they would have no future in case of regime collapse. This makes North Korea different from many other dictatorships. A clerk in Mubarak's Egypt, for instance, could assume that, Democrats or not, Islamists or not, under a new regime he would still sit at his desk and continue the old routine of, say, issuing permits for house construction. Ditto a high-ranking military officer, who also would expect that under a new government in Cairo he would still command his battalion. Consequently, they did not see the revolution as a personal threat, and might have even been supportive of the movement.

In North Korea things are different: the elite—pretty much everybody who is somebody—believe that it has nothing to gain and much to lose through unification with the South. These fears might be—and, indeed, are—exaggerated, but they are by no means groundless. It is important that their predicament stems from the existence of a successful South, not from particular policies followed by a specific Seoul administration. Even if the most pro–North Korean administration imaginable will come to power in Seoul, it will not make South Korea less dangerous (perhaps, as we will see later, a friendly South is actually *more* dangerous—even though this fact might not be currently appreciated in Pyongyang).

This reconstruction of the Pyongyang elite's thinking is necessarily hypothetical, but an impressive confirmation of this hypothesis has emerged recently. This confirmation came from Kim Jong Nam, Kim Jong Il's oldest son who lives overseas in semi-exile (largely in Macao and continental China). Kim Jong Nam is the only member of the Kim family who talks to foreign journalists. They occasionally manage to intercept him in an airport or a lobby of an expensive hotel. With the passage of time, his short interviews have become more substantive in content and more politically frank. In 2010 he even went so far as to openly voice his disapproval of the hereditary power transfer at that point developing in Pyongyang.

His remarks became even more candid in recent years, and in January 2011 he gave a lengthy interview to Yoji Gomi, a journalist for *Tokyo Shimbun*. Soon afterward it was revealed that since 2004, the maverick North Korean prince had maintained e-mail exchanges with Gomi, who published these e-mails in a book.

The single-most important topic in this book is the (im)possibility of Chinese-style reforms in North Korea. Kim Jong Nam has clearly stated his belief that market-oriented reforms would probably revive the North Korean economy. In one case, addressing his half-brother Kim Jong Un (by that time already the successor to Kim Jong Il), he implored him to "have pity on the common people" and follow the Chinese example.

However, in many other cases, Kim Jong Nam is far less certain about the potential positive impact of reforms. In his January 2011 interview, he said, "I personally believe that economic reforms and openness are the best ways to make life better for the North Korean people. However, taking North Korea's unique position into account, there is a fear that economic reforms and openness will lead to the collapse of the present system."

In the same interview, Kim Jong Nam repeated the same point: "The North Korean leadership is stuck in a bind. Without reforms the country's economy will go bankrupt, but reforms are fraught with the danger of systemic collapse."[9] This is a remarkably forthright—but completely reasonable—admission, and unfortunately it confirms that the North Korean leaders understand perfectly well how dangerous the reforms would be for their survival.

In such a case, what is the best policy choice for the North Korean elite? The optimal course of action appears to be a continuation of the policies the current leaders and their predecessors have followed for the last two decades. Domestically, the regime's policy aim has been to keep the North Korean population under control, compartmentalized, and, above all, isolated from the outside world. Internationally, the safest solution is an aid-maximizing strategy, which includes attempts to squeeze more aid from outside through diplomacy and blackmail.[10] This foreign aid helps to keep the inherently inefficient economy afloat, prevents another major famine, and allows the country's tiny elite to live a reasonably luxurious lifestyle while buying at least some support from "strategically important" social groups (the aid was first distributed to the military, the police, and the populations of major urban centers).[11]

Judged from the point of view of leaders in Pyongyang, this policy has been a success: they remain in control and enjoy a privileged life even today, in 2013, while a majority of more liberal and permissive Communist regimes have long been overthrown. By keeping the system unchanged and restraining the spontaneous growth of the private, market-based economy, the North Korean elite has probably forfeited the chance to achieve sustainable economic growth. However, growth is not their major concern. They do not mind growth, to be sure, but only as long as it does not jeopardize more important goals of maintaining the political stability and their own domination. They would be happy to see a North Korean economic boom—as long as they are not going to enjoy this wonderful picture through the window grate of their cell.

The international media often engage in the endless (and useless) speculations about the factional struggle in Pyongyang, telling us about the technocrats, also known as "pragmatists," who allegedly fight the conservative ideologues and military hard-liners. Such struggle might indeed go on even though most media reports are often based on speculations and unreliable hearsay. However, the oft-repeated description of the alleged reformers as "pragmatists" is misleading. If such people actually exist, they are better described as "dangerous idealists" or "starry-eyed romanticists" whose reformist program, if ever carried out, will hasten the regime's demise and lead to their own downfall (which would be good for a majority of the North Koreans—but this is an altogether different matter).

Pyongyang reformers will face a sad (should we say tragic?) paradox: no matter how successful their reforms will be if judged in objective terms, the majority of North Koreans would still perceive even the most brilliant success as a failure when using the fabulously rich South as the natural benchmark.

However, even if reform-minded individuals exist, they are a minority. What the mainstream North Korean elite want is to return to the year 1984—not that of the Orwellian dystopia, but the last year when Kim Il Sung's system was still functioning properly (though admittedly, the properly functioning Kim Il Sung society had a number of remarkable similarities with an Orwellian dystopia). The economic policies of the regime are largely driven by the desire to revive the hyper-Stalinist model of the past. It is possible that many people on the top sincerely hope that this model might somehow work, but even if they do not succumb to such fantasies, they still have no choice: due to the existence of the rich South, the hyper-centralized and highly controlled Stalinist economy seems to be the only type compatible with maintaining political stability.

PUTTING THE GENIE BACK IN THE BOTTLE: (NOT-SO-SUCCESSFUL) CRACKDOWNS ON MARKET ACTIVITY

When we described the North Korean "capitalism from below," it is important to remember that most of the new entrepreneurial activities have been technically illegal, even if the government is willing to turn a blind eye to what is happening at the marketplace. In the midst of the famine, North Korean authorities still sporadically cracked down both on markets and on so-called capitalist profiteering. Usually, such crackdowns ended in naught, being quietly sabotaged by the low-level officials who either depended on markets themselves or understood that excessive pressure was likely to further aggravate the already disastrous situation.

In 2002, however, Pyongyang's negative attitude toward the emerging market economy appeared to change. On July 1, 2002, North Korean leaders introduced a set of measures that are frequently described in the foreign media as the "2002 reforms." With the word "reform" regarded as too radical, even subversive, the state media never accepted this description and the policy is officially known in North Korea as the "7.1 measures" (that is, "July 1 measures").[12]

As usually happens at the first sight of any change in North Korea's policies, the measures were heralded overseas as the sign of the long-awaited reforms and received an enthusiastic reception in the international media. This started a wave of the usual speculations about North Korea finally doing the right thing and turning the Chinese way. Newspaper headlines were sanguine: "With Little Choice, Stalinist North Korea Lets Markets Emerge," "Signs That North Korea Is Coming to Market," and "North Korea Experiments, With China as Its Model."[13] This optimism was completely unfounded, as we see later.

The 7.1 measures in fact included several different sets of policies. First, consumer prices were raised dramatically. For example, for decades rice was "sold" within the PDS at the purely token price of 0.08 North Korean won per kilogram. After the reforms, the price increased by a multiple of 550 (!) to 44 won per kg, approximating the market price at the time. Official wages increased as well, albeit on a smaller scale. According to Yim Kyong-hun's calculations, retail prices on average increased by a multiple of 25, whereas wages increased merely by a multiple of 18.[14]

Second, the 7.1 measures introduced changes in the management of state companies that increased the power and independence of company managers. Not only were managers allowed to use the market to acquire resources and sell finished products, but they were also given more freedom to design incentives for workers—like, say, a right to pay performance bonuses.

Third, the 7.1 measures envisioned the establishment of "general markets" (*chonghap sichang*), a move that in the foreign media was often described (misleadingly) as "lifting the ban on private market trade." Of course, one could not possibly lift a ban that never existed, as by 2002 a majority of North Koreans were already earning their living through private market activity of some kind.

The formal establishment of general markets was less significant a change than it might have appeared. Essentially, it was a belated and grudging acceptance of what the government knew it could not control. One might be surprised to learn that the majority of the market vendors whom the present author interviews regularly (many dozens of people) simply have no idea about any reform happening in 2002! They did not hear about the measures that supposedly legalized their businesses and changed their lives—and with good reason: the much-hyped measures had little impact on the actual working of the markets, apart from changing their official name and making them (eventually) a bit more regulated. The vendors continued to do what they had been doing for years.

Nonetheless, the 7.1 measures and associated policies indicated that the Pyongyang leadership acknowledged and, to an extent, accepted spontaneous "de-Stalinization from below." This relaxation did not last long, however. Soon afterward, the North Korean authorities began their attempts to reverse the changes that had spontaneously occurred in the previous decade.

This approach might be bad for the economic growth, but it is good for the political stability that is Pyongyang's overwhelming concern. The North Korean leaders understand that spontaneous liberalization was dangerous and never felt at ease about the markets. Thus, in 2005 they decided that this was the time to launch a decisive offensive against the informal economy.

By that time, the famine was over, even though malnourishment remained widespread (and still is). A large role in the economic recovery was played by the generous foreign aid. However, it would be an oversimplification to think that it was foreign aid alone that put an end to the disaster of the late 1990s—the partial recovery was helped by the emergence of the private economy (private fields in particular) and the adjustment of what remained of the state sector. Improved harvests played a role, too. The North Korean government saw this mild but palpable improvement as a sign that it could do what it wanted to do—revive the pre-crisis system.

As an interesting illustration of this attitude, consider a remark made by a North Korean official in October 2005. When asked by a visiting South Korean scholar whether the government indeed had restarted the rationing system, the official replied: "Now, when we have a good harvest and plentiful reserves of rice, are the private sales of rice at the market necessary?"[15] The underlying assumption is clear: ideally, the economy should be based on administrative distribution and rationing, whereas markets and retail trade should be tolerated only as a means of coping with emergencies.

In October 2005, roughly when the above-quoted conversation took place, the government announced that the long-defunct PDS would be restored in full, albeit with some modifications. The North Korean populace was assured that from now on everybody would be given standard rations on a regular basis, as had occurred under Kim Il Sung. The price of rations was fixed at the post-2002 official level—rice, for example, was 44 won per kg. By the time of the announcement, however, the actual market price for rice had already reached 800–900 won, and by 2009 was fluctuating around the 2,000 won mark, so the new PDS price of 44 won per kg still remained a token.[16] The decision to reinstate the PDS was accompanied by the revival of the government's monopoly on grain purchases. It was said that private trade in grain would be banned—or, rather, authorities reconfirmed the ban that had technically existed since 1957, was never formally lifted, but ceased to be enforced in the early 1990s.

The attempted revival of the PDS was presented as a sign of a "return to normality" and was officially referred to in the North Korean parlance as the "normalization of food distribution" (*siklyang konkup chongsanghwa*). Most of the North Korean populace would agree with this description: after all, a majority of the North Koreans would have lived most of their lives under the PDS and indeed would perceive the system as "normal."

The revival proved to be a very partial success. In subsequent years the rations began to diminish again. As of 2012 anyone living outside of Pyongyang has to be an official or work at a military plant in order to get a full or nearly full ration. The ban on the private sale of grain lasted for merely a few months. By late 2006 rice and corn were again sold and bought freely, as the police and low-level officials were unwilling to enforce the new regulations. As we will see below, this was a typical outcome of many attempts to revive the old patterns: the government efforts seldom meet open resistance, but are quietly sabotaged by the low-ranking officials and population alike.

Attempts to regulate or limit market activities intensified after 2005. In December 2006 authorities prohibited able-bodied males from engaging in market trade. Men were allowed to trade at the markets only if the aspiring vendor was not the primary breadwinner of the household but a dependent.[17] Indeed, in Kim Il Sung's North Korea all men were expected to work a "proper" job—that is, be employed in the government sector.

There is a rational (indeed, very rational) reason behind the seemingly bizarre policy of keeping workers at nonfunctioning factories: the North Korean surveillance system operates on the assumption that every adult has a proper job with a state-run enterprise; thus, indoctrination and police surveillance are centered on the workplace, where the entire "organizational life" takes place.

The ban did not have much impact, however, on actual market activities, since men seldom trade in North Korea. Conversely, the government's decision a year later, in December 2007, to extend the ban on market trade to women below 50 years of age was much more important.[18] The decision reportedly led to riots in March 2008, particularly in the city of Chongjin.[19]

For a brief while the police and officials tried to enforce the ban, so the younger female vendors had to use a number of tricks. The most common way to evade regulations was to bring along an elderly mother-in-law or other aged female relative when going to the market. If police asked questions, the vendor explained that it was actually her highly esteemed mother-in-law who did trading, while she just dropped by to briefly help the old lady. This ruse could work, admittedly, only as long as the police were not too serious about enforcing the ban—and this was actually the case. Within a few months the ban was forgotten completely. Once again, the quiet resistance won.

Nonetheless, the North Korean government did not give up and in late 2008 prepared a decisive move against the markets. In November the local authorities were officially notified that beginning in 2009, the private markets would be allowed to operate only three days every month. No sales of industrial goods would be allowed on the markets, either. The leadership made explicitly clear that improvement in the North Korean economic and social situation would make markets obsolete.[20] At the last moment, however, the plan was cancelled.

The backlash, however, was not limited to the markets. After 2005 the authorities increased control over the porous border with China. This led to a dramatic decline in the number of refugees hiding in China, falling from estimates of 200,000 in 1998 to a mere 20,000 to 40,000 in 2010.[21] Although a number of factors, including improvement of the food situation, contributed to this dramatic drop in refugees, increased efficiency of the North Korean border control played a major role. It has become far more difficult to cross the border river without bribing the border guards.

The antimarket policies of the North Korean authorities culminated in the currency reform of 2009. It was designed to destroy the unruly markets once and forever. However, it shared the fate of the earlier antimarket measures: it failed, and this failure was quite a spectacle.

SALARIES

What was the average income of a North Korean in the 1980s and how much does he or she earn nowadays? These two questions sound natural and commonplace, but are rather difficult to answer — largely because wages in the North play a dramatically different role to that of wages in a capitalist (or even a Soviet-style Socialist) economy.

That said, in nominal terms the question is simple enough. In the 1980s the average monthly salary in North Korea was 70 to 80 North Korean won. In subsequent years it rose to a level of some 100 won in 2000. After the 2002 reform, salaries were increased dramatically, reaching the average level of 3,000 won, and have remained at that level ever since. Nowadays, North Korean workers draw salaries in the range from 1,500 to 6,000 won.

The official exchange rate of the North Korean won is now fixed at 135 won per US dollar, but the market rate seems to be far more indicative. Since currently the market rate fluctuates around the 3,400 won per US dollar mark, the official salary is equivalent to between $0.5 and $1.75 a month. For the Kim Il Sung era, the application of the then market exchange rate would mean that an average salary of 70 won would be roughly equivalent to some $20. But these figures are essentially meaningless and even misleading.

Under Kim Il Sung, North Korea was a rationing economy par excellence. Everything was rationed and the state, being the sole employer in the nation's economy, decided how much grain a worker should eat every day (usually 700g), how much soy sauce he or she should be allowed to have, and how often pork or fresh apples should appear on the average Korean's table. Markets existed, but the vast majority of North Koreans in Kim Il Sung's era satisfied their consumption demands through the state-run distribution system.

The North Koreans of the era, however, did not necessarily see the public distribution system (PDS) as a system of control. For them, it was often seen as a social welfare system, because rations were subsidized heavily, almost to the point of being free.

For example, the price of grain within the public distribution system was fixed between 0.04 and 0.08 won. The entire standard food ration (cereals, soy sauce, some vegetables, and a few eggs and fish) would in the 1980s cost between 5 and 10 won a month or, in other words, some 10 percent of the then-average monthly salary.

In the North Korea of the Kim Il Sung era (that is, before the early 1990s), a wage was little different from pocket money. People could use it to buy stationery or movie tickets, or satisfy other supplementary needs, while essential goods and services were provided all but exclusively through the rationing system. The best equivalent might be military service: a soldier in a conscript army is supposed to fight and work, while the state is expected to take care of his reasonable consumption needs and also provide him with a certain amount of pocket money.

Among other things, this system created a remarkable degree of material equality. No doubt, even in the Kim Il Sung era, officials lived much better than the average person. But in most cases, living standards were remarkably uniform across the country and social groups. Even for officials, their privileges came not from higher salaries, but from access to special distribution points. There, they were issued items unavailable to normal people, like chocolate and cigarettes with filters.

Rations stopped being delivered between 1993 and 1995, with people discovering that in the new situation they had to rely on the market in order to obtain all food. This was not easy because from the mid-1990s, the average monthly salary would suffice to buy merely two kilos of rice.

In 2002 the state attempted to change the situation by increasing the official price of rice to the then market level, while also dramatically increasing salaries to partially compensate for the hike. Obviously, North Korea's economic planners did not realize the consequences of a dramatic increase in the supply of money. After a few months of hyperinflation, the price of rice stabilized to compensate for the increase in cash supply and North Korean workers, now paid some 3,000 won instead of 100 won a month, discovered that they could afford to buy the same two or three kilos of rice.

(continued)

No wonder that North Koreans turned to a great variety of activities to earn the necessary cash to buy the necessities of life. Now, in 2012, refugees agree that the survival income for a family of three or four is 50,000 won (some $15 according to the current exchange rate)—roughly 10 times the official salary. So, it is no surprise that salary is not seen as a major indicator of one's income and prosperity.

A DISASTER THAT ALMOST HAPPENED: THE CURRENCY REFORM OF 2009

In late 2009 North Korean leaders decided to inflict a major blow to the market system, wiping out capitalistic activities and punishing independent entrepreneurs (also known as "shameless anti-Socialist profiteers"), while also rewarding those few who remained loyal to the Party and Leader in the midst of turmoil. Judging by some peculiarities that occurred during the subsequent events, it seems that it was not so much the faceless "leadership" but rather Kim Jong Il himself who was the mastermind behind the botched counterreform of 2009.

In 2009 the North Korean leaders used a well-known policy device—currency reform. Such reforms have been part of life in all Communist countries, but similar measures have been used in market economies to curb hyperinflation. The Soviet currency reform of 1947 initiated by Joseph Stalin himself can be seen as an archetypical operation of this type. The Soviet reform was later emulated by other Communist regimes, including North Korea, which underwent reforms of this type in 1959, 1979, and 1992.

The reform scenario is well known. One day, usually in the morning, the population suddenly learns that old banknotes are to become useless in a few days, and should be swapped for new banknotes. For note exchange, strict limits are set. For cash the limits are usually equal to a couple of monthly salaries, while money in bank accounts usually is treated with greater leniency and can be exchanged in somewhat greater quantities—but still within limits. The exchange period is made

The birth of the regime: Kim Il Sung and General Ivan Chistiakov, 1947 (Russian State Archive of Film and Photo Documents, 0-216988)

Voting on the first North Korean elections, 1947 (Russian State Archive of Film and Photo Documents, 0-216991)

North Korea in the late 1940s: portrait of young Kim Il Sung, above the slogan, "Long live the liberator of small nations Generalissimo Stalin!" (Russian State Archive of Film and Photo Documents, 0-216883)

A US air raid, Pyongyang, 1950 (Russian State Archive of Film and Photo Documents, 0-232460)

Ruins of Sinuiju, 1951 (Russian State Archive of Film and Photo Documents, 1-7677)

Pyongyang street in 1985 (Photo by Sergei Kurbanov, author's collection)

Pyongyang street in 2005 (Photo by author)

Anti-American poster on Pyongyang street (Moravius)

Street vendors on Ongnyu Bridge, Pyongyang (Moravius)

At a bus stop (Moravius)

Building an apartment bloc in Pyongyang (Moravius)

Anglers at Wonsan pier (Moravius)

Construction works at the countryside (Moravius)

Oxcart, the major means of transportation in the countryside (Moravius)

Pyongyang outskirts in winter (Moravius)

Well-tended private plots near Nampo (Moravius)

Roadside market—Chongdan County (Moravius)

Road construction works (Moravius)

deliberately short, usually a few days only, and the number of places where exchanges can be made is also limited.

The intended result of such a policy is a dramatic reduction in the money supply, which is very good for curbing inflation. In Communist countries, which tended to embrace this kind of currency reform, the policy had an important added benefit: it wiped out illegal savings of black market operators. People who lived on their official salaries and/or tended to keep money in government-controlled banks suffered as well, but to a far lesser extent when compared to the sorry fate of those involved in unsanctioned economic activities.

Accordingly, on the morning of November 30 (at 11:00 a.m., to be exact), the North Korean populace learned that old banknotes would go out of circulation. As was often the case with such reforms, it was accompanied with devaluation: two zeroes from the North Korean paper currency, the won, had to be lopped off, so 100 "new" won were supposed to buy as much merchandise as 10,000 "old" won. This would make the prices roughly similar to what they used to be in the early 1990s, just before the collapse of the state-run economy. The change of the banknotes had to be completed within less than a week and the exchange limit was initially set at 100,000 "old" won per person—equivalent to $30 on the then-ongoing exchange rate. Panic ensued, since many North Koreans, especially those involved in private economic activities, had significant amounts of cash holdings in North Korean currency. Many a private company faced collapse (as was intended by the reform planners).

The North Korean currency reform of 2009 had one striking peculiarity, however, which made it different from its prototypes and doomed it to failure. It was declared that all people who were employed by state-run factories and institutions—that is, virtually all those legally employed in the economy—would receive the same amount in the new currency in wages as they did in the old currency. This measure effectively constituted a hundredfold (that is, 10,000 percent) overnight increase in salaries and wages. Take, for example, the case of a skilled worker who dutifully attended his or her nonfunctioning factory and was before the currency reform paid 3,500 won per month. After the reform, the worker was still to be paid 3,500 won per month. At the same time, the price of all goods and services was supposed to go down a hundredfold—for example, the price of rice was officially fixed at the level of 22 new won per kilo, instead of the prereform level of 1,800–2,000. This—theoretically!—implied that his "new" 3,500 won would buy as much as "old" 350,000 won.

For a while, foreign observers were taken aback by such a seemingly irrational move and speculated about secret designs behind the plan—or even refused to believe the first reports about the promised 10,000 percent rise of wages. However, it soon became clear that no secret design existed, and that reports were true indeed. Obviously, the people who approved the plan did not quite understand that by increasing salaries a hundredfold overnight they would produce a tidal wave of inflation, and not a dramatic increase in living standards.

North Korea has undergone currency reforms a number of times, and its financial experts are aware of similar reforms elsewhere—so one cannot help but wonder how such a bizarre feature made its way into the reform plan. One can speculate that planners initially intended to follow the well-established pattern and launch a standard confiscatory currency reform—that is, a reform in which most of the cash deposits would be appropriated by the state, and both salaries and retail prices would be decreased in equal proportions. However, it seems likely that at the last moment somebody intervened and ordered a dramatic revision of the plan, suggesting to dramatically increase official salaries.

The person who suggested this was unbelievably naïve, not to say ignorant, about the fundamental workings of an economy, where human beings have to divide limited resources and are not able to simply create resources with paper alone. One should not be so surprised by such naiveté. Taking into consideration the mechanics of the North Korean state, such a decision had to be initiated (or at least personally approved) by Kim Jong Il himself. The North Korean ruler has never in his life had to worry about paying for groceries or saving for a new car (let alone for a rainy day). Kim Jong Il was indeed a brilliant power broker and a world-class diplomatic manipulator, but he had a reputation for being almost comically incompetent in matters of economic management—and the 2009 reform confirmed this widespread opinion.

One can easily imagine how the Dear Leader would look through a currency reform plan and say: "And what about poor wage-earners? Should we not reward the people who remained loyal to the socialist industry and did not go for black markets? Why not increase their salaries, so they will become affluent, more affluent than those anti-socialist profiteers of the black market?" One would imagine that few, if any, officials would dare to explain the dire economic consequences of such generosity to the Dear Leader.

From the first hours, the currency reforms took a very messy turn indeed. People rushed to save their earnings and savings, and panic buying ensued. In a sense, this was expected to happen, but the scale of panic was unusual. To placate the situation, the authorities adjusted the rules, increasing the maximum exchange limits, but this did not help. Unfortunately, further actions merely exacerbated the crisis.

The authorities obviously supposed that the PDS would start functioning immediately, delivering the rations to the masses, but this did not (and could not) happen. As one would expect, inflation began to speed up. For a while the government kept issuing restrictions on the maximum market price for essential goods—for example, rice should not be sold for more than 24 won per kilo. The market ignored these regulations. In rare cases when the regulations were enforced by police, nobody was going to sell at the price that was well below the market equilibrium, so goods disappeared. In an attempt to rein in the chaos (and, perhaps, to "punish" the stubborn merchants and vendors), the regime closed all markets in December. In early January 2010, hard currency shops, where the elite and new rich could buy quality goods, were closed as well. This latter decision delivered a blow to the highly privileged groups of the population. In January it did not necessarily help to be an army general, a spy master, or a successful antiques dealer—even these people would have trouble getting daily food for their families.

For a brief while in January and February 2010, a major outbreak of public discontent seemed to be within the limits of the possible. The dissatisfaction was expressed with unprecedented frankness. It was the first time in decades even highly privileged members of the Pyongyang elite openly

criticized their government's actions when talking to foreigners. Russian
students in Pyongyang were approached by their classmates who did not
bother to hide their anger about the currency reform, and North Korean
diplomats sometimes made pointed comments to their foreign opposite
numbers. A military attaché of one Western country (not exactly friendly
from the North Korean point of view) told me that his opposite numbers
related that the North Korean government "doesn't quite understand what
it's doing." One can imagine how angry a military intelligence officer in
one of the world's most controlled societies has to be in order to share his
frustration with an imperialist outsider.

It is not coincidental that around this time rumors about the impend-
ing collapse of North Korea began to spread. To an extent these rumors
were probably circulated by South Korean conservatives then in control in
Seoul, but the sense of insecurity was briefly shared by many people who
had firsthand access to Pyongyang (not least by the Chinese whose unease
was palpable in those days).

But nothing serious happened. By April, it was business as usual
(almost). Foreign currency shops and private markets were reopened in
February, the rich and powerful stopped complaining, and the humbler
folks resumed their usual economic activities, which lay well outside the
shrinking government-controlled sphere.

In the aftermath of the reform fiasco, the government withdrew all
restrictions that had been introduced in the 2005–2009 antimarket campaigns. The local authorities were explicitly ordered in May 2010 not to
intervene with the daily working of markets—as long as politically
dangerous items, like South Korean DVDs, were not on sale. It was again
unofficially permitted to sell grain at the market price, and traders regardless of age or gender were allowed to conduct business much as they liked.
Obviously, the government again implicitly admitted that North Korea in
its present shape could not exist without active markets—its hyper-Stalinist rhetoric notwithstanding.

There were talks that the North Korean premier, soon to be ousted from
his job, apologized for "mistakes" when talking behind closed doors to a
gathering of officials in Pyongyang. There were also widespread rumors

that Pak Nam-gi (a high-level KWP official, responsible for economic policy) was executed for his "counter revolutionary activities and espionage." Allegedly, the old bureaucrat was accused of being a lifelong American spy who deliberately mishandled the reform in order to inflict damage to the North Korean economy. Both rumors were widely reported in the international media, and might be true indeed, but one should keep in mind that neither was confirmed by North Korean official sources.

There is nothing surprising about this silence. However strange it might appear to a reader, the entire issue of the currency reform was *never* mentioned in the open-access North Korean media. When the entire country was in an unprecedented state of chaos, not a single article in the official newspapers even mentioned what was going on. All information and instructions reached the North Korean populace through classified channels: notices were put on the boards at the banks, markets, and shops, and announcements were occasionally made over cable radio whose programming could not be heard by outsiders (and often differed from one neighborhood to another). References to the currency reform in the official media could be found only in the types of media that are inaccessible to the average North Korean and exclusively target a foreign audience—like, for instance, the pro-North newspaper in Japan (*Choson Shinbo*).

The government succeeded in getting the political situation under control, but it could not do much about the law of supply and demand. Thus, a tidal wave of inflation rose immediately after the reform—and what else would one expect after an effective 10,000 percent overnight increase in all wages and salaries? Within a few months, the four-digit inflation wiped out whatever little gains state employees had received from the entire operation. By late 2010 the price of food and consumption goods stabilized at roughly the same level as before the currency reform (which could have been predicted by anyone who ever took Economics 101).

In essence, the bold attempt to deny the law of supply and demand ended pretty much like a challenge to the law of gravity would. It remains to be seen, however, whether North Korean leaders have learned their lesson. The level of economic ignorance they have demonstrated in 2009 makes one suspect that the Kim family (and, perhaps, many of their top

advisers) cannot grasp even the basic mechanisms that govern a functioning economic system. Admittedly, this ignorance about modern economics does not prevent them from being shrewd politicians who
recognize what they need to do in order to stay in power. They know how
to maintain a world where they and their families will have no need to
worry about such mundane matters as paying their bills.

Nevertheless, it is possible that the North Korean leaders have learned
a thing or two from their dangerous encounter with the world of the market economy. Beginning in May 2010 attempts to reverse the marketiza-
tion were abruptly stopped, and for the following years the markets were
left alone. In essence, the government, burned by their 2009 failure,
returned to the policy of the late 1990s: while markets are not endorsed,
they are for all practical purposes tolerated.

THE BELATED RISE OF A "NEW STAR GENERAL"

Since the early 1970s North Korea has been a family dictatorship, an
absolute monarchy in everything but name. Consequently, it was almost
universally expected that in order to maintain the stability of the Kim
family regime, Kim Jong Il would eventually anoint one of his sons as
successor. Rumors about a coming succession have widely circulated in
the media since the mid-1990s. International media outlets occasionally
run stories where, whilst citing "well-informed sources" inside North
Korea, they claimed that Kim Jong Il had "just made a decision" about the
succession.

In discussing Kim Jong Il's alleged choice, the media named a number
of allegedly approved candidates—including all three known sons of Kim
Jong Il, his brother-in-law, his sister, his daughter, and his current mistress. But until 2008 all these reports were proven to be false. For some
reason, Kim Jong Il was not in a hurry to anoint an heir designate until
almost the end of his reign.

For a while during the 1990s, most people expected that Kim Jong Il
would choose his eldest son Kim Jong Nam as a successor. This didn't

happen, however. In May 2001 Kim Jong Nam was apprehended by the Japanese immigration service when he tried to enter Japan on a fake Dominican passport. He was accompanied by two women, one of whom was obviously his wife while another was likely to be a servant, as well as by a child. When questioned by the immigration authorities, Kim Jong Nam admitted his true identity and explained that he just wanted to visit Disneyland.

It was widely reported that this incident led to a falling out between Kim Jong Nam and his father, but these claims are based on hearsay. It is clear, however, that over the last decade Kim Jong Nam has spent most of his time in Macao and China, seldom visiting Pyongyang. He was not even seen at his father's funeral in December 2011. Reputedly, he runs the Kim family's finances from these locations, but the exact nature of his activities in Macao remains murky.

When Kim Jong Il finally made his choice for successor, he decided to promote his youngest son, Kim Jong Un, who was probably born in 1983—his exact age was never known with certainty. Kim Jong Un was educated in Switzerland, where all children of Marshal Kim attended high school. Not much is known about the youngest Kim—even his name for a long time was misspelled in the media. Obviously, after a few years in Switzerland, Kim Jong Un was brought back home and received some individual training at Kim Il Sung University.

Kim Jong Il finally made up his mind in late 2008, soon after he suffered a serious health problem—apparently, a stroke. This might have reminded him about his own mortality, so in early 2009 he spread word among North Korea's bureaucrats and the party faithful that a new genius of leadership had emerged from within the ancient lands of Korea. By the summer of 2009, the propaganda began to target virtually everybody and the name of the "Young General Kim" or "New Star General" was frequently invoked at regular indoctrination sessions. Propagandists did not explicitly state that the new shining star of political wisdom was somehow related to Kim Jong Il and Kim Il Sung.

The succession became semiofficial in September 2010, when the Korean Workers' Party held its conference, the first official convention of the party top-brass since the 1980 KWP Congress. On the eve of the conference, Kim Jong Un and his aunt Kim Kyŏng-hŭi were promoted to the rank of four-star general (becoming, perhaps, the world's youngest person and the world's only woman, respectively, to hold such rank). At the same conference, Kim Jong Un was appointed deputy chairman of the Central Military Committee of the Party, a previously unimportant institution that has now been brought to the administrative forefront of the North Korean government.

Since then, the North Korean media began to report Kim Jong Un's activities. He often appeared in the company of his father while visiting military units and model factories, or chatting with steel workers and tractor drivers. Paeans to his wisdom and talent began to appear in the media with increasing frequency.

When Kim Jong Un was first introduced to the North Korean public in September 2010, he appeared clad in a Mao suit, which was completely identical to the attire his grandfather used to sport in the 1950s. Nowadays such a suit is decisively out of fashion, so the Young General's choice of clothes had clear political connotations—it showed that he was a rightful successor to the dynasty once founded by his grandfather. It helps, of course, that Kim the Third has a striking resemblance to Kim Il Sung (and not just because he is also unusually stout for a North Korean). To emphasize Kim Jong Un's connections to his father, a similar visual message was employed. In winter the youngest Kim appeared before cameras in a gray parka and fur hat that were completely identical to those of his father. In such ways, the average North Koreans were reminded that their country would eventually be run by a reincarnation of Kim Il Sung and Kim Jong Il.

The choice of Kim Jong Un as the successor was somewhat unexpected. Prior to 2008 his candidacy was not seriously considered by Pyongyangologists, since he was seen as excessively young and lacking in tangible experience. He spent a large part of his childhood overseas, while as a youngster he led a secluded life in the palaces of the Kim family. He probably doesn't know much about the country he has to run, and most of the top North Korean dignitaries, in their late 60s, 70s, and 80s, could easily be his grandparents. It was most likely assumed that for a while, Kim Jong Un would remain a figurehead, assisted by a team of experienced advisers.

It is important that 2009– 2010 was a time when Kim Jong Il's sister, Kim Kyŏng-hŭi, and her husband, Chang Song-t'aek, rose to the summit of political power in North Korea. Kim Kyŏng-hŭi, who spent most of her life as the top manager of North Korea's light industry (not exactly a success area), was in 2010 promoted to the rank of full (four-star) general. In all probability Kim Jong Il reasoned that the relatively young Kim-Chang couple (they are in their mid-60s) would make the best regents for his inexperienced son.

Probably such an arrangement was also welcomed by the entire old guard, who assumed that a young and inexperienced leader would have no choice but to hew to their advice—so that even after Kim Jong Il's death, they would run the country as they pleased, at least for a few years.

Not everyone was happy about the decision, but no sane North Korean would express his or her doubts openly. The only exception was Kim Jong Un's semi-exiled half-brother Kim Jong Nam, who hinted that the decision might be problematic while still confirming his loyalty toward the family. In October 2010, during an unusually long and frank interview with the Japanese Asahi TV, he said: "Personally I oppose the hereditary succession for three generations, but I presume there were internal reasons. We should abide by such reasons if there are any."[22] In January 2011, during a short interview with *Tokyo Shimbun*, he was even more frank. Reportedly, he said: "Even Chairman Mao Zedong of China did not enforce hereditary succession. [Hereditary succession] does not fit with socialism, and my father was against it as well. [. . .] My understanding is that [the power succession] is intended to stabilize the internal system. North Korea's in-stability leads to instability in the region."[23] In the second half of the same interview he allegedly added that "in the peculiar situation of North Korea," reforms and openness might lead to the regime collapse.

THE SUDDEN BEGINNING OF A NEW ERA

When, at noon on December 19, 2011, the people of North Korea saw the clothes of the new anchorwoman from their TV set, they probably guessed instantly what had happened. Clad in mourning attire and tearful, the

announcer delivered the big news. North Koreans were informed that
Kim Jong Il had died two days earlier, during the morning of December
17. It was stated that he was on his famous palatial train en route to provide on-the-spot guidance somewhere in the countryside. This statement
has since been put into doubt, but the exact circumstances of his death are
not that important. Whenever and however he died, the 17-odd years of
his rule came to an abrupt end.

At the time of Kim Jong Il's demise few doubted that Kim Jong Un
was meant to become his successor. Nonetheless, it was by no means a
foregone conclusion that the second dynastic transition would go
smoothly. It seems that Kim Jong Il had been expecting to live a few
years longer than he actually did. Obviously he and his entourage assumed that they would have three to seven years at their disposal to
prepare a smooth transition and train Kim Jong Un for his new duties
and responsibilities.

It is often overlooked that Kim Jong Un had not been explicitly proclaimed the successor to his father. Of course, the way the media treated
him left no doubt about his destiny. Nonetheless, at the moment of Kim
Jong Il's death, Kim Jong Un was technically merely a four-star general,
one of a dozen top military officers, four-star generals, vice marshals, and
marshals of the Korean People's Army (even though, admittedly, by far the
youngest of them all). He was also a vice chairman of the Party's Central
Military Commission, a rather obscure part of the Korean Workers' Party
structure, which has played only a minor political role since the mid-
1970s. Obviously, it was assumed that in the near future Kim Jong Un
would be finally proclaimed successor and officially made second-in-
command to his father.

It might be surmised that Kim Jong Un's official promotion to heir designate was initially scheduled to take place amidst the expected gala cele-
brations of Kim Il Sung's 100th birthday in April 2012. However, Kim Jong
Il died before these plans could be brought to fruition.

However, this uncertainty had little immediate impact on subsequent
events. Within days after Kim Jong Il's death, the North Korean media
extolled the masses to switch their loyalty to Kim Jong Un. In quick

succession, Kim Jong Un was immediately made Supreme Commander of the Korean People's Army and acquired the title of Supreme Leader. His name began to appear in bold script in the official publications. In a curious and Orwellian twist, the North Korean propagandists edited the older copies of the regime's official newspaper, so in the online PDF archive the name of the Supreme Leader appears in bold even in the issues from early 2011 when it was not actually spelled this way.

Perhaps the most surprising thing about the dynastic transition is that it went so smoothly, without anything unexpected occurring. Everything happened more or less completely in line with what was predicted by Pyongyangologists. Kim Jong Un inherited power without any visible challenge—even though his immediate inferiors in the hierarchy could easily be his parents and even grandparents. As expected, for the first months of his rule Kim Jong Un was surrounded by a trio of advisers, Chang Song-t'aek, Kim Kyong Hee, and Lee Yong Ho (Kim Kyong Hee has been slightly pushed aside by her husband and has featured less prominently than most experts expected).

In most other dictatorships, such an embarrassingly young and politically inexperienced dictator would almost certainly face a challenge from within the inner circle. This did not happen in North Korea (so far), and with good reason: the Pyongyang decision makers are aware that any instability might have grave consequences for all members of the elite. An open clash at the top is likely to provoke political chaos, in which winners and losers alike will perish. In other words, it seems that North Korean leaders have internalized the dictum of Benjamin Franklin, who famously said, "Gentlemen, we must now all hang together, or we shall most assuredly all hang separately."

With his own shortcomings, this young and somewhat comical-looking, rotund man is the embodiment of legitimacy in North Korea. He belongs to the Paekdu bloodline and he is the son and grandson of the top leaders. In the modern world, this might appear to be a weak, even bizarre foundation to build a political power structure upon. But the North Korean leadership, surrounded by a hostile world and presiding over potentially dangerous subjects, have nothing better.

The North Korean media had no time to build up a sufficiently impressive personality cult of their new leader. After all, Kim Jong Il was successor for 20 years before his father's death but Kim Jong Un had just over a year. So one should not be surprised that Kim Jong Il still remains the most frequently mentioned personality in the North Korean media, and soon after his death, Marshal Kim Jong Il even got a promotion—on February 14, 2012, he became a Generalissimo.

Kim Jong Un began to follow his father's routine. He has been frequently shown doing on-the-spot guidance in military units and collective farms across the country. His wisdom and warmth have been much extolled and North Korean TV has hastily produced a documentary about his greatness. This is where we can see footage of the "Supreme Leader" getting out of a tank and toying with a rifle. In other words, everything has continued much as before—the only difference initially being that Kim Jong Un, unlike his father, was quite willing to deliver public speeches.

Soon after Kim Jong Un's ascension, on December 30, the National Defense Commission issued a statement where the North Korean top leadership said explicitly: "We declare solemnly and confidently that the foolish politicians around the world, including the puppet group in South Korea, should not expect any change from us."

There were some unusual occurrences nonetheless. For instance, on February 29, 2012, North Korea signed what became known as the "Leap Day Agreement" with the US representatives in Beijing. This agreement was concluded after years of near complete breakdown in the lines of communication between Pyongyang and Washington. The agreement gave North Korea 240,000 tons of food aid in exchange for their assurances that they would refrain from testing nuclear devices and/or missiles. To the great surprise of all observers, and to the great annoyance of the doves in Washington, North Korea almost immediately reneged on the agreement and announced what it called a "peaceful satellite launch." The test was carried out on April 13. The reasoning behind the launch following such an agreement remains unclear. The agreement was broken within weeks of it being signed and did not seemingly bring any benefit to Pyongyang—not a single ton of food was delivered. Infighting in the bureaucracy or a lack of communication between different agencies in the North Korean government seem to be plausible explanations.

The missile launch, along with the fallout following its failure, was rather unusual in and of itself. North Korea announced its intention to launch a satellite into space well in advance and even invited foreign journalists to come and witness these momentous events. The rocket failed 90 seconds after launch. In an unprecedented move, the North Korean government explicitly and almost immediately admitted the failure.

This was quite remarkable. Three previous launches (1998, 2006, 2009) of long-range missiles had all ended in failure as well, but the North Korean authorities had officially insisted that the 1998 and 2009 launches were both successes, while the attempted 2006 launch was never mentioned in the North Korean media. By openly admitting this time that the satellite did not reach the orbit, Kim Jong Un took an unprecedented step—in effect acknowledging that technical failures are possible even in his country, blessed with Juche science though it is.

The real changes, however, could only be observed somewhat later, in summer. In July 2012, Kim Jong Un came to the concert of a newly established pop music group named Moranbong (which is also the name of a very famous scenic hill park in downtown Pyongyang). The official media reported that the group would greatly contribute to the "further development and construction in People's Korea." Well, perhaps, but the group's first concert was rather unlike anything North Korea has ever seen. To start with, the female performers who comprised the group were dressed rather risqué by North Korean standards. The music performed included the theme from the Hollywood movie *Rocky* and a song by Frank Sinatra. While this music was being performed, actors dressed as Mickey and Minnie Mouse, Winnie the Pooh, and Tigger, too (to quote A. A. Milne) were on the stage. Disney lawyers even felt obliged to release a statement soon afterward confirming that they had not been involved nor received prior permission for the concert.

There was no doubt that this display of cuddly creatures on national TV was supposed to be a media event. Kim Jong Un himself was present, and his august presence left little doubt that this combination of risqué dress and American pop cultural icons had his unconditional approval. Up until now, America has been presented as a source of capitalist decadence, lust, and sleaze, with its popular culture vilified as an embodiment of abnormal and immoral qualities.

Admittedly, icons of Disney cartoons are by no means unknown to many North Koreans living in major cities. They are often present on kids' apparel and toys imported from China and sold in the marketplace. But there is a difference between tolerating the presence of Mickey "imperialist" Mouse on personal property and promoting him to stardom via national TV.

Kim Jong Un was not alone at the concert. He was accompanied by a mysterious, beautiful woman, dressed impeccably in black. Soon after, the same woman would be seen on a number of other public occasions by the side of the Supreme Leader. Many Pyongyang watchers began to speculate about who she was, the vast majority quickly concluding that she was likely to be Kim's wife. Speculation was not to last long, however, as North Korean media soon explained who she was. Her name was Ri Sol Ju and Kim Jong Un had indeed married her. She has subsequently accompanied her husband quite a few times, talking to kids in a kindergarten, greeting generals at a military meeting, riding a roller coaster, and enjoying the company of a young seal in Pyongyang Zoo (often sporting the latest Dior bag).

By North Korean standards this is all but unprecedented. Kim Il Sung's first wife Kim Jong Suk was eventually made into a major object of personality cult, but she was completely unknown in her lifetime. His second wife would enjoy a brief spell of political prominence and perhaps had major political ambitions in the 1970s, but she would soon fade into obscurity and would only appear in public when her husband met visiting foreign dignitaries who happened to come to North Korea with their spouses. Kim Jong Il was even more strict in this regard, so none of his numerous wives and live-in girlfriends ever appeared in public in that role. His last mistress, Kim Ok, occasionally accompanied him during overseas trips, but her true identity was never admitted and she was officially just a member of the delegation.

Both the open endorsement of Western pop culture and the willingness to show off his beautiful wife might be attributable to Kim Jong Un's less than advanced age, as well as his desire to make his country into a less boring place. After all, he had just recently been a Swiss schoolboy, an admirer of gadgets and pop music. However, these actions also indicate that he is at least willing to experiment with new ideas and challenge the existing norms of public behavior.

It has subsequently become clear that Kim Jong Un does not merely want to change cultural and symbolic things alone. On July 17, the first visible crack appeared in the seemingly cohesive North Korean elite. On that day, at a special meeting of the Politburo, Vice Marshal Lee Yong Ho, a member of the de facto regency trio, was suddenly ousted from all his official posts. The official explanation was health problems, but almost nobody took this seriously. Lee Yong Ho's removal was probably another sign of the ongoing rise of party apparatchiks and industrial managers who are pushing aside the generals. Some of these people are probably more inclined to experiment than are the top brass in the military.

Around the same time, reports about changes in agricultural management began to appear. From the little that is known about the new agricultural policies it appears that these reforms are relatively piecemeal if compared to Chinese reforms of the 1980s, but quite similar to the initial experiments that took place in the late 1970s. Under the system that is to be implemented in a small number of trial areas, farmers will be permitted to dispose of (at market price) all that they produce in excess of government quotas. Concurrently, rumors about imminent changes in industrial management began to circulate as well.

Does this mean that Kim Jong Un is inclined to steer North Korea toward Chinese-style reforms? It is of course too early to say for certain, but it seems that the young dictator wants to run things somewhat differently. He wants to break with at least some of the established traditions of his father's regime. He seemingly does not share the fear his father and his father's advisers had about the likely political consequences of reform.

Of course, this does not mean that these fears were and are unfounded and paranoid. On the contrary, it might be that the behavior of a former pupil at a Swiss private school is indeed reckless and dangerously adventurous (if judged from the elite point of view). It is too early to say whether Kim Jong Un will be able to proceed with more changes (even though it seems likely) and whether his desire for change will be translated into a comprehensive reformist strategy. Opponents of reform may succeed in removing him from power or persuade him that, in the peculiar case of North Korea, reforms are too risky (as reforms indeed seem to be). And, of course, if young Kim succeeds in thwarting the opposition, he will still have to face the forces his policy will unleash. His well-experienced and street-smart father avoided changes because he believed that such forces would be too powerful to control. It remains to be seen whether much younger Kim Jong Un, who probably learned a significant part of his politics from computer games, will be able to control these forces of popular discontent and escalating political expectations.

Be that as it may, the second succession in North Korea is sure to bring us more surprises than the first did in 1994.

THE CITY OF MONUMENTS

Pyongyang is usually presented as an ancient city. And this, in a sense, is really the case. The area has been the site of a major settlement for nearly two millennia. However, the present Pyongyang was built almost from scratch in the mid-1950s.

This was largely the result of a major US bombing campaign that reached its height in 1952. The US command had hoped to bomb the North Korean government into submission, and by the end of the war, some 90 percent of the city ceased to exist and most of its population had fled to the countryside.

Reconstruction began in the 1950s. From the very beginning, the new government wanted to build an exemplary Communist city free from reactionary traces of the feudal and imperialist past (Kim Il Sung was quite explicit when he said, "There were many defects in Pyongyang because it was built in an uncultured and lopsided way, under Japanese imperial rule"). The skyline that emerged owed much to the late Stalin's Soviet

Union. Indeed, many parts of the 1950s and 1960s Pyongyang look exactly like a Soviet provincial city of the same period. At the time, many important positions in the construction industry were occupied by Soviet Koreans who would later be purged and accused of "wrecking."

The center of 1960s Pyongyang was called Stalin Street (eventually renamed Victory Street). However, a new round of major construction began in Pyongyang in the 1970s. This was a time when most of the major landmarks of modern North Korea were erected. On the hill overlooking the Taedong River, a great statue of Kim Il Sung was erected. Behind that, the museum of Korean Revolution was built. Not far from there one could see the Mansudae Theater, where the exemplary revolutionary operas were performed in the 1970s. The large central square, predictably named after Kim Il Sung, was topped off with a mammoth People's Study House. Most of these structures broke with earlier Soviet heritage and were built in a mock traditional style (but still with a touch of characteristic megalomania).

On the opposite side of the Taedong River, a Tower to the Juche Idea was erected in 1982. The general shape of the Chuch'e Tower duplicates that of the Washington monument in the US capital, but exceeds it in size. The tower is 150 meters high and is crowned with a 20-meter-high torch that is illuminated at night. The tower includes 25,550 granite blocks—one for each day Kim Il Sung had lived by the time the monument was unveiled.

And of course there were a great many high-rise apartment buildings constructed in the 1970s and 1980s. Some of these high-rise quarters are actually off-limits for normal Pyongyangites, including a large district near the 35-story Koryo Hotel. This is where Central Committee officials live behind high fences.

However, contrary to what a short-term visitor might think, the majority of Pyongyangites do not live in these apartments. One merely has to go to the Juche Tower in order to get a real idea about how the living quarters of Pyongyang are structured. With the exception of government residence areas, multistory apartment buildings serve as screens that stand on the perimeter of districts, inside of which one can see clusters of

(continued)

humble traditional dwellings that are not so different from village houses. On the outskirts of the city, no one bothered to try to disguise these houses and they are readily visible.

The construction boom ended abruptly in the late 1980s, when Soviet subsidies dried up. The sad, if somewhat comical, history of the Ryugyong Hotel is a reminder of it. This 110-story, as yet unfinished, hotel was meant to be the largest hotel in East Asia. Initially it was meant to be completed in 1989, but due to economic crisis, work stopped and for two decades the skyline of Pyongyang was dominated by a gigantic concrete pyramid (official photographers worked hard to make sure it was never seen in official photographs).

But very recently a new construction boom has begun in Pyongynag. New high-rise buildings and monuments started to appear after 2007, and even the ugly Ryugyong Hotel was finally glassed—thanks to a deal with an Egyptian mobile phone company. However, it remains to be seen whether the Ryugyong will ever be opened to the public. It might just be for show, like other things in Pyongyang.

The city of Pyongyang was built to be a visual representation of paradise as imagined by Kim Il Sung and his fellow guerrilla partisans. They have probably achieved what they wanted but one cannot be sure whether outsiders are sufficiently impressed by the results of their efforts.

CHAPTER 4

Survival Diplomacy

The North Korean elite of today finds itself in a peculiar and unenviable position. It cannot reform itself because in a divided nation, Chinese-style reforms are likely to trigger regime collapse, which in turn will bring ruin to the current elite. North Korea is therefore stuck with an outdated economic system that cannot generate growth and sometimes cannot even provide for the sheer physical survival of the country's population. Hence, the North Korean government has no choice but to seek outside aid just to stay afloat.

This is difficult, since such aid cannot be sought through the channels usually employed by poorer countries—that is, by lobbying international organizations and NGOs. "Normal" aid is not of help to North Korea's rulers because such aid always comes with conditions that are seldom compatible with their policy goals.

North Korean leaders know that they are unlikely to attract enough aid on politically acceptable conditions if they follow the established explicit and implicit rules of aid-seeking. They have thus decided to bend the rules, playing a myriad of games and using a variety of tools to seek aid on their own terms. While the outside world tends to concentrate on the nuclear issue, one should not forget that while the nuclear card is the best known and most powerful of these diplomatic tools, it is by no means the only one. The diplomatic survival games are played by the North Korean regime with admirable skill, but also with remarkable disregard for humanitarian concerns.

PLAYING THE NUCLEAR CARD

A discussion of North Korea's foreign policy should start with the nuclear issue, which has dominated all Western discourse about North Korea for two decades. Former Deputy Assistant Secretary of Defense Gregory Schulte recently described this attitude as a "fixation with nuclear diplomacy."[1] A Vietnamese diplomat, posted to the United States, once joked that he would have to work hard to explain to Americans that Vietnam is not a war. I'm not sure whether he's succeeded as yet, but it's certain that for the vast majority of Americans and Europeans, North Korea is a nuclear device.

This overemphasis on the nuclear issue has obscured the fact that for the North Korean leaders, the nuclear weapons program is not an end in itself but rather one of many strategies they use to achieve their overriding goal of regime survival. Like their unwillingness to reform themselves, their costly decision to go nuclear is anything but irrational. Instead, it is deeply related to the peculiarities of their domestic and international situation and unlikely to ever be reconsidered.

The United States and other major Western countries have good reason to worry about the North Korean nuclear program. But contrary to what North Korean propagandists now tell their domestic audience, US leaders do not lose sleep in fear of a North Korean nuclear attack on the United States. The North Korean nuclear potential is small and its delivery systems unreliable or nonexistent. Thus, at least in the foreseeable future, the chances of an attack are very low, and chances of a success lower still.

Admittedly, the North Korean military can be very creative and could compensate for the technological shortcomings through ingenious tricks—for example, a nuclear device can be hidden in an ordinary-looking fishing boat and then detonated somewhere in San Francisco Bay.

It might be argued that in the event of a war between the United States and North Korea, the trawler in question would probably arrive at its destination long after hostilities are over and the North Korean regime has ceased to exist. This is true, but a device might be detonated closer, like in Tokyo Bay or Incheon, a couple of dozen miles away from Seoul. Such a (relatively) low-tech revenge operation will not merely kill tens of thousands of people but also close down these important transportation hubs, creating an economic shockwave of global proportions.

Nonetheless, the probability of such a doomsday scenario is not high, so the North Korean threat is largely indirect—but still serious. North Korea's bold defiance of international counter-proliferation regimes sets a very dangerous precedent. If North Korea were to get away with its nuclear program, it would likely be followed by other rogue states.

Another worry of Washington is the threat of proliferation itself. Indeed, the North Korean government might be willing to sell nuclear technology or fissile materials to the highest bidder. Nuclear proliferation and cooperation between Pakistan and North Korea is a well-known fact and seemingly reliable intelligence indicates that North Korean nuclear weapons experts have maintained links with Iran, Burma, and Syria.[2]

Consequently, for the United States, denuclearization is the overwhelming concern while all other matters are seen as marginal. Had North Korean nukes not existed, few Washington movers and shakers would care about North Korea. Pyongyang decision makers rightly assume that nukes are their major leverage in dealing with the developed world—and they have made great use of this leverage in the last two decades.

The North Korean nuclear program has a long history: as early as 1959, the Soviet Union and North Korea signed their first agreement on cooperation in nuclear research. A similar agreement was soon concluded with China as well (Pyongyang never put all its eggs in one basket).

In the 1960s the North Korean version of Los Alamos began to take shape in the city of Yongbyon, some 90 kilometers to the north of Pyongyang. For reasons of greater secrecy, the nuclear research facility was called the "Yongbyon furniture factory." The major article of equipment of this "furniture factory" was not a sawmill but a small Soviet-designed research reactor, the IRT-2000, completed in 1965. In the 1970s the North Korean scientists independently modernized the reactor, increasing its output.

There are few doubts that from the early stages Pyongyang leaders considered the military applications of their nuclear program, but it seems that the decisive turn happened in the 1970s. At that time, South Korea was working hard to develop nuclear weapons of its own—and came quite close to success.[3] For the North, which has always had good intelligence about its archenemy, Seoul's nuclear ambitions were a well-known secret. As a result, in approximately 1975, the North Korean political leaders decided to speed up their own military nuclear program.

The chief political obstacle was the position of the former Soviet Union, the major supplier of nuclear know-how. Moscow took non-proliferation seriously, and had no intention of seeing its nuclear monopoly erode—let alone creating conditions where its rogue and unruly quasi-allies would be able to provoke serious trouble. Sensing the true intentions of Pyongyang, the Soviet Union made nuclear cooperation conditional on a number of measures that would seriously hinder the development of nuclear weapons. Incidentally, Washington treated South Korea's nuclear plans in much the same manner and eventually ended the nuclear ambitions of Seoul. China also did not want a nuclear power across its border, so the usual North Korean strategy of playing Beijing against Moscow didn't work as it usually did.

Nonetheless, Pyongyang tried hard. As Walter Clemens writes in his research on the history of the North Korean nuclear program:

> [S]everal features of its diplomatic behavior are of more than historical interest. First, Pyongyang was aggressive and insistent in seeking foreign aid and assistance for nuclear purposes [. . . .] Second, [. . .] North Korea's leadership consistently evaded commitments to allies on nuclear matters, particularly constraints on its nuclear ambitions or even the provision of information. Third, North Korea's words and deeds evoked substantial concerns in Moscow and other Communist capitals.[4]

The Soviets made their continuing cooperation conditional on North Korea's participation in the non-proliferation regime. In exchange for compliance, North Korea was promised technical assistance in building a nuclear power station of its own. Pyongyang bowed to Soviet pressure and in 1985 signed the Non-Proliferation Treaty.[5]

But the world changed. The Communist bloc that both controlled Pyongyang's nuclear ambitions and provided it with aid collapsed and the North Korean economy nose-dived immediately. North Korea also ceased to be a part of the uncomfortable but sometimes reassuring Cold War alliance system, so it had to take security far more seriously. To meet the new challenges, the nuclear program had to be sped up.

When promoting their nuclear program, North Korean leaders essentially had two main goals in mind.

First, the North Korean nuclear program serves military purposes. Nuclear weapons can be seen as the ultimate deterrent, so North Korean leaders believe that as long as they have a credible nuclear potential they are unlikely to be attacked by any foreign power, above all the United States. Theoretically, it could be argued that an alliance with China would provide North Korea with a measure of security. However, the Pyongyang leaders might be afraid that China would not be willing to get into a major confrontation in order to save the Kim family from annihilation—the world has changed much since 1950, when Chinese forces had crossed the Yalu.

Needless to say, this fear of being attacked was amplified by the experiences of the 1990s and 2000s, when a number of states were the subject of US military actions. After the Iraq War, North Korean diplomats and politicians frequently said to their foreigner interlocutors: "Had Saddam Hussein really had nukes he would probably still be in his palace." This opinion was further reinforced by events in Libya—after all, Colonel Gadaffi's willingness to surrender nukes did not prevent the West from a military intervention when Gadaffi's regime was challenged by the local opposition forces.

Second, Pyongyang requires nuclear weapons for diplomatic purposes—frankly, as an efficient tool for diplomatic blackmail. On balance, this goal seems to be even more important than using the nukes as a strategic deterrent.

Indeed, they do in fact necessitate such a blackmail tool. If we look at the geographic and macroeconomic indicators, the one of closest similarity to North Korea is Ghana. If the CIA Factbook is to be believed, in 2010 North Korea's and Ghana's populations were 24.4 and 24.7 million, respectively, while their per capita GDP were $1,800 and $1,700, respectively. Still, North Korea is light years ahead of Ghana when it comes to international attention and ability to manipulate the external environment. In terms of aid volume, North Korea punches above its weight.

The aid-monitoring regime in North Korea is remarkably lax by any accepted international standard. It has to be lax, since North Korea does not merely need foreign aid: it needs the aid that will come without too many conditions, and whose distribution the donors will not monitor too carefully. Contrary to what some extreme critics of the regime say, it does not want to starve its population to death. Kim Jong Il and his son Kim Jong Un, as well as their advisers, would probably much prefer to see North Korean farmers alive and well (and extolling the leadership's wisdom and benevolence), but their survival is not very high on the regime's political agenda. Thus, uncontrolled aid can be distributed to the chosen groups of the population whose support or, at least, docility is vital for the political stability—above all, to the military, police, officials, and the population of Pyongyang and other major cities. Therefore, the irritating presence of foreign monitors is not welcomed. Needless to say, political demands of the donors—like, say, a suggestion of changes to the economic management—are not acceptable, either.

So far, North Korean diplomats have been remarkably successful in getting aid on conditions that would be seen as unacceptable from another country—and there is little doubt that the nuclear program played a key role in this success.

AID-MAXIMIZING DIPLOMACY

The first nuclear blackmail campaign (aka, "the first nuclear crisis") was launched around 1990. Evidence of Pyongyang's nuclear weapons program began to surface, despite the fact that North Korean officials denied the very existence of such a program. Nonetheless, the evidence mounted, and North Korean diplomats did not really mind: the growing unease served their interests quite well (one cannot rule out that some leaks were even arranged by the North). As tensions mounted, North Korea threatened to withdraw from the Non-Proliferation Treaty, and at one point Pyongyang diplomats even promised to turn Seoul into a "sea of fire" if the necessary concessions were not made.

The blackmail brought success. After much saber rattling and diplomatic maneuvering, in 1994 the oddly named "Agreed Framework" treaty was signed in Geneva. According to the Agreed Framework, North Korea promised to freeze its military nuclear program and accept international monitoring of its nuclear facilities. North Korea also agreed to suspend construction of two additional nuclear reactors and ship some spent nuclear fuel rods out of the country.

In exchange, it got hefty payments. To handle the issues, an international consortium known as KEDO was created (KEDO stands for "Korean Energy Development Organization"). By far the chief donors to the KEDO budget were South Korea, Japan, and the United States (in 1995–2005 they provided $1,450, $498, and $405 million, respectively).[6] KEDO was to build in North Korea two light water reactors that are good for power generation but not particularly useful for production of weapons-grade plutonium. It was also promised that until the completion of the reactors, KEDO would regularly ship significant quantities of heavy fuel oil to North Korea, free of charge.[7]

It is widely rumored that the US negotiators were ready to be so generous because at that time they assumed the North Korean regime would not last long and thus the promised aid and concessions would not need to be delivered. For example, in 1994 Jeffrey Smith of the *Washington Post* quoted unnamed US officials who assured him that the implementation period of the Agreed Framework "is almost certainly a sufficient period of time for their regime to have collapsed."[8]

Apart from the light water reactors, North Korea also received a lot of foreign aid without too many conditions. To a large extent this reflected the mood that remained dominant during the Clinton administration. At the time, a number of US policy makers believed that by providing aid and pursuing the KEDO agreement, the United States might eventually build enough trust to persuade North Korean leaders to surrender their nuclear program completely—or at least keep the situation under control until the collapse of the Kim family regime, which they thought would happen soon.

It was against such a backdrop that North Korea, then in the grip of a disastrous famine, became a major recipient of foreign aid beginning in 1995–1996. Most of the aid was presented as purely humanitarian in nature and unrelated to the ongoing crisis, but there are good reasons to think that North Korean officials saw the aid as a kind of tribute, an additional reward for their willingness to ostensibly freeze their nuclear program. This might be a cynical view, but a look at the statistics confirms that North Korean officials might have been right in their hard-nosed assessment. As we'll see below, as soon as relations with the United States deteriorated in 2002, the American aid all but disappeared. The same thing happened to Japanese aid after a crisis in relations caused by revelations about the abduction of Japanese citizens. This hardly supports the view that the aid was driven exclusively by lofty humanitarian considerations.

Throughout the 1996–2001 period (the time when the food crisis was most acute) North Korea received a total of 5.94 million metric tons of food aid. Most of this aid came from countries described by Pyongyang's official propaganda as the "mortal enemies of Korean people"— the United States, South Korea, and Japan. The United States provided 1.7 million metric tons (28.6 percent of the total), South Korea provided 0.67 million metric tons (11 percent), and Japan provided 0.81 million metric tons (13.6 percent). Of the ostensibly "friendly" countries, only China was a major provider of aid throughout the 1996–2001 period, with 1.3 million metric tons of food shipped to the North.[9] The food shipments played a major role in mitigating the humanitarian disaster.

North Korean diplomats not merely succeeded in acquiring a large amount of aid, but also ensured that the aid came without too much obtrusive control, and hence could be channeled to those people whose compliance and support were vital for the regime's survival. Foreign monitors were denied any access to a significant part of the country, including areas that were hit hardest by the 1996–1999 famine. Even in the most permissive period, around 2004, the foreign monitors were allowed to supervise distribution only in 167 (of 201) counties.

No Korean speakers were allowed into the country, and until 2004 the authorities even banned World Food Program (WFP) personnel from attending Korean language classes. Monitoring teams were always accompanied by the government-assigned interpreters who filtered all questions and answers. North Koreans often assumed—probably correctly—that these people were by default on the payroll of the political police, so they were unlikely to say anything dangerous in this menacing atmosphere. The number of WFP monitors was kept small, and their inspection trips had to be approved by the authorities well in advance—so everything could be arranged and monitors usually saw only what their handlers wanted them to see.[10]

Things changed after the so-called second nuclear crisis. The crisis erupted in October 2002 when Assistant Secretary of State James Kelly was visiting Pyongyang. By that time the US government had acquired intelligence indicating that North Koreans were cheating, and that Pyongyang was secretly pursuing a uranium enrichment program. In Pyongyang, James Kelly confronted North Korean officials. What followed is not exactly clear: according to Kelly, the North Korean deputy foreign minister admitted the existence of the highly enriched uranium (HEU) program, but the North Koreans eventually denied that such admission had taken place. They came out with a different interpretation: according to Pyongyang's version of the story, the North Korean diplomat in question merely said that North Korea was entitled to have an HEU program since it was facing a hostile superpower—implying that the entitlement was more or less theoretical. At any rate, this exchange was taken as proof of the clandestine HEU program. With the wisdom of hindsight, this seems to be a correct assumption, since in 2009, after years of denial, Pyongyang admitted that it had the HEU program. In November 2010 North Korean officials proudly showed off a huge uranium enrichment facility to visiting US nuclear scientists.

It is possible that North Koreans hoped to acquire an additional source of income by negotiating a buyout of their HEU program for a hefty price—a scheme somewhat similar to the buyout of plutonium program in 1994. However, even if it was indeed the initial plan, it did not work as intended. With George W. Bush and his neoconservative advisers in the White House, things took a different turn. Instead of bargaining for another buyout, the United States cited the HEU program as proof that North Koreans should not be trusted. Large-scale aid was discontinued. The KEDO project was closed down, with all personnel being withdrawn from the construction sites between 2005 and 2006. In 2003 North Korea formally withdrew from the Non-Proliferation Treaty, becoming the first state to ever do so (and, actually, creating a dangerous precedent).

Obviously some Washington hard-liners assumed that without US aid North Korea would soon collapse. However, North Korean diplomats have been successful in finding substitutes for the US aid—from 2002 to 2010 aid shipments came from South Korea and, later, China compensated for the sudden halt of the US food and economic assistance. Indeed, the North Korean economy actually began its partial recovery right around the time when US aid was halted. At any rate, the Bush administration was not in the mood to talk to Kim Jong Il, whom Bush despised and once even described as a "pigmy" (North Korea itself was described as a part of the "axis of evil").

As an important part of efforts aimed at pressing the North Korean regime and driving it to denuclearization and/or collapse, the US government used Section 311 of the Patriot Act and targeted financial institutions it knew handled the money of the North Korean government and Kim family. They were accused of money laundering—an accusation not completely unfounded but perhaps exaggerated, as only a relatively small part of the Pyongyang income comes from illegal activities. In September 2005 a small bank in Macao, Banco Delta Asia (BDA), was singled out as a "money laundering outlet"—indeed, it was very involved in dubious transactions with Pyongyang. As a result, $25 million of North Korean funds were frozen and US banking institutions ended operations with the BDA.

Obviously, the US government wanted to set a precedent by issuing a warning to all banks that might wish to become too cozy with the North Korean regime. When it comes to state finances, $25 million is not a large sum of money even for a poor state like North Korea, but the decision produced a surprisingly strong reaction from Pyongyang—perhaps because the funds seemed to be the private treasure of the Kim family. For a brief while, international bankers avoided any interaction with their North Korean peers, and in some cases large transactions had to be conducted in cash. It was argued that such measures interrupted the supply of perks to the Kim family and top North Korean bureaucrats, whose appreciation for Swiss cheese and French cognac is well known.

An important byproduct of the "second nuclear crisis" was the launch of the six-party talks, which began in 2003 with the stated goal of laying the ground for the eventual denuclearization of the Korean peninsula. The talks were attended by the six powers involved in the ongoing nuclear crisis—the United States, China (the host of the talks), South Korea, Russia, Japan, and, of course, North Korea. From the very beginning there was little doubt that the talks were not going to achieve their stated goal, since the Kim family regime has never had the slightest intention to surrender its nuclear program. Nonetheless, the six-party talks were not useless: negotiations helped to ameliorate tensions and created a useful forum where Korea-related security issues could be discussed freely.

However, because the United States provided so little aid to Pyongyang between 2002 and 2006, relations between North Korea and the United States remained very tense. North Korean leaders therefore decided that it was time to dramatically raise the stakes.

By that time North Korea had amassed enough plutonium to produce a few crude nuclear devices. In early 2010 it was estimated that North Korea had manufactured 40 to 60 kg of weapons-grade plutonium, of which 24 to 42 kg was available for weapons production. Siegfried Hecker believes that North Korea is "most likely to possess a nuclear arsenal of four to eight primitive weapons," even though it still "appears a long way from developing both a missile and a warhead to launch a nuclear weapon to great distance."[11]

What followed was yet another exercise of Pyongyang's favorite tactics. When North Korean strategists are not happy about the situation and suspect that more aid and concessions can (and therefore should) be squeezed from the outside world, they follow the same routine. They first manufacture a crisis and drive tensions as high as possible. They launch missiles, test nukes, dispatch commandos, and drop all sorts of menacing hints. When tensions are sufficiently high, with newspaper headlines across the globe telling readers that the "Korean peninsula is on the brink of war," and foreign diplomats feeling a bit uneasy, the North Korean government suggests negotiations. The offer is accepted with a sigh of relief, giving North Korean diplomats the leverage to squeeze maximum concessions out of their negotiating partners as a reward for Pyongyang's willingness to restore the precrisis status quo. Usually, they succeed.

This policy was applied to Moscow and Beijing during the 1960s and 1970s (without missile launches, of course—but different and subtler ways were used to manipulate Moscow and Beijing). It also worked well during the first nuclear crisis of 1990–1994.

Consequently, during October 2006, North Korean leaders decided to make a point by conducting their first nuclear test. The yield was surprisingly low and it is possible that the nuclear device did not work as intended, but the underground explosion in remote northern mountains was enough to demonstrate that North Korea was indeed moving toward creating an effective nuclear weapons capability.

After the test, the UN Security Council immediately passed a properly stern Resolution 1718, which was supported by all permanent members (including Russia and China). At the time, optimists cheered the news and began to persuade themselves and everybody around that China had finally done the right thing and from now on would be in the same boat as the United States and major developed countries. This was not the case, of course: China was not in the same boat—and never will be. While unhappy about nuclear proliferation, China is not going to do anything that might trigger an acute domestic crisis in North Korea. Even though they professed to participate in the sanctions regime, the Chinese did not let it influence their position: on the contrary, 2006, the year of the first nuclear test, also marked an upsurge in the scale of Chinese aid to and economic cooperation with Pyongyang—and this scale has been increasing ever since.

As we will see below, South Korea, with left-leaning administrations in control from 1998 to 2008, was even more willing to shower North Korea with aid without asking too many questions about aid use and distribution.

The Bush administration belatedly realized that sanctions and pressure had not achieved the desired result. On February 13, 2007, a joint statement was produced during another round of the six-party talks. The joint statement promised the resumption of US and foreign aid in exchange for North Korea's theoretical commitment to eventual denuclearization. Around the same time, the State Department effectively halted the measures aimed at Banco Delta Asia and scaled down the operations against the real or alleged money laundering by the North Korean regime.

The present author learned about the 2007 joint statement while in Moscow, eating lunch with a group of Russian diplomats. An ambassador who was sitting next to me read the faxed text of the statement and said: "Well, from now on the North Koreans will know what to do when they run out of money next time." This was a really perceptive remark: the return to talks might have been a correct (or, at least, an unavoidable) decision, but the timing of the February 2007 joint statement was most inappropriate. Indeed, from the North Korean point of view, it did not merely confirm that blackmail works, but rather confirmed that blackmail works wonders. One could hardly find a better confirmation of the efficiency of Pyongyang's usual tactics—first make a crisis, then escalate tensions, and finally extract payments and concessions for the restoration of the status quo.

MEANWHILE, IN SOUTH KOREA . . . (THE RISE OF 386ERS AND ITS CONSEQUENCES)

Under the George W. Bush administration, Washington discovered that the US approach to North Korean issues seriously differed from that of the South Korean government, hitherto the United States' most reliable ally in East Asia. Some people even argued that the US-led sanctions were derailed by a soft-line policy that dominated the South Korean approach in the years between 1998 and 2008. This is probably not the case, since the hard-line stance was likely to fail anyway, but the discord between Seoul and Washington was nonetheless all too open and real. Needless to say, North Korean diplomats have made the most of these disagreements.

This discord has, above all, domestic roots, being brought about by slow but important changes within South Korean society. It makes sense to have a look at these changes—not least because they are likely to influence the situation for years to come.

From the end of the Korean War and until around 1980, South Korean politics and ideology were almost completely dominated by the Right. South Korean rightists were hard-line anti-Communists; they favored a long-term alliance with the United States as the cornerstone of their nation's foreign policy and saw the eventual unification of Korea under a capitalist and liberal regime as their primary long-term goal (although as time went on, their commitment to and interest in the unification began to wane slightly). These views were predominant among the political and intellectual elite, and were widely shared by the broader South Korean population. There were dissenters, of course, and some individuals, especially in academia, might have secretly held leftist views, up to the point of being orthodox Leninists. However, these people had almost no impact on the general political climate—living under a repressive and militantly anti-Communist regime, they had to keep their opinions to themselves.

Things began to change in the early 1980s, following a generational shift. The new generation of Koreans did not have firsthand memories of the Korean War and the destitution of the 1950s. They did not survive on cans of US food aid and they came to see three daily meals of rice (an unattainable dream for their parents' generation) as a natural and unexciting part of one's daily life. They also were the first generation in Korean history that had almost universal access to secondary education—and many of them proceeded to college as well. Much later, in the 1990s, this group was nicknamed the "386 generation," since they were born in the 1960s, attended universities in the 1980s, and were in their 30s in the 1990s when this term was coined.

This "386 generation" took spectacular economic growth for granted, despised the military dictatorships, and were skeptical about the market economy. They were a generation that managed to live through one of the greatest success stories in the history of capitalism without even noticing it. Where their once-starving parents saw growth, prosperity, and security, they saw inequality, social injustice, and subservience to foreign powers. The new generation of young Koreans—or rather its politically active minority—was passionately anti-authoritarian, but also anti-American, nationalist, and left wing.

The trademark combination of nationalism and hard-core leftism, as well as their deep disgust with the military regimes in Seoul, made a significant number of the 386ers into North Korean sympathizers. The early 1980s was an era when the works of Marx and Lenin were much perused by young South Korean intellectuals. Some of them went further: they read treatises on Juche thought and exchanged smuggled North Korean publications and transcripts of North Korean radio broadcasts. The more radical of these young dissenters began to imagine the North as a land of social justice, unspoiled Koreanness, and, somehow, democracy.

Leftist activists played a major role in the pro-democracy movement that in 1987 brought an end to decades of authoritarianism in South Korea. However, soon after this triumph, the more radical factions of the nascent South Korean radical Left suffered two major blows.

First, between 1989 and 1990, the Communist bloc disintegrated. It instantly became clear that neither the Soviet Union nor Eastern Europe were what South Korean student radicals somehow believed them to be, namely a paradise of workers' rights, general well-being, and true democracy, lands where happy peoples enjoyed an eternal bliss of a near-perfect social system.

Second, in the mid-1990s, the dramatic increases in contact and interaction with North Korea (both direct and indirect, via China) made it impossible to dismiss reports of North Korea's destitution as "fabrications of the reactionary forces" and "lies of CIA-paid hacks." It began to dawn on South Korean leftists that North Korea was a very poor Third World country run by an authoritarian government (they still cannot make themselves utter the word "dictatorship" when talking about the Kim dynasty). Up until now, many of South Korea's self-styled "progressive intellectuals" have remained remarkably willing to overlook even the most repulsive features of the Pyongyang regime, while being unforgiving when it comes to abuses committed by the South Korean military dictators.

Nonetheless, their initial enthusiasm for a Juche utopia vanished by the mid-1990s.

In the heyday of South Korean student radicalism, during the late 1980s, a vocal minority of activists believed that the country should be unified under some version of Leninist Socialism, more or less similar to the then-current North Korean system. The majority, however, preferred a less radical solution and talked of a confederative state where both parts of Korea would keep their peculiarities whilst moving toward a compromise in social and political terms. Theoretically, the South Korean Left, including its moderate factions, still prefers a confederation, obviously in the hope that within such a confederation a sufficiently "progressive" (read: non-market) model could prevail somehow.

Meanwhile, the mainstream also moved far away from the anti-Communism of former times while discovering important reasons to be skeptical about the prospect of unification as it had been understood before. Since the mid-1990s a growing number of younger South Koreans have began to quietly entertain doubts as to whether unification at the first opportunity would be such a good idea.

This ongoing shift of opinions reflected changes in South Korean society. The number of people in the South who have ever had direct personal connection with the North is dwindling. As of 2010, people born before 1940 constituted merely 9.8 percent of South Korea's population.[12] They are the only people, however, who might possibly have some first hand memories of the North or North Korean relatives and family members.

The bitter German experience also played a major role in the reassessment of a once rosy attitude toward the unification. News from Germany made Seoul decision makers and the general public realize that the unification of the North and South would be vastly more expensive than anybody had imagined. The difference in per capita income between East and West Germany was 1:2 or 1:3, while in Korea, even if one believes the most optimistic estimate, the ratio is 1:15 (pessimists think it is closer to 1:40). The ratio of the population is also less favorable than in Germany. Taking into consideration the ongoing German troubles, well known in Seoul, this sounds like a recipe for disaster.

The generational shift contributed to changes as well. The politically active youngsters of the 1980s (now in their 40s or even early 50s) wanted unification because they were both leftist and nationalist. Their fathers (now in their 60s and older) wanted unification because they were anti-Communist and nationalist. However, the youngest generation—the 386ers' children and younger siblings—are different. Born in the 1980s and 1990s, they are less nationalistic, less anti-American, more pro-market, and, most significantly, they do not really see North Korea as a part of their national community and tend to associate unification with economic hardship, not with the realization of some great national dream.

This slow-motion decline of the once-universal enthusiasm for unification is reflected by public opinion polls. In 1994 91.6 percent of South Koreans said they considered unification "necessary." In 2007, according to a poll conducted by Seoul National University, the number of such people shrank to 63.8 percent.

It is especially important that age matters: the younger a South Korean is, the less likely he or she will be enthusiastic about unification. A 2010 Seoul National University study of attitudes about unification indicated that 48.8 percent of South Koreans in their 20s said that "unification is necessary." These youngest participants actually constitute the only age group where the unification idea was supported only by a minority. Among people in their 30s, 55.4 percent of the participants agreed that "unification is necessary," and among those over 50, 67.3 percent favored unification.[13] This is not a surprise—everybody who interacts with younger South Koreans is aware that serious doubts about unification are common and indeed almost universal in this milieu. These people know that unification will be very expensive, and they do not quite understand why they should pay this money.

Even older people are having doubts these days. A Korean businessman in his early 70s, himself born in what is now North Korea, and with a long experience of interacting with Northerners because of his manifold business projects, recently described his feeling about the unification to the present author: "Well, the Northerners say they are so happy under the wise guidance of their Dear General. Let them be happy there, if they like it so much. They are so different from us by now. Even their physical appearance is different, they are so short! So, the later we'll have unification, the better. In a hundred years, perhaps."

It is remarkable that nowadays even supporters of unification seldom rely on nationalist or other idealism-driven rhetoric—obviously on assumption that such idealism is unlikely to be shared by their compatriots. Instead, they talk about the economic advantages of unification, which will give the South Korean economy access to the "cheap labor and rich mineral resources" of the North. Irrespective of whether such statements are true, they clearly reek of a quasi-colonial attitude toward the supposed "brethren"— and this attitude does not bode well for North Koreans' post-unification future.

However, there is one interesting peculiarity: these changes in public opinion are seldom reflected in public discourse. This silence is understandable. All "ideological packages" that exist in South Korea include ethnic nationalism as a key ingredient and the idea of unification is an inseparable part of all varieties of Korean nationalism. For any Korean public figure it would be politically suicidal to openly question the need of eventual unification. Any good Korean citizen, regardless of his/her views on any other issue, is expected to believe in the shared historic destiny of the North and South. This contradiction between professed beliefs and actual feelings makes many people look for excuses that would justify postponing unification into a distant undetermined future—but without falling into the heresy of openly challenging the need for unification as such.

A DECADE OF SUNSHINE

Against such a backdrop, in late 1997, Kim Dae Jung, a lifelong dissenter and pro-democracy activist, was elected president of South Korea. His campaign was based on a critique of the old right-leaning establishment. Kim Dae Jung promised more social security, a softer policy in dealing with North Korea, and a harsher approach to big business. Aging Kim Dae Jung was old enough to belong to the generation of the 386ers' parents, but the "386 generation" embraced his candidacy with much enthusiasm. The next elections in 2002 were won by another candidate who clearly associated himself with the South Korean nationalist left—Roh Moo Hyun, a former human rights lawyer and pro-democracy activist.

The conservative South Korean media sometimes described both presidents as if they were closet Communists. This was clearly not the case, and their opinions on the economy or welfare were not that much different from that of German Social Democrats or the British Labor Party (even though they and their supporters were remarkably nationalist by the current standards of the European Left). However, in dealing with the North, the left-leaning administrations were prepared to jettison the old hard line. To an extent their approach reflected the ideological biases of the 386ers, some of whom held important jobs in both administrations. At the same time this soft approach reflected the increasingly strong doubts the average South Korean had with regard to a German-style unification-by-absorption.

This is how the Sunshine Policy was born. This policy was launched by Kim Dae Jung's government in 1997 and continued by Roh throughout his term of 2002–2008. The stated goal of the Sunshine Policy was to encourage the gradual evolution of North Korea through unilateral aid and political concessions. The policy's name refers to one of Aesop's fables, "The North Wind and the Sun." In the fable, the North Wind and the Sun argue about who is able to remove a cloak from a traveler. The North Wind blows hard but fails to succeed, since the traveler wraps his cloak even more tightly to protect himself. The Sun, however, warms the air, thus forcing the traveler to remove the unnecessary cloak.

The policy was based on the belief that a soft approach would persuade the North to institute large-scale reforms, more or less similar to those undertaken in China and Vietnam, thus opening the way to a gradual and manageable unification, perhaps through some form of a North-South confederation. An important aspect of the underlying assumptions of this policy was a belief (in all probability, erroneous) that reform would prolong the existence of the North Korean state and make possible a gradual elimination of the huge economic and social gap between the two Koreas.

As Korea expert Aidan Foster-Carter has noted, "Despite the rhetoric of unification, the immediate aim [of the "Sunshine" policy] was to retain two states, but encourage them to get on better."[14]

After 1997 the South began to provide the starving North with considerable amounts of aid, but the breakthrough in relations between the two Koreas was achieved in September 2000, when President Kim Dae Jung went to Pyongyang to meet Kim Jong Il in the first-ever intra-Korean summit. Kim Dae Jung had to pay a political as well as financial price to achieve this success—it was later discovered that North Korea demanded a payment of $500 million as a preliminary condition for accepting the proposed summit. The payment was promptly delivered, and only then did the summit take place.

These concessions annoyed South Korean rightists, who often claim that "Kim Dae Jung paid $500 million in order to purchase a Nobel Peace Prize for himself." Indeed, the South Korean president became the Nobel Peace Prize winner in 2000, "for his work for democracy and human rights in South Korea and in East Asia in general, and for peace and reconciliation with North Korea in particular." There might be some kernel of truth in these accusations since Kim Dae Jung, being a lifelong politician, never forgot about self-promotion. But at the same time, the 2000 summit did open channels for a truly astonishing increase in inter-Korean exchanges.

As we remember, between 1996 and 2001, the United States and Japan were among the main providers of food aid to North Korea. By 2002 the United States dramatically reduced its aid after the "second nuclear crisis," while the South significantly increased its own aid to the North. During the period between 2002 and 2007, the North received 5.1 million metric tons of overseas food aid—some 850,000 tons in an average year. South Korea shipped to the North 2.41 million metric tons of food aid (nearly half of the total—47.1 percent). During the same years, China provided 1.60 million metric tons (31.3 percent of the total amount of foreign aid) while the United States shipped 0.57 million metric tons (11.2 percent).[15] The combined contribution of all other countries was marginal—yet another reminder of the essentially policy-motivated nature of the "humanitarian" aid to North Korea. Actually, the South Korean contribution was even larger than the figures suggest, since in the years of sunshine it also shipped huge quantities of chemical fertilizer (between 200,000 and 350,000 tons a year throughout 2000–2007, or some 35 percent to 45 percent of all fertilizer used in North Korean agriculture). Without these shipments, North Korean harvests would have been far lower.[16]

A great number of North-South economic projects, big and small, were launched during the years of 1998 through 2008. Most of them were officially described as "cooperative projects," but in actuality they tended to be lopsided. South Korean companies that dealt with the North were directly and indirectly subsidized by the South Korean government.

Among these projects three were of special importance—the Kŭmgang Mountain tourist zone, the Kaesŏng industrial zone, and the Kaesŏng City Tours. All these projects were politically acceptable for North Korea's leader, always worried about the possible political consequences of unrestricted interaction between Northerners and Southerners.

From this point of view, the Kŭmgang Mountain tourist zone, the first of the "Big Three" projects, can be seen as an ideal undertaking. It is, essentially, a fenced-off ghetto for South Korean tourists and hence politically safe.

The project was conceived as early as 1989, when Chung Ju-yung, the founding chairman of Hyundai Group, the largest South Korean business conglomerate, first met with the Pyongyang leaders, including Kim Il Sung himself. Chung Ju-yung was born in what is now North Korea, and in the last years of his long and eventful life he demonstrated a sentimental attachment to his native land. This seems to be the reason why his Hyundai Group (or, to be more exact, its Asan subsidiary) took on all three major intra-Korean projects.

Chung Ju-yung's proposal envisioned an establishment of a South Korean resort in North Korea. The resort was to be located in the Kŭmgang ("Diamond") Mountains, which for centuries have been seen in Korean culture as the embodiment of scenic beauty. The mountains conveniently lay near the DMZ.

In November 1998 the Kŭmgang project commenced operations. As with the majority of North-South "cooperation" projects, the South did most of the work while the North received the lion's share of the project's benefits. For the South Korean side, the project could hardly be called a success story. In January 1999 Hyundai predicted that by the end of 2004, there would have been a cumulative 4.9 million visits to the North. The actual figure was merely 0.9 million. Hyundai Asan also said in 1999 that by 2004 some 1.2 million South Korean tourists would visit the project annually. Yet the actual number of visits in 2004 was 274,000—four times below the initial expectations. In 2007 the number of visitors peaked at 350,000—an impressive figure, but still well below the rosy expectations of the late 1990s.[17] Between 2001 and 2002 the project nearly went bankrupt and only a massive infusion of the South Korean government funds saved it from capsizing.

The South Koreans did not rush to the new resort. This lack of enthusiasm was easy to explain, since the trips were not cheap: a tour to Kŭmgang would cost almost as much as cheaper tours to China or Southeast Asia. At the same time, the allure of North Korea, once clearly a "forbidden fruit," was diminishing in the South.

Once in the resort, South Korean visitors were not allowed to venture outside the fenced area. The local population was removed from this area completely, and only a few hundred North Korean minders and plainclothes "guides" were present there. Most of the semiskilled personnel at the project were ethnic Koreans recruited from China—they were willing to work for low wages, and they were politically safe for the North Korean authorities (like the tourists themselves, Chinese-Korean personnel were not allowed to leave the resort).

Nonetheless, some "ideological damage" is possible even in such circumstances. One of my North Korean interlocutors was sent to work at the resort construction during a labor mobilization in the early 2000s. During his stay, he had no contact with South Korean tourists whatsoever, and did not see them even from afar, but later, after his defection to the South, he mentioned this trip as a turning point in his ideas about the South. He could see some South Korean equipment, and also some buildings erected by the Southerners, and it was enough. He said: "I knew that the South was ahead of the North, but only after my trip to Kŭmgang tourist zone I realized how much ahead they actually are."

Much in line with the Kŭmgang tourist zone was the decision to start tours to the ancient city of Kaesŏng, which is located near the DMZ and has great historic significance for all Koreans. Compared to the Kŭmgang tourist zone, Kaesŏng city tours meant a greater level of exposure. Every day, the inhabitants of Kaesŏng could see dozens of large, shiny South Korean buses, which crisscrossed a small historical downtown. Each bus, apart from a driver, had two or three minders, whose job was to make sure that visitors would not take shots of the everyday life of the city. Pictures could be taken only at designated stops. Upon departure, all digital cameras (only digital cameras were allowed on tours) had to be checked frame by frame, and those visitors who dared to take politically incorrect pictures—of, say, an ox-cart on a city street—would have to pay a fine.

Nevertheless, the North Korean authorities obviously did not have enough money to ensure sufficient segregation of the South Korean tourists. The police did not allow North Koreans to get within a few dozen yards of tourists, but even from such a distance Northerners could see that Southerners were well dressed and unusually tall by Northerner standards.

Interaction with minders was also allowed and even frequently initiated by the minders themselves. Obviously, these young police and intelligence officers were supposed to do their job—that is, gain intelligence. Nonetheless, there is no doubt that in the process they also discovered many interesting things about actual life in the South. One might argue that the secret police personnel would know the truth anyway, but this is hardly the case: normally such people would be far too low in the pecking order of the North Korean bureaucracy to be allowed that much access to subversive knowledge about the "other Korea."

Of all the "three projects," the Kaesŏng industrial zone (KIZ) is by far the most significant both economically and politically. The idea of the KIZ is based on the increasingly common assumption that the interests of both Koreas can be served by a combination of Southern capital and technologies with Northern cheap labor. So, it was decided to develop an industrial park in the vicinity of the DMZ. In this industrial park South Korean companies would employ North Korean workers who, laboring under the supervision of South Korean managers, would produce cheap items for sale in South Korea and overseas.

The KIZ construction began in 2003, and by late 2004 the first production lines began to operate in the complex. Big business did not show much interest in the idea, so only small- and medium-sized South Korean companies chose to move into the KIZ. For them, the South Korean government provided generous inducements, which included, among other things, cheap loans and guarantees. The guarantees were especially important, since even in the early days of the Roh administration, when the North-South relations went through a short honeymoon, South Korean businessmen were afraid that overinvesting in the KIZ would one day make them hostages to the policies of both Seoul and Pyongyang.

Contrary to earlier worries, the KIZ was remarkably successful. Admittedly, as was the case with the Kŭmgang tours, the initial estimates were proven to be overoptimistic: in 2003 it was promised that as early as 2007 some 100,000 North Korean workers would be employed by some 250–300 South Korean companies in the area. The actual results were less impressive: by late 2010, some 120 South Korean companies operated at the KIZ, with 47,000 North Korean workers employed. Over half of the companies (71, to be exact) dealt with clothing and textiles. In 2010 the KIZ-based companies produced goods worth $323.3 million (again, slightly over half consisted of textiles and clothing). For the mammoth South Korean economy, this is small change, but for the North this income is significant enough.[18]

The KIZ is located some 10 kilometers away from the DMZ, so the South Korean personnel commute daily, but some of them stay there overnight (thus creating an ever-present possibility of a hostage situation in case of a crisis). As of 2010 there were about 800–900 South Korean technicians and managers who supervise the North Korean workers.

Theoretically, the South Korean companies pay their North Korean workers the agreed basic monthly wages of $61 (as of 2010), but this figure does not include overtime premiums and special incentives, so the actual monthly payment seems to be close to $90–100 per worker. However, this salary is paid to a North Korean government agency that makes a number of deductions, so only a fraction of the total—less than 35 percent—reaches the workers' pockets. Indeed, the KIZ is a major cash cow for the North Korean state, providing an estimated annual revenue of $25–40 million. This allowed the numerous critics of the project to describe it as a "slave labor camp." The description is grossly unfair: even after the deductions, the KIZ jobs are by far the best-paid regular jobs in North Korea, so the locals strive hard to be accepted to a KIZ-based factory.

Any interaction between North Korean workers and South Korean managers is discouraged. In one incident, a South Korean manager was kept under arrest for a few months, allegedly for criticizing North Korea and encouraging a female North Korean worker to defect.

Nonetheless, one should not underestimate the impact that the KIZ has on the city of Kaesŏng and the surrounding area. By now a significant part of the local population are employed in the KIZ. It looks like the average South Korean industrial district and, as such, would probably be described as monotonous and faceless by visiting aesthetes from other parts of the world. But for the North Koreans themselves, the area looks stunningly unusual and beautiful. The streets are lined with trees, roads are paved, and bright electric lights are on every night. Standard prefabricated buildings are clean and brightly colored. This is not what the average North Korean has seen in the typical industrial district in his country. As a matter of fact, first-time visiting North Korean officials cannot hide their surprise—even though such improper emotions might be politically dangerous.

North Korean workers in the KIZ need not talk to South Koreans to get an idea of what life in South Korea looks like. The South Koreans are tall, well dressed, and their skin testifies to the fact that they don't spend much time on labor mobilization, neither planting rice with bare hands nor pushing cement blocks around. Even small talk might not be that innocent, since hints about daily life in the South—both intentional and incidental—are bound to be dropped and North Koreans will certainly take notice. No amount of police surveillance will prevent this from happening.

Even smuggling from the KIZ has a remarkable impact on minds in surrounding areas. For snacks, many North Koreans are given Choco Pies, a seriously unhealthy, sugar-rich but delicious snack, popular in the South. It is known that most of them get the Choco Pies from the KIZ to share with their families. These Choco Pies become carriers of highly subversive messages about South Korea's sophistication and prosperity—like pretty much everything that is taken from the KIZ, legally or otherwise (and theft is a big problem).

The KIZ does fill the regime coffers, no doubt, but it also serves as a conduit for new and uncensored knowledge about the outside world. We can be sure that thanks to the KIZ, an overwhelming majority of some quarter-million people who live in its vicinity have come to understand that most of what they read about South Korea in the official media is completely false. Even minders and political police agents are not immune from the effects of these discoveries.

IN SEARCH OF A GULLIBLE INVESTOR

In 1991 the North Korean government established a special economic zone (SEZ) in the remote northwestern corner of the country. The Rason SEZ, as it became known later, was to be located where the borders of China, Russia, and North Korea meet, and become a business hub of the region.

News of the establishment of North Korea's first SEZ produced much enthusiasm in the international media. As usual, there was no shortage of pundits who saw the decision as a sure sign that Chinese-style reforms soon would be launched in North Korea. After all, in China of the early 1980s, similar SEZs—islands of the market economy in an ocean of state socialism and central planning—played a major role in the early stages of the reform. Surely, the optimists claimed, the introduction of the SEZ was a sign that North Korea would soon emulate China.

As subsequent developments demonstrated quite well, the Rason SEZ was not a sign of reform. Neither was it a success. By the year 2000, the total volume of foreign investment in the area was a paltry US$35 million even though initially, in 1991–1992, there were talks of about US$2 billion of investment.

The major problem was the location. The Rason area is underdeveloped even by North Korean standards. The only paved road in the area connects Rajin and Sonbong, and even this is only a single lane. The bridge that connects the area with China has remained unchanged since colonial days. Obviously, Pyongyang expected that rich foreign investors would pay for the upgrading of the infrastructure. They did, but only on a very limited scale.

So for two decades the Rason SEZ has largely remained dormant, serving essentially as a large marketplace where North Korean merchants have been able to buy Chinese goods for further resale in the inner regions of North Korea. (The merchants needed a special pass to get in since the area is fenced off and off-limits to ordinary North Koreans, but nowadays a small bribe can solve this problem with ease.) For a brief time it also served as a gambling enclave for rich Chinese, but after some ugly embezzlement incidents, the Chinese demanded the closure of the local casino. The zone slipped into obscurity, even though its small port was sometimes used by the Russian and Chinese companies for cargo transit.

In 2002 the North Korean government made another attempt to launch an SEZ—this time in the border city of Sinuiju.

In 2002 the proposed policies looked fairly radical. It was stated that the entire population of Sinuiju, some 350,000 people, would be relocated to other areas, to be replaced by 200,000 model workers, handpicked by the authorities for their skill and perceived political reliability.

The most unusual act was the decision to appoint a foreigner as the SEZ governor. The choice was Yang Bin, a Chinese entrepreneur with Dutch citizenship, then reputedly the second richest man in China. He was 39 years old at the time.

On September 12, 2002, the Supreme People's Assembly, the North Korean rubber-stamp parliament, adopted the Basic Law of the Sinuiju Special Administrative Region. The Law consisted of six chapters (government, economy, culture, fundamental rights and duties of residents, structure, and the emblem and flag of the region), with an impressive 101 articles.

(continued)

The Basic Law proclaimed that the legal system would remain unchanged for 50 years, and that foreigners would enjoy the same rights as North Koreans in the area. Foreign judges were to be invited to solve disputes and oversee the enforcement of the laws.

It looked too good to be true, and for a while there was a great deal of media hype about a "breakthrough." The North Korean vice minister for foreign trade called the SEZ "a new historical miracle."

However, "new historical miracle" Sinuiju hardly lasted 50 weeks, let alone the promised 50 years.

It was probably the Chinese who sank the project. Beijing was not amused by the turn of events. Yang Bin wanted to transform the city into a gambling center, a "Macao of the North." This was not welcome. It is also likely that China did not want competition between Sinuiju and its northeastern cities. It did not help that the North Koreans, following their modus operandi, did not bother to liaise with the Chinese beforehand.

Yang Bin was already under investigation at that time. Soon he was arrested for fraud and sentenced to 18 years in prison. No one heard about the Sinuiju SEZ for another decade.

In 2011 an announcement about a new SEZ in the vicinity of Sinuiju was made—largely on the assumption that it would attract Chinese businesses. It might indeed become a success, but taking into consideration the track record of the North Korean SEZ, one should remain careful.

THE SUN SETS

By late 2007, North Korea's strategists had good reason to feel happy about results of their diplomacy and brinkmanship. The US administration had given in, resumed aid, and even the revival of KEDO seemed likely after the February 13 declaration. Aid from the South helped to make up for the innate inefficiencies in the North Korean economy. In the long run, the Sunshine Policy might not have been as good for the North Korean regime as Kim Jong Il and his lieutenants seemingly assumed, but its destabilizing potential was unlikely to be noticed until much later. In addition, China had become increasingly involved in the North Korean situation, so North Korean diplomats could and obviously did hope to resume their old game of skillfully manipulating rival sponsors. But then things suddenly took an ugly turn.

To a large extent the new North Korean crisis was a result of Pyong-yang's own miscalculations, but political changes within South Korea also played a major role in creating a new challenge for the North Korean regime.

By 2005–2006, the South Korean public was increasingly dissatisfied with the Roh Moo Hyun administration. Rightly or wrongly, Roh's government was seen as responsible for an economic slowdown. It also became clear that the noble past of pro-democracy fighters did not shield them from the scent of corruption. The political Right at the same time acquired charismatic leadership in the shape of the former Seoul Major Lee Myung Bak (nick-named "the bulldozer," due to his passion for demolition and construction). By late 2007 few doubted that the Right was well positioned to win the next elections by a landslide. In a last-ditch attempt to save his legacy and the Sunshine Policy, President Roh rushed for a second summit with the North, which took place in Pyongyang in October 2007. Among other things, he promised to open another industrial zone similar to that of Kaesŏng. But it was too late: elections were won by the Right and in February 2008, Lee Myung Bak became the new president of the Republic of Korea. Tellingly, the domestic North Korean media did not report the results of the elections for some two months.

The issue of North Korea remained marginal during the campaign. The foreign media usually only bother to mention Korea in relation to some North Korea—induced crisis, so people outside the Korean peninsula tend to assume that South Koreans see the North Korean issue as a de-fining or at least very important part of their country's political agenda. This has long ceased to be the case. A poll taken before the 2007 presiden-tial elections encapsulates this spirit quite well. In the poll, would-be South Korean voters were asked to name "the most important task of the next president." Of the participants, 36.1 percent said that this should be "eco-nomic development and creation of jobs"; 27.4 percent said "closing the income gap and improving welfare"; 22.4 percent wanted "political and social unity"; 11.2 percent wanted "political reform and leadership"; and only a meager 2.4 percent said that the would-be president should, first of all, concentrate on "improving inter-Korean relations."[19]

The results of the 2007 elections are often interpreted as a sign of the 386ers' demise, and the Kim-Roh decade as a deviation from the "normal" state of affairs. Such views are especially common among US conservatives—those few, of course, who care about Korea at all. However, this is an overly simplistic interpretation. In spite of the 2007 setback, the nationalist Left—with its instinctual anti-Americanism and measured sympathy for the Pyongyang dictatorship—is bound to remain an important force in Korean politics for decades to come. For better or worse, the old Right-leaning consensus is dead, and South Korean politics will likely see the pendulum-like movement from the Right to the Left and back.

Even though the North Korean issue was secondary for his politics, the Lee Myung Bak administration had rather different ideas about how to deal with the North. He accused the two previous administrations of propping up the North Korean regime and making it even more dangerous. He also emphasized the need for strict reciprocity in dealing with North Korea—aid should be conditioned on meaningful political concessions from the North.

These views were epitomized in the "Vision 3000" plan, officially known as "Vision 3000, Denuclearization, Openness." Vision 3000 describes what will become possible if North Korea surrenders its nuclear weapons. In such a case, the South promises, the North will see a flood of aid on a hitherto unthinkable scale. Within merely a decade, South Korean aid will help to increase the average per-capita annual income to the level of US$3,000, some three times the current level (which, by the way, would be achievable only with annual growth exceeding the 20 percent mark—hardly a realistic assumption). As the name itself suggested, the North Korean government was expected to improve economic efficiency by initiating Chinese-style reforms.

Needless to say, this proposal was clearly a nonstarter and was rejected outright. On May 30, 2008, the official North Korean wire agency, KCNA, described the "No nukes, opening and 3,000 dollars" (this is how the official name of the "Vision 3000" plan is rendered into North Korean English newspeak) in its highly idiosyncratic English:

> No nukes, opening and 3,000 dollars peddled by traitor Lee Myung-bak as a policy toward the north suffices to prove that he is desperately pursuing the confrontation between the north and the south in ideology [. . .] Lee's pragmatism is little short of a hideous act of treachery as it is intended to sell off the national interests to the outsiders and make the dignity and sovereignty of the nation their plaything.

Soon afterward, President Barack Obama took office. It was initially assumed that Obama would pay little attention to the North—and this was bad news for Pyongyang, too.

Faced with this new and unfavorable situation, the North Koreans resorted to the tactics they had used in the past with so much success. Obviously, North Korean strategists decided that it was time to manufacture a new crisis—as usual, to squeeze necessary concessions from their adversaries/donors.

The first incident took place in July 2008, when a South Korean housewife was shot dead during the early morning while walking on the beach in the Kŭmgang tourist zone. It remains an open question as to whether the shooting was indeed an accident or a part of a North Korean tension-building strategy. At any rate, the North Koreans took an unusually tough stance when it came to investigating the incident and the Kŭmgang resort's operations were halted.

In November 2008 it was the turn of the Kaesŏng city tours. At the time, anti-Pyongyang activist groups had begun to send balloons with leaflets into North Korean territory. The North Korean government demanded the immediate cessation of such activities and when Seoul refused to take measures, the North Korean authorities halted tours to Kaesŏng. In order to further increase the pressure on Seoul, they also introduced measures that greatly restricted the activities of the Kaesŏng industrial zone.

North Korean strategists seemingly assumed that the deterioration in North-South relations would make the South Korean public uneasy, and therefore would force the Lee administration into a softer approach toward the North. This was a miscalculation. None of the tourist projects are of economic importance to the South and the average South Korean voter cares about the North much less than North Korean policy makers presumed. Hints of the possible closure of the Kaesŏng industrial zone failed to produce the desired result as well, since the project is very marginal within the South Korean economy.

At the same time North Korean strategists began to raise the stakes in their deals with the United States. In April 2009 they again launched a long-distance missile that could theoretically have hit targets in Alaska and Hawaii—that is, if it worked properly. The launch, like the previous long-range missile tests, was a failure. Nonetheless, the North Korean media told the public that Juche science again succeeded in putting a satellite in space.

To further emphasize the message, the North went one step further and in May 2009 conducted a second nuclear test. Unlike the 2006 test, the second nuclear test was a technical success and demonstrated to the world that North Korea has indeed developed a workable nuclear device.

The UN Security Council produced another stern resolution (Resolution 1874), once again duly supported by the Chinese. However, merely a few months later Chinese Prime Minister Wen Jiabao visited Pyongyang, and Chinese aid to the North was increased further. After the nuclear test the volume of trade between China and North Korea began to grow with remarkable speed, tripling throughout between 2006 and 2011.

As was expected by those who are accustomed to North Korea's negotiation style, the barrage of threats and bellicosity was followed by a charm offensive. In July 2009 the flood of macabre abuse aimed at Seoul and Washington suddenly ceased and, all of a sudden, the North Korean media started to express their goodwill toward both South Korea and the United States.

As a sign of goodwill, Pyongyang agreed to release two US journalists who in the spring of 2009 had crossed the Sino-Korean border. They had spent a few months under arrest, and then an "unofficial" US delegation led by former President Clinton flew to Pyongyang and negotiated their release. The Hyundai Group chairwoman also came back from Pyongyang with a Hyundai employee who had allegedly plotted the defection of a North Korean female employee.

The "crisis manufacturing strategy" has worked well in the past, but by 2008–2009 both Washington and Seoul had had enough. This time, neither was going to reward North Korea merely for its willingness to reduce tension and return to the status quo.

To a very large extent, earlier US willingness to give concessions was based on the assumption that the North Korean nuclear issue could be solved through diplomacy. In other words, it was assumed by many in Washington that the North Korean government could be convinced and/or bribed into surrendering its nukes. This was a misconception, of course, since the North Korean government has neither the intention nor, frankly, a valid reason to surrender its nuclear weapons. However, for a while this illusion was shared by many in Washington, making negotiations and concessions possible. But such hopes disappeared by 2008.

The United States has taken an approach often described as "strategic patience" (also known as "benign neglect"). The term implies that the United States will not do anything of significance until the North demonstrates its sincere commitment to denuclearization by taking certain measures that will clearly and irreversibly diminish its nuclear capabilities. The approach of Seoul has been even harsher.

By early 2010, the North found itself in a new and unfavorable situation, with both major adversaries-cum-donors suddenly becoming unreceptive to the customary mixture of threats, tension-building provocations, charm offensives, and minor concessions. Pyongyang's strategists therefore decided to increase pressure by reminding the world of their ability to create additional problems for the United States and the ROK.

This might seem illogical, but such an approach is rational, since North Korea does not risk too much by driving tensions higher. Certainly, North Korean policy planners know that if a war were to break out they would lose it quickly. But they also know that war would be prohibitively costly for democratically elected politicians in Seoul and Washington.

At the same time, North Korea might actually have advantages over the South at the level of border skirmishes and small-scale raids. The North is aware that the South is incapable of inflicting damage on anything of value to the North Korean regime. If a major exchange of fire were to occur in the DMZ or the NLL (the latter is a disputed maritime border that divides the two Koreas in the Yellow Sea), the South Korean military might be perfectly capable of sinking a few North Korean warships or wiping out a coastal defense battery or two; or, perhaps even destroying a command headquarters, complete with a few dozen unlucky colonels and a couple of one-star generals. However, neither the rusty warships of World War II vintage nor the lives of humble colonels are of much significance to Pyongyang. The domestic political impact of such a military misadventure is also not going to be large since the government-controlled media will either hide a disaster or even present a humiliating defeat as a great triumph.

At the same time, such an exchange of strikes and counterstrikes might have a significant political impact on South Korea. First of all, South Korean voters are not fond of tension, and they might, in the long run, penalize their government for its inability to keep North Koreans quiet and nonthreatening. Second, the South Korean economy is very dependent on foreign markets and foreign businessmen who don't like media reports about a war that is, allegedly, "likely to erupt in Korea next week." Such reports are gross exaggerations, to be sure, but overseas car importers are not supposed to understand the intricacies of the inter-Korean politics better than your average journalist.

This asymmetry means that North Korea can raise the stakes with relative impunity when it chooses to do so—as long as the risk of skirmishes escalating to a full-scale war remains low.

With this in mind, in 2010, Pyongyang simultaneously pursued two tension-building programs, one directed at Seoul and another targeting Washington. The message they wanted to deliver was still the same, however: Pyongyang wanted to show that it cannot just be ignored and neglected, and that it is cheaper and safer to pay North Korea off than suffer the trouble it is capable of creating.

In order to drive this message home in Seoul, the North Korean military undertook two important and somewhat unprecedented operations. In March 2010, in a bold raid, North Korean submariners torpedoed the South Korean naval corvette, the *Cheonan*. It sank immediately, taking 46 lives, roughly half of its crew. A few months later in November, North Korean artillery shelled the island of Yeongpyeong, located in disputed waters near the NLL (South Korea's claim to the island itself is not disputed by the North). It was the first major artillery attack on South Korean territory in decades.

In dealing with the United States, Pyongyang chose to target Washington's usual weak spot—that is, fear of nuclear proliferation. In 2002 accusations of uranium enrichment led to the repudiation of previous US-NK agreements. Until 2009 North Korea vehemently denied the very existence of a highly enriched uranium (HEU) program. In 2009 the existence of the HEU program was acknowledged and in November 2010 Pyongyang extended an invitation to Dr. Hecker, former director of the US Department of Energy Nuclear research site at Los Alamos, to visit their nuclear facilities. They showed him around a modern, fully operational (and very large) uranium enrichment facility. Of course, this once again demonstrated that North Koreans had been lying all those years. Hardly anybody was surprised by such a discovery, however.

THE ENTRY OF CHINA

Another important change of the last decade was the reemergence of China in North Korean politics. In the early 1990s, China obviously wrote Pyongyang off and perhaps did not expect the Kim family regime to last for more than a few years. But from around 2001, trade and general economic interactions between North Korea and China began to grow, and this growth accelerated around 2006, when the first nuclear test led to a tightening of the sanctions regime. Chinese dignitaries began to frequent Pyongyang, and in the last years of his life Kim Jong Il visited China at least once a year. By 2010 annual trade between North Korea and China had exceeded North Korea's trade with all other countries combined.

China is often described in the media as "North Korea's ally." This is not really the case, since in reality the Chinese—general public and officials alike—tend to look at North Korea with bemused disdain. It reminds them of parts of their own past few if any Chinese want to return to. The Chinese are often annoyed by North Korea's provocative behavior that jeopardizes stability in the region. Most Chinese scholars and scholar-officials behind closed doors agree that *in the long run* unification of Korea under Seoul's control appears to be likely, and almost inevitable (this position was confirmed by WikiLeaks cables, but this was hardly a revelation for those who interact with the Chinese frequently). However, China would prefer this long run to be very long indeed—and with good reason. For Chinese policy makers, all things considered, a nuclear-armed North Korea seems to be a lesser evil than an unstable or collapsing North Korea (and, perhaps, even less an evil than a Korea unified under a US-friendly Seoul government).

Chinese goals on the Korean peninsula fall along a hierarchy. To simplify things a bit, first of all, China needs stability in and around Korea. Second, China would prefer to see the Korean peninsula divided. The desire to stop North Korea from developing nukes comes as a rather distant third.

Beijing's greatest fear seems to be the instability that would be caused by North Korea's implosion. China sees such a prospect as dangerous because it will have to deal with refugee flows, the threat of WMD proliferation, and geopolitical uncertainties of different kinds—like, say, smuggling of the nuclear material to (or through) Chinese territory.

The Chinese government also has valid domestic reasons to prefer the status quo. Chinese leaders are well aware that the domestic support for their own regime overwhelmingly depends on their ability to maintain a very high level of economic growth. Any disturbances in adjacent areas might divert resources and in the worst case scenario might even trigger some unrest in China itself.

The second most important concern of Beijing's policy makers is to keep Korea divided (if not forever, at least for the longest possible time). North Korea constitutes a buffer zone on the borders of China, and, the official pro-unification rhetoric notwithstanding, the emergence of a unified Korean state will not serve Beijing's long-term interests. There is little if any doubt that such a unified state would be dominated by South Korea, so unification will produce a democratic and strongly nationalist state, likely to be a US ally, on China's borders.

The continued division of Korea also provides China with manifold economic advantages. The dire economic situation of the North Korean state allows Chinese companies to get access to North Korean mineral resources and transport infrastructure at minimal cost. It is also possible that over the next decade, China will begin to make use of North Korea's cheap but relatively skilled labor. Needless to say, in a unified Korea labor will not remain cheap and it will be much more difficult for Chinese businesses to acquire mining rights.

Last but not least China also worries about the influence such a unified Korean state would exercise on the ethnic Korean minority in China—and quasi-official territorial claims, frequently voiced in Seoul,[20] do not help to quell these worries, either. One should remember that a significant number of South Koreans, including several politicians, have openly expressed reservations about the 1909 Treaty between Korea (then under Japanese domination) and China that defines the current land border between the two countries. They claim that a large area of Kando (Jiandao in Chinese), in Northeast China, should rightfully belong to Korea—the area is currently home to millions of Chinese citizens. In 2004 up to a dozen ROK National Assembly members established a group solely dedicated to the promotion of the Kando claims.[21] More radical nationalist Korean groups continue to make loud territorial claims to even greater parts of Manchuria and Russia's Maritime Provinces.[22]

The third Chinese strategic aim in dealing with North Korea is denuclearization. Admittedly, the nuclear issue is less important to China than to the United States. Nonetheless, it is still significant. According to the Nuclear Non-Proliferation Treaty of 1968, China is one of five recognized nuclear weapon possessing states. This makes China a member of a small and highly exclusive international club, giving it little reason to welcome dilution of the power accorded by nuclear weapon possession.

In addition to this, North Korea's nuclear ambitions could potentially trigger a nuclear arms race in East Asia, with South Korea and Japan developing nuclear weapons as well—a prospect that would not be welcomed by Beijing.

Economic considerations are often discussed when it comes to Chinese goals in Korea. Indeed, China dominates North Korea's foreign trade almost completely. In 1995 the trade volume between the two countries was $0.55 billion. By 2000 it had decreased slightly, to $0.49 billion. From there growth began. By 2005 the volume had tripled, reaching $1.6 billion; in the next five years it tripled again, reaching the level of $5.6 billion by 2011, increasing from $3.4 billion in 2010.[23]

Currently it is difficult to know to what extent such a growth is driven by the strategic considerations of Beijing, and to what extent it comes "naturally," as a byproduct of China's own unstoppable growth and its appetite for natural resources. It seems that both the strategic considerations of the Chinese state and the purely economic interests of Chinese businesses have conspired to bring about this growth.

However, in spite of the impressive growth in trade volume, in purely economic terms North Korea is of very secondary importance to China. Loud talk of a Chinese "economic takeover of North Korea" should not obscure the fact that the volume of trade between the North and China is a paltry $5.6 billion, while the volume of trade between South Korea and China is $246 billion—an impressive 44-fold difference.[24] To put things in a more global perspective, China's trade with Chile ($29 billion in 2011) is roughly five times larger than its trade with North Korea, even though Chile has a smaller population and, needless to say, is far more distant both politically and geographically.

To the extent China's economic interests exist, they can be divided into three groups. First, Chinese companies are interested in North Korea's mineral resources. North Korean deposits of coal, iron ore, and copper might not be exceptionally rich by world standards, but nonetheless are of considerable value to the resource-hungry China. Thus, over the last decade Chinese companies have negotiated a number of concessions on mining rights issues.

Second, China is interested in the use of North Korea's transportation infrastructure. Three North Eastern Provinces of China are landlocked, so if a Chinese company in the vast and populous area wants to ship goods overseas, the nearest port is either Dandong or Dalian, about 1,000 km away. If China obtains the right to use port facilities on Korea's East Coast, it will dramatically shorten the land routes and save much in transportation costs. It seems that the June 2011 decision to revitalize the special economic zone in Rason is related to this goal.

Third, Chinese small businesses are increasingly interested in outsourcing to North Korea, where wages are well below what would be acceptable for Chinese unskilled and semiskilled workers. In North Korea, local girls are willing to work at a Chinese-operated sweatshop for $20–25 a month. In China, an entrepreneur would have to pay some $100 a month for the same job.[25]

Growing economic dependency on China worries Pyongyang. For decades, the North Korean government has been very good at avoiding exclusive dependence on just one donor, since Pyongyang politicians liked to use the donor countries' rivalry to its advantage.

Therefore, one should not be surprised that China is not treated too favorably by internal North Korean propaganda (this was also the case for the Soviet Union when it was the major donor to North Korea in the 1980s), and the North Korean minders do express their dislike for the Chinese even to trusted (sort of) foreign visitors. The North Korean public and, especially, North Korean officials are frequently reminded by their superiors that they should not get too cozy with the Chinese. In 2007 North Korea's state media reported on alleged spies of an unnamed foreign country being unmasked by the North Korean security service. No details were given at the time, but hints indicate that these real or alleged spies were working for China.

The North Korean elite has good reason to be cautious. It is true that China would prefer to see Korea divided and hence favor a separate regime in Pyongyang, but this does not mean China has to maintain the Kim family in power. China seems to be the only power that has the potential to intervene in North Korean domestic affairs when and if it sees some serious need to do so. The North Korean leadership seems to take seriously the probability of another Chinese-backed conspiracy, somewhat similar to the August conspiracy of 1956. China is not eager to intervene directly in the internal politics of Pyongyang, since it has no reason to jeopardize the status quo that, on balance, serves China's interests reasonably well. But things may very well change eventually.

As we will see later, there might be situations in which the North Korean elite changes its attitude toward China. However, that will most likely be a last resort—if, for instance, an acute domestic crisis arises. For the time being, however, Pyongyang clearly prefers to keep Beijing at arm's length.

The degree of not-so-hidden mistrust between Pyongyang and Beijing is well demonstrated by what David Straub once aptly described as "the strategic partnership fantasy," quite widespread in North Korean ruling circles. In spite of all the anti-American rhetoric, frequently of almost comical bellicosity, in confidential talks North Korean dignitaries often suggest that North Korea does not really mind becoming an ally of the United States, thus helping Washington to deter China (for a hefty reward, needless to say). When I myself first heard such remarks from a North Korean official, I was taken aback, but then it became clear that such hopes are regularly expressed to foreign interlocutors, including influential Western diplomats or ex-diplomats (of whom David Straub is one). This dramatic reorientation is not going to happen, to be sure, but the existence of such unrealistic expectations speaks volumes about the actual attitude toward China in Pyongyang's ruling circles.

Many in the United States, especially in the last few years, have expressed a hope that China can use its alleged influence in Pyongyang in order to somehow press North Korea into denuclearization. Alas, this hope is unfounded since China has very limited leverage when it comes to dealing with North Korea. As all major partners of North Korea (including Seoul, Moscow, and Washington) have learned to their dismay, significant economic involvement with and assistance to North Korea does not translate into comparable political leverage.

Theoretically China could make the economic situation of North Korea extremely difficult by halting aid and putting severe restrictions on cross-border trade. If China wished to do so, it could plunge North Korea into another economic disaster that might even exceed the Arduous March of the late 1990s. However, China cannot fine-tune North Korean politics and squeeze concessions on the issues North Korean leaders see as vital for their survival. A senior South Korean diplomat once told the present author, "China doesn't have leverage when it comes to dealing with North Korea. What it has is not a lever, but rather a hammer. China can knock North Korea unconscious if it wishes, but it cannot really manage its behavior."

Contrary to the expectations of some optimists in Washington and Seoul, China has little reason to use this "hammer." The problems created by North Korea's risky behavior and its nuclear program are seen in Beijing as less significant than the problems likely to be created by a serious domestic crisis in North Korea and/or by the emergence of a unified Korean state on China's border. China prefers to maintain a status quo, which has many downsides, but on balance seems to be better than any of the likely alternatives.

The Contours of a Future: What Might Happen to North Korea in the Next Two Decades

Let's be frank: it is beyond humans' power to predict the future. History has a very long (and still growing) list of prophets whose confident predictions have been proven completely wrong. Many widely anticipated events never happened, while a number of pivotal changes came absolutely out of the blue.

Having made these necessary precautionary remarks, the author nonetheless intends to engage in some speculations on the likely future (or rather futures) of North Korea. Of course, the reader should not forget that this discussion is speculative by its very nature, so the author will make generous use of such adverbs as "plausibly," "probably," and "perhaps" as well as such verbs as "might" and "seem."

It seems that the future development of North Korea will consist of three stages. The first stage is the present stage of stability. It might be called "Kim Jong Il's stability" but it is likely to continue for a while under Kim Jong Un as well. However, the current system is both unsustainable and unreformable, so "Kim Jong Il's stability" is likely to end in a dramatic crisis.

There are a number of triggers that might unleash this crisis, as well as a number of ways in which it may unfold. However, North Korea will not, probably, remain unstable for any length of time. There are good reasons to believe that the crisis period, as chaotic and dangerous and violent as it might be, will be relatively short, so some sort of new and relatively stable political and economic regime will emerge.

WHY NORTH KOREA IS LIKELY TO CONTINUE FOR A
WHILE (BUT NOT FOREVER)

If one reads newspaper reports about North Korea, one cannot help but get a very dire picture of an insane dictatorship whose leaders enjoy a seemingly meaningless saber-rattling while their subjects live under the constant threat of another murderous famine. This is not true: in North Korea, the saber-rattling is actually a carefully premeditated component of diplomacy, and the internal economic and political situation is not as grim and unstable as most newspaper reports tell us (but grim nonetheless).

From time to time newspapers shower readers with the predictions of a looming mass starvation in North Korea (often with an implicit— and unfounded—assumption that it might provoke regime collapse). These headlines come out more or less every year, usually in spring. In March 2011 the *New York Times* wrote: "North Korea: 6 Million Are Hungry." One year earlier, in March 2010, the *Times* of London warned: "Catastrophe in North Korea; China must pressure Pyongyang to allow food aid to millions threatened by famine." In March 2009, the *Washington Post* headline said: "At the Heart of North Korea's Troubles, an Intractable Hunger Crisis." In March 2008, the *International Herald Tribune* ran a predictable headline: "Food Shortage Looms in North Korea"[1] The predictions of the gloom come every year, but famine does not.

Indeed, over the last years there have been times when the food situation deteriorated, perhaps nearly to the point of another famine outbreak. Nonetheless, on balance the last 5 to 10 years can be described as a time of modest but undeniable improvement of the economic situation in North Korea.

Economic statistics are murky, but they seemingly indicate that by 2005 North Korean GDP has roughly returned to the pre-crisis level of the late 1980s. According to the estimates of the Bank of Korea, widely believed to be the most reliable (or, better, the least unreliable) assessments of the North Korean economy, the GDP growth in 2000–2011 averaged 1.4 percent per annum.[2] A moderate increase, to be sure, but an increase nonetheless. Of course, one can and should be skeptical about the exactness of the figure—Marcus Noland, one of the world's best experts on the North Korean economy, loves to repeat: "Never trust a datum about the North Korean economy that comes with a decimal point attached." However, anecdotal evidence and observations generally support such mildly optimistic estimates.

Malnourishment remains common (this has been the case for decades), but after 2000, few if any North Koreans have starved to death. "Capitalism from below" brought social stratification, but the new middle class can now afford items that were unheard of in Kim Il Sung's time. DVD players are common. Refrigerators remain rare, but are no longer exceptional, and even a computer in a private house is not seen any more as a sign of extreme luxury.

The improvement is especially noticeable in Pyongyang. The huge avenues of the North Korean capital, once infamous for their complete lack of traffic, are now reminiscent of the streets of 1970s Moscow—traffic is not too heavy, but clearly present. In older parts of the city, where streets are not that wide, one can occasionally even encounter traffic jams, once completely unthinkable. Visitors and richer Pyongyangites alike can feast on numerous delicacies in a multitude of posh restaurants, which have popped up around the city in recent years. Expensive shops stocking luxury goods are becoming more numerous as well. Gone are the days when a bottle of cheap Chinese shampoo was seen as a great luxury, since nowadays one can easily buy Chanel in a Pyongyang boutique.

This slow improvement of the economic situation might actually prove to be dangerous for the regime. Without radical reforms North Korea might grow moderately, but it is not going to achieve a growth rate that would be compatible with that of China or South Korea. Therefore the huge income gap, the major potential source of political trouble, will keep growing. At the same time, less daily economic pressure means more time to think, talk, and socialize for the North Korean citizens—and this is not good news for the regime. Contrary to the common perception, people seldom start revolutions when they are really desperate: in such times they are too busy fighting for physical survival. A minor but insufficient improvement in people's lives is what authoritarian regimes should fear most.

As we have seen before, the most rational survival strategy for the North Korean government is to avoid reforms, to continue the zero tolerance policy in dealing with internal dissent, and to inhibit and, whenever possible, roll back the spontaneous growth of the capitalist institutions. Kim Jong Il seemingly understood this well enough, but it remains to be seen whether his young successor will fully realize the importance of these requirements.

It is quite possible that for a decade or two the regime will succeed in its efforts to maintain the status quo. However, this political success will come with a deadly price: it will prolong economic stagnation. The longer the center will hold, the greater the gap between the North and its neighbors—above all South Korea—and the greater the potential for a future explosion.

It seems that no amount of government effort can possibly roll the situation back to what it used to be under Kim Il Sung in the 1960s and 1970s. In those days, North Korea's version of "national Stalinism" was viable because at that time many North Koreans were willing to accept and even support the system and because Korea still had a lot of untapped resources that could be mobilized for the needs of the industrial economy. The international environment was also very different half a century ago. In the 1950s North Korea then boasted the most advanced economy of continental Asia and was surrounded by poor and dictatorial regimes. Last but not least, it was so much easier to keep people isolated and ill-informed before the advent of the digital age.

The situation has changed. The initial popular enthusiasm for the promises of Stalinism has long evaporated. North Korea is lagging hopelessly behind all its neighbors in terms of both economic performance and individual freedoms (even China looks like a true democracy to the average North Korean). Information is getting inside the country thanks to the development of new media—DVD players, tapes, transistor radios, and, increasingly, computers. The North Koreans are slowly losing their fear of the government and are increasingly willing to raise dangerous political topics in their private interactions. This does not bode well for the long-term future of the regime. Its final crisis can be postponed but by no means prevented.

The ongoing generation shift might be especially dangerous for the regime. Those North Koreans who are now below the age of 35 are very different from their elders. They have not been subjected to intense ideological indoctrination, and they lived in a world where everybody knew that newspapers were not telling the complete and only truth. They do not remember the times when the state was seen as a natural giver of all things—for many of them, the state and its officials are merely a swarm of parasites. They know that the outside countries are doing well, and most of them are aware that the North is lagging hopelessly behind the South. They also grew up in more relaxed times, when state terror was scaled down, and hence they are less afraid to speak about dangerous topics. This new generation might constitute a serious problem for the Kim family, but it will take a decade or two before this problem will become acute.

CONTOURS OF A COMING CRISIS

Currently it seems that there are four likely scenarios that might bring an end to the era of "Kim Jong Il's stability," triggering a dramatic crisis. These scenarios are attempted reforms, factional clashes in the leadership, spontaneous uprisings, and the contagion of a revolt in China.

The first scenario of the final crisis is an attempt at reforms more or less similar with those of China and Vietnam. This statement might appear to contradict what I said earlier: I have argued that the North Korean leadership understands the inherent danger of Chinese-style reforms and will not take the risk.

However this was said in the context of the Kim Jong Il era's North Korean leadership—and this leadership is changing. It is true that Kim Jong Un inherited most of his advisers from his father, but these people are now well in their 70s if not 80s, so they are likely to be replaced in the near future. Indeed, it has been reported that some very young North Korean princelings, grandchildren of Kim Il Sung's comrades-in-arms, have begun their meteoric ascendancies to high-level positions. Even though Kim Jong Un's advisers and confidants will be largely children or close blood relations of his father's advisers, this does not preclude them from having vastly different views on many important issues. These people—including, above all, Kim Jong Un himself—might be seduced by the glamour of Chinese reforms. They might hope to emulate the success of the great neighbor while enriching and empowering themselves in the process (pretty much like the Chinese party cadres have done). They also might feel sorry for the plight of North Korean commoners—after all, the history of many an aristocracy has shown that the descendants of brutal robber barons and sadistic warlords sometimes have surprising bleeding hearts.

Therefore, these people might take the risks their fathers considered unacceptable. A "Pyongyang Spring" might be initiated by the new rulers, out of greed, idealism, and naivety. Such a "Pyongyang Spring" will surely generate a great wave of enthusiasm and rosy hopes in the international media. One can easily imagine CNN journalists running enthusiastic reports about, say, a McDonald's outlet opening next to Kim Il Sung Square or, perhaps, broadcasting an interview with an iconoclastic North Korean academic who will courageously tell his students that Kim Il Sung occasionally made mild mistakes, so the Great Leader's policy should be considered as merely 85 percent correct.

Such changes are likely to be greeted with much enthusiasm by the international media, which will perceive (and present) these news items as a proof that the North Korean problem is solving itself. But one should not be fooled by this hype and rosy expectations. A reforming North Korea will be less, not more stable than the repressive and stagnant North Korea of the late Kim Il Sung and Kim Jong Il eras.

It is not completely impossible that the future reformist government will manage to find the right balance of terror, persuasion, and material incentives that will keep their regime stable for a long time. It will help if the reformers somehow manage to persuade China to bankroll the entire experiment—of course, major political concessions, bordering on partial surrender of sovereignty, will be necessary to get a really massive influx of the Chinese funds (otherwise, the Chinese will see such investment as too risky). And, last but not least, a more positive approach to the market dealers will help. It is often overlooked that the black market dealers and party apparatchiks share one basic interest: they are only two major groups who want North Korea to continue as a separate state for the foreseeable future. If the North Korean state turns capitalist, an owner of a few food stalls has the chance to end up as the CEO of a supermarket chain—but only as long as his or her enterprise will remain shielded from the South Korean retail giants. And the best way to achieve this is, of course, to keep two countries separated as long as possible (or indefinitely).

If such a "developmental dictatorship" is to emerge in North Korea, the present author would welcome it almost wholeheartedly—with full understanding that many will accuse him of being cynical and heartless. No system is perfect, and dictatorship, developmental or not, is bound to be nasty. Nonetheless, the lives of the average North Koreans will greatly improve under such a regime that is also less likely to be provocative on the international scene. In a sense, it might be even preferable to an instant switch to full-scale democracy, which is bound to be very traumatic, as we will see later. However, maintaining such a reformist authoritarian regime will be a permanent exercise in tight rope walking—due, as we have said, to the existence of the rich, free, and very attractive South. Therefore to the present author it appears more probable that the future North Korean reformer—be it Kim Jong Un or whoever else—will face not the fate of Deng Xiaoping but rather that of Mikhail Gorbachev. First admired and adored by the North Korean public, as well as by the South Koreans and Western media, North Korean reformers would soon be seen as an obstacle on the way to more radical change and, eventually, unification with the fabulously rich South.

Such mounting pressure is likely to lead to an outbreak of popular discontent against unlucky reformers and, perhaps, regime collapse. The difference with the Soviet Union of 1991 is that in the case of North Korea there are much higher risks of an endgame becoming violent, so one can only hope that the naïve reformer will be lucky enough to escape with his life.

Another possible trigger of the final crisis is the outbreak of serious factional infighting within the top leadership. This is the second scenario. Such an outbreak might take the form of a purge of prominent officials, or it might lead to an attempted coup (successful or not—does not really matter). The probability of such a factional clash doesn't appear to be high at the time of writing. Admittedly the international media loves to run stories about alleged factional infighting in Pyongyang, but these stories are based on hearsay.

Nonetheless, common sense suggests that factions are likely to exist, even though the North Korean leaders have understood the need to maintain unity and not to rock the boat. But nothing is eternal and the next generation of leaders might lack an understanding of how dangerous an open feud can become. Alternatively, a loser in a factional clash might decide to go down fighting and make the conflict quite public and even violent. Understandably, if a general believes that he will face an execution squad tomorrow, he is not going to care a great deal about the regime's long-term stability. In another twist of the same scenario, some foreign power (in all probability, China—nobody else is in a position to stage such an operation) might decide to encourage a group of ambitious people to challenge the seemingly irrational old guard.

Whatever the reason, such an open clash might jeopardize the regime's stability. The lack of unity at the top will be perceived as a sign of the elite's inability to keep the situation under control. In this situation many people who would otherwise remain docile will start expressing their grievances— with predictably dangerous consequences for the regime's future.

The third possible scenario of the endgame is a spontaneous outbreak of popular discontent—a local riot quickly developing into a nationwide revolutionary movement, somewhat similar to what we have seen in 2011 in the Arab world. A public suicide by an unsuccessful fruit peddler in a countryside Tunisian town sparked a revolt that in no time wiped out some Arab dictatorships and damaged others. The Ceausescu regime in Romania, arguably the most repressive of all the Communist regimes of the late 1980s in Eastern Europe, was doomed when the security police attempted to arrest a popular priest in the small town of Temisoara.

Nowadays, North Koreans appear to be too terrified, isolated, and distrustful of one another to emulate Tunisians of 2011 or Romanians of 1989. Nonetheless, the control is steadily getting weaker, the fear is diminishing, and the knowledge of available alternatives is spreading, so in the long run (and we are talking long-term prospects here—the 2020s, perhaps), a similar scenario will not be impossible in North Korea.

The fourth scenario is a contagion of some unrest in China—the only country where an outbreak of civilian disobedience or a riot might produce some impact on North Korea. Right now the Chinese "developmental dictatorship" appears to be stable, but if a major challenge to the regime is going to arise there, it is likely to produce a deep impact on North Korea as well.

Of course the above-mentioned scenarios can combine, and the present author is not sufficiently vain to believe that he has listed all the possibilities in this short sketch. On top of that, neighboring powers might get entangled with such developments as well, even though at the current stage outside players would prefer to steer clear of North Korean perils. Nonetheless, one thing appears to be almost certain: due to the peculiarities of North Korea's domestic and international situation, neither a gradual and manageable transformation of the regime nor its perpetual survival appears to be a likely outcome. Sooner or later, it will go down in crisis—in all probability, suddenly and, alas, violently.

There are at least two pieces of bad news that relate to the scenarios outlined above.

First, unfortunately for us outside observers, the above-listed scenarios imply that the warning time will be short or absent, so North Korea might look perfectly stable on one Monday morning only to become a chaotic mess by Friday afternoon. The only exception is a reformist scenario: it will probably take a few years before attempted benevolent reforms will turn ugly.

A second piece of bad news is that the coming collapse might become quite violent—there is little reason to expect a North Korean revolution to be "velvet." The major factor is the difference between the interests of the ruling elite and a majority of the population. One might expect that in the event of a crisis a majority of common North Koreans will expect and demand unification with the prosperous and free South. They will probably act not so much due to their democratic or nationalist idealism (even though both are likely to be present), but out of material considerations.

Since the gap in living standards between South Korea and the North is at least the same as the current gap between the United States and Vietnam—and perhaps much larger—the pull of glittering South Korean prosperity will become irresistible. Common North Koreans will expect (wrongly) that in case of unification they will immediately enjoy a lifestyle equivalent to that of their southern brethren.

However, the North Korean elite is likely to have very different opinions about the subject. As has been mentioned above, these people understand that in case of the regime collapse they will not be able to maintain their privileges. Many of them are afraid that if unification happens they will be persecuted by the victorious southerners or perhaps even lynched by angry mobs of their own compatriots. These fears might be exaggerated but they're not completely unfounded.

Therefore the elite might choose to fight, assuming that they will be fighting for their lives and the lives of their loved ones. The elite constitute only a small part of the population—if we include the security police, elite units of the military, and mid- to high-level party functionaries as well as their families, the total is likely to be one to two million people or some 5 to 7 percent of the entire population. However, these people know how to handle arms, have an organizational infrastructure, and, on balance, they are also better informed and have more social skills than humble commoners. There are also good reasons to suspect that they have already made some preparation for guerilla war, so a fair amount of arms are at their ready disposal (and they might make good use of the army arsenals as well).

The elite's initial instinct will be to put down disturbances, slaughter the ringleaders, and attempt to restore what the Kim family regime defines as "law and order." If unsuccessful, they will beg for Chinese help.

STABILITY WILL RETURN, BUT HOW?

However, there is good news: the instability in North Korea, while highly probable in the long run, is unlikely to last for a long period of time. For a while the country might even look a bit like Somalia, where rival cliques wage a violent struggle for the control over a few remaining objects of economic or strategic value. But even if that were to be North Korea's fate, it would not last long.

North Korea is no Somalia. It is located in the middle of a highly developed region, while its small size and long coastline make projection of force much easier. It has considerable nuclear stockpiles and a large WMD arsenal that no major international player would like to see unattended. In other words, it seems that a major crisis in North Korea will be seen by the international community and nearby powers as a clear and present danger. So, an international or unilateral peacekeeping operation of some kind seems to be likely—even though currently none of the potential "pacifiers" is too happy about such a prospect.

In the current situation there are three possible scenarios for a peacekeeping operation in what is now North Korea. First, such an operation could be launched by South Korea unilaterally (probably with some US involvement). Secondly, a unilateral Chinese action is possible. Finally, a peacekeeping operation might be a joint international one, perhaps mandated by the UN.

Prospects for a unilateral South Korean operation is the first option that can be considered. Few people outside the Korean peninsula realize this, but from Seoul's official point of view no North Korean state ever existed. According to Article 3 of the ROK Constitution, "the territory of the Republic of Korea shall consist of the Korean peninsula and its adjacent islands." Therefore, the northern part of the Korean peninsula is legally the sovereign territory of ROK, with the DPRK (North Korea's official name) a self-proclaimed entity. Officially, South Korea goes to great lengths to emphasize that North Korea is not actually another state, but merely a special region within the borders of ROK (North Korea does the same in regard to the South). Suffice it to say, even economic exchanges between the two Korean states are not officially described as "exports" and "imports"—a special word had to be coined, to emphasize that such exchanges are not, really, international in nature.

This sounds fine on paper, but it may become quite complex in practice—not least because the profound changes that have happened within the

South Korean society over the last decades. The South Korean public is still committed to unification, but this commitment is increasingly theoretical. There is little doubt that the South Korean public will approve a unilateral action if a mild and non violent "velvet revolution" erupts in Pyongyang, so the people of the North will welcome South Korean tanks waving ROK national flags and showering them with azaleas.

However, such a rosy outcome is unlikely to occur. South Korean forces might have to fight their way to Pyongyang against the determined resistance of the Kim loyalists. This will not look pretty, and taking into consideration the current mood in South Korean society, one cannot help but doubt whether a South Korean government will have the political will to dispatch troops to Pyongyang if the troops suffer significant casualties. The present author has privately asked a number of South Korean officials and military officers whether, in their opinion, a unilateral operation would be possible under such circumstances. Nearly all of them think that chances are relatively low.

Chinese unilateral intervention is another possible outcome of the likely crisis in North Korea. So far, Chinese policy on the Korean peninsula has been largely aimed at keeping the North afloat at a moderate cost. However, if the situation in the North were to destabilize, China would have to decide whether it is willing to get the North out of trouble by committing many more resources and perhaps even military force to this task. As we have said above, if a crisis were to occur, a very significant part of the current North Korean elite is bound to side with China, begging the Chinese government for help. They would much prefer a Chinese-controlled satellite regime to a unification under South Korean tutelage.

Will China listen to these demands? It is difficult to say now, since such a move could bring short-term benefits to Beijing, but in the longer run it will also produce manifold complications. Chinese intervention will restore law and order in North Korea, thus preventing a refugee crisis and greatly curtailing the likelihood of uncontrolled nuclear proliferation. It will also ensure that North Korea will continue to exist as a strategically useful buffer zone and that Chinese corporations will be able to maintain their privileged access to North Korea's resources.

However, for China these geopolitical gains come with a large price tag. It was Chinese analysts themselves who, during private conversations with the present author, have explicitly described the possible sources of complications.

To start with, a Chinese takeover of the North and emergence of a Beijing-controlled regime there will produce a tidal wave of anti-Chinese sentiment in South Korea. Even as the South Korean public demonstrate little actual enthusiasm for unification, they are still likely to be outraged by a Chinese intervention in the North. China may instantly become the major target of Korea's nationalist passions and the ROK-US alliance will be strengthened dramatically.

Inside North Korea, nationalism will emerge as well. It is almost certain that a China-controlled satellite regime will embark on a path of market-orientated reforms. Being backed by Chinese subsidies (and Chinese tanks), such a regime can afford to take political risks that are prohibitively high for the present North Korean government. Reforms will likely lead to an economic revival of the country and a dramatic improvement of living standards of the North Korean population. Nonetheless, this new wealth and new individual freedoms—however considerable—will not transform the majority of North Koreans into supporters of the regime, let alone admirers of their Chinese overlords.

If anything, the Soviet experience in Eastern Europe serves as a good guide in this regard. In 1956 Soviet tanks crushed a popular rebellion and installed a pro-Soviet client regime in Hungary. This regime was more successful than anyone had anticipated and soon made Hungary, according to a popular joke of the time, "the merriest barrack of the Soviet camp." Soviet subsidies played a major role in this consumerist boom, but this did not make either the Soviet Union or its Hungarian clients popular with the Hungarian people. Common Hungarians still despised their government and blamed the Russians for more or less everything that didn't go right in Hungary. A similar, albeit less pronounced, picture could be found in other parts of Soviet-controlled Eastern Europe, and we have little reason to believe that Chinese intervention in North Korea will be any more popular (more so since the average North Korean will be looking to the free, prosperous, and "purely national" South with admiration—and the gap between the two Koreas will remain huge for a couple of decades at least).

Last but not least, an open intervention into a North Korean domestic crisis will deliver a blow to the myth of a "peaceful rise of China" that plays such an important role in Beijing's global image-building efforts. All of China's neighbors will be very concerned by the news about Chinese intervention, since they will see themselves as possible next victims of China's rediscovered "imperial ambitions." This will lead many of them to improve their relations with the United States. They will take measures to ensure that the Chinese will not have leverage over their domestic political situations. Needless to say, Beijing will not welcome these developments.

These grave problems might cause Beijing to embrace the third option—that is, an international peace-keeping operation in what is now North Korea. Technically such an operation could be authorized by the United Nations, but in practice the slow and unwieldy UN bureaucracy is hardly able to handle the unpredictable situation fast enough. Therefore for all practical purposes such an operation will probably be best handled by the Six-Party talks mechanism—in other words, by coordinated efforts of South Korea, China, the United States, Russia, and Japan (a UN mandate might still be a good way to make the operation sufficiently legitimate).

Such an international peacekeeping operation might be acceptable to all major players, since it will help to address the major concerns of all parties involved. China will be protected from the threat of refugee flows and WMD smuggling. The political damage will be mitigated, too: even if China is clearly in the driver's seat, the UN mandate will largely protect it from the accusation of "neo-imperialist designs."

For South Korea, an international peace-keeping operation might be acceptable as well. The mandate of the peacekeeping forces is likely to be explicitly restricted, so that after a certain period of time, the forces would be withdrawn. Considering current circumstances, one can be almost certain that North Koreans will overwhelmingly support unification with the South (or, at least, for some federation with the South). In other words, a UN-mandated operation will ensure that Chinese forces, in due time, would leave the peninsula.

For the United States, an international operation would also be preferable to a unilateral Chinese intervention. It would deliver both outcomes that the United States needs most in Northeast Asia: first, it will denuclearize the North; second, it will eventually lead to the emergence of a Seoul-dominated Korean state.

For both the long-term strategic interests of South Korea and the United States, as well as for the majority of the North Korean population, the emergence of a pro-Chinese satellite regime in North Korea will still be better than indefinite continuation of the status quo. Nonetheless, a unification of Korea still should be seen as the most preferable outcome. Therefore one should be ready to consider measures that will persuade China that a unified Korea is less unacceptable than an intervention.

First of all, China should be assured that a unified Korea will not become a strategic bridgehead for US military influence in continental Northeast Asia. For example, if the ROK and United States make a joint statement promising that upon unification no US forces and/or US military installations will ever be located north of the present-day DMZ area, it will help to ameliorate Chinese strategic concerns.

The United States will probably find such concessions acceptable. On balance, the United States will gain much from an ROK-led unification of the Korean peninsula. Among other things, it will solve the nuclear issue and will put to rest fears of proliferation. The emergence of a unified democratic (and nationalist) state on the Chinese border will also be conducive to US national interests. Therefore, relatively minor concessions in regard to the troops' number and location are likely to be seen as an acceptable price to pay.

There is another problem that should be taken care of in case of a "unification crisis." Recurrent support of irredentism in Northeastern China and semi-official claims about alleged Korean territorial rights to large chunks of Chinese territory does not escape the notice of Beijing—and strengthens the suspicions that a unified Korea would strive to seed discontent in the borderland areas of China. In case of a unification crisis, it will help if the ROK government explicitly states that earlier agreements pertaining to Sino-Korean borders will be respected by a unified Korea.

It will also be necessary to explicitly assure Beijing that the government of a unified Korea will respect and honor all Chinese concessions and mining rights that were granted by the North Korean state. Many of these deals were signed under dubious circumstances and might look redolent of the unequal treaties of the 19th century. Nonetheless, it still remains an important step towards winning Chinese support—and this support is vital in case of unification.

Alas, the widespread hope that the emergence of reformist groups in Pyongyang will finally bring about a non nuclear, non threatening, and developing North Korea seems to be wishful thinking. Such an outcome, while not completely impossible, is not particularly probable, since the hypothetical reforms are likely to make North Korean politics dangerously unstable. The current regime will survive as long as it does not change much, but in the long run it is not sustainable, so sooner or later it will go down—likely, in a dramatic and dangerous crisis. However, it seems that there are only two possible long-term outcomes of this crisis: either a unification of Korea under the auspices of Seoul or an emergence of a relatively stable China-controlled satellite regime (the latter scenario might also mean that the division of Korea will become permanent).

CHAPTER 5

What to Do about the North?

Let's start from the bad news: the North Korean problem has no simple or quick solutions. Negotiations and concession will not help much, while pressure and sanctions will be even less useful. We should therefore brace ourselves for a long, winding, and, occasionally, dangerous drive.

This does not mean that the situation is beyond hope and control. The North Korean leaders are fighting a losing battle, trying to save what is, essentially, unsustainable. Sooner or later they will lose, and the outside world (well, those in the outside world who want North Korea to change) can do something to facilitate the developments and also make sure that the unavoidable changes will be less rough and violent. The useful measures are simple and cheap, but will require a great deal of long-term commitment and some touch of counterintuitive thinking. Alas, both qualities are somewhat lacking in modern-day democracies.

WHY THE STICKS ARE NOT BIG ENOUGH

Throughout the two decades that have passed since the emergence of the North Korean nuclear issue, the US strategy has oscillated between two positions.

There have been soft-liners who believe that, if the Pyongyang regime is given sufficient monetary rewards, political concessions, and security guarantees, it will ultimately abandon its nuclear ambitions and, perhaps, revive its economy through Chinese-style reforms—thus becoming a "normal state." They insist that Pyongyang should be treated gently, given concessions and monetary rewards, and persuaded that compromise will serve its own best interests. Under the impact of the second nuclear test and other recent events, the doves' numbers in Washington and Seoul shrank dramatically, but the soft-line option still remains on the sideline and might eventually regain popularity.

Their opponents are hard-liners, hawkish believers in the power of sanctions and pressure (these beliefs are often strengthened by the recurrent hope that the Pyongyang regime is just on the brink of collapse). They assume that pressure will eventually cause Pyongyang to denuclearize or push it to extinction (or both). They believe that economic hardship and perhaps even fear of military reprisals will make the North Korean leaders surrender their nuclear program.

Taking into consideration the nature of democratic politics, which regularly brings new (and not necessarily experienced) people to important jobs, there is little doubt that both approaches will keep competing in the foreseeable future. Consequently, US policy (and, for that matter, the policy of Seoul) will continue to oscillate between these two extremes. This is not good news since so far the experience has demonstrated that neither approach is going to work. Neither pressure nor concessions will speed up the delivery of the desired outcome—a nonnuclear and developing North Korea.

Regardless of what the hawks say, the threatened use of military force against North Korea is not credible—even if one forgets moral considerations that would clearly define such an undertaking as an act of aggression. Surgical strikes and air raids against nuclear installations (akin to the Israeli air raid on Iraq's nuclear research center in 1981) will not work. It is too late for this now. The weapons-grade plutonium and nuclear devices have been manufactured, and now they are safely hidden in some of the underground facilities for which North Korea is so famous. It is virtually impossible to locate all of the North's nuclear devices at the moment, and even if by some miracle reliable intelligence is obtained, it will be difficult to destroy these massive underground fortifications.

For a number of reasons, a large-scale invasion by ground forces is also a nonstarter. North Korea has a rugged, mountainous terrain and a large, if poorly equipped, army. It has no chances to win a major war, but it is perfectly capable of making its adversaries pay a very high price for their eventual victory.

An additional—and very important—problem is the vulnerability of Greater Seoul. The so-called metropolitan area is home to nearly half of the entire ROK populations (some 24 out of 50 million), but is located merely 25–30 km away from the DMZ. To make the most of this strategic advantage, the North Korean military built heavily fortified artillery positions, with some 250–300 long-range artillery pieces that can hit targets within an entire city. In case of an open war, North Korean heavy guns and multiple rocket launchers will inflict heavy damage on the South Korean capital. A fast evacuation of the mammoth city is virtually impossible. This ensures that war, irrespective of its final outcome, is bound to be bloody and will bring a large-scale destruction to South Korea's major city.

The North Korean strategic planners know that they are going to lose a full-scale war, and this is why they will never start it. However, they also realize that Seoul would not start such a war unless seriously provoked. In spite of the expected outbursts of rhetoric, losing a passenger airliner to a North Korean bomb or a naval warship to a torpedo attack is not seen in Seoul as a serious enough provocation.

After the 2010 attacks, the Seoul government often talks about a decisive retaliation, a powerful counter strike that would follow another North Korean attack. As political rhetoric, it sounds good and sells well with the public, but it is completely unrealistic. It is worth remembering that in the past, South Korea has ignored far more outrageous North Korean provocations. After all, in 2010 the North Koreans conducted a stealth torpedo attack against a warship in disputed waters. This is unacceptable, but much less so than bombing a passenger airliner—and such a bombing is what the North Koreans did in 1987, seemingly with impunity. There are good reasons why Seoul used to be patient in the past: it understood that retaliation would not be a good idea.

With its impressive technological superiority, the South Korean military could probably sink half the North Korean navy or wipe out a number of their artillery positions within a few hours. In most places, that sort of defeat would have serious political consequences—but not in North Korea.

The lives of North Korean soldiers and sailors are of no value to the Pyongyang decision makers: their scions do not serve in the military, they shop in Paris instead. The death of a few hundred soldiers will be seen as a sorry but fully acceptable price—and will not deter Pyongyang from planning a new round of provocations.

Some argue that such a military disaster would damage the regime's credentials, which are connected to a "military first" policy. But Kim's regime controls the media so completely that even the most humiliating defeat would be presented as a great victory, a spectacular triumph of North Korean arms. Only a handful of generals will know the ugly truth, and these generals understand that they would have no future without the current regime, so they are unlikely to protest.

In the worst-case scenario, the chain of retaliation and counterretaliation might escalate into a general war with disastrous consequences. Far more likely, though, is that this chain of strikes, counterstrikes, and counter-counterstrikes will remain under control. In this case, the supposed retaliation will merely help the North Korean leaders to achieve their goals. News reports about exchanges of fire are certain to increase the sense of crisis. This is exactly what the Pyongyang strategists want.

This peculiar situation is also understood by the more reasonable hard-liners in Washington and Seoul, who are thus left with sanctions alone. But the efficiency of such sanctions is doubtful. First of all, strict and comprehensive sanctions are difficult to impose, since China, and to a lesser degree Russia, will be unwilling to be party to a truly rigorous (read: efficient) sanctions regime. Neither Russia nor China wants North Korea to go nuclear, but they both have other issues on their agenda, and some of those issues are more pressing than the Korean nuclear question.

The use of financial sanctions, a ban of the activity of North Korean banks, more or less along the lines of the Banco Delta Asia (BDA) problem, is an option to which North Korea seems to be relatively vulnerable. However, the efficiency of such sanctions has never really been tested.

To make things worse, North Korean society is designed in such a way as to make even efficient sanctions politically irrelevant.

Normally, sanctions work in an indirect way. In most cases, sanctions impact the populations of target nations, making their lives less comfortable and more stressful. This leads to a growing discontent as the public begins to blame their government for their declining living standards and other associated problems. The strategy of economic sanctions is based on the assumption that dissatisfied people will press for change in the policy, or even remove their government via popular revolution (or, in the case of a more democratic and tolerant regime, at the ballot box). Alternatively, dissatisfied and/or ambitious members of the ruling elite might also use the crisis as an opportunity to overthrow the regime, peacefully or not. Once these dissatisfied elite members take power, they might make concessions to have the sanctions removed.

However, none of these mechanisms is likely to work in the peculiar case of North Korea. Despite the significant relaxation of the past two decades, North Korea is not liberal enough for its people to have any influence in matters of governance. North Koreans do not vote (well, they do vote with a predictable 100-percent approval rate for a single government-appointed candidate). They are terrified and isolated, they do not have the rudimentary self-organization necessary for creating a resistance movement, and they are still to a large extent unaware of any alternative to their mode of life. A popular revolt, Tunisia-style, might be possible in the long run, but is unlikely to happen any time soon.

At times it has been suggested that the sanctions (especially financial sanctions) will deprive the regime of the funds that are used to reward the top brass with small perks, like bottles of Hennessy cognac and Mercedes cars. It is assumed that as a result of such deprivation the North Korean generals and dignitaries will become restive and exercise some pressure on the government, demanding the surrender of nukes and/or reforms. This is an unrealistic expectation as well. The entire upper crust of the North Korean elite is likely to share the belief that regime stability is a basic condition for their survival. So we might presume that they would be willing to put up with locally produced liquors and used Toyotas if the alternative is a regime disintegration that will (or so they believe) send them to clean the floors of their prison cells, if not straight to the lampposts.

In other words, in the highly unlikely case that China sincerely cooperated with a sanctions regime (the only way such sanctions would really have any teeth), the sanctions would merely help to starve to death another few hundred thousand North Korean commoners without producing any of the desired political effects. The Pyongyang elite would see the death of a few hundred thousand as a regrettable but necessary price to pay for the survival of their regime.

WHY THE CARROTS ARE NOT SWEET ENOUGH (AND WHY "STRATEGIC PATIENCE" IS NOT A GREAT IDEA, EITHER)

Thus, as we have made clear, the hard-line policy is not going to have much impact on North Korea. Alas, the same is applicable to its major alternative, the policy of engagement. The Washington soft-liners usually cite three major incentives that can be put on the table as a reward for denuclearization: aid; security guarantees; and normalization of relations with the United States. To borrow the expression of Wade Huntley, an influential soft-liner, US administrations should just "sit down and talk" in order to resolve the nuclear issue.[1] The root of the current problems, the soft-liners insist, is America's unwillingness to be flexible and generous enough and its adherence to an approach that is too militant and/or excessively idealistic. This approach is what Wade Huntley describes as "emancipatory militant idealism"—the belief that the United States might and must use force for achieving the benevolent goals of emancipating suppressed peoples worldwide.[2]

The aid would be most welcome in Pyongyang, no doubt. However, even a large lump-sum payment is not necessarily a long-term solution. Once the money is spent (and it will be spent quite quickly), a nonnuclear Pyongyang regime will have great difficulties in obtaining additional aid. Without nukes, North Korea would be just another impoverished country that must compete for donor attention with such places as Sudan or Zimbabwe. Even though some aid would probably come its way, it would be on a smaller scale than is currently being received. It also would be strictly conditional and its distribution carefully monitored. However, in order to survive, the Kim family regime needs to be able to distribute its foreign aid according to its own priorities, without excessive interference from the donors. The North Korean leaders need money, but only the kind of money they can control. They prefer payments and giveaways to investment, since the latter implies a great deal of interaction between foreign investors and North Koreans. As well, it cannot be directly channeled to the programs the regime considers necessary for its own survival. It is the existence of the nuclear program that allows Pyongyang politicians to determine the conditions on which aid should be delivered and distributed.

The promises of the US security guarantee—even if such promises are to be believed—are also not sufficiently attractive to change Pyongyang's behavior. Few people would doubt that North Korean leaders are sincerely afraid of a large-scale US-led invasion, and this fear is justified, as the fate of Iraq, a fellow member of the "axis of evil," has demonstrated. However, there are at least two reasons why such security guarantees might be irrelevant.

First, North Koreans deeply distrust Americans (and, more broadly speaking, all foreigners), and they do not believe in the value of foreigners' promises, especially when such promises are made in democratic systems where leaders and policies are bound to change every few years and where the moralistic outbursts of public opinion might outweigh all earlier agreements.

Second, North Korean leaders know that in the final analysis, their major security threat is internal, not external. They are afraid of a US-led invasion, Iraq-style, but they are even more afraid of a domestic coup or revolution. Needless to say, neither the United States nor any other outside player can provide them with a guarantee against such an outcome—indeed, as events in Libya demonstrated, they are likely to actively encourage such an outcome. One cannot imagine a US president who promises to send the US Marines to suppress a pro-democracy rebellion in Pyongyang (but one can easily imagine a president who dispatches marines—or, more likely, jets— to save the rebels from slaughter by the Kim loyalists). At the same time, their nuclear status at least increases Pyongyang leaders' ability to fend off unwanted intervention in the event of a domestic crisis as well as their ability to extract foreign aid under their conditions (and control over aid distribution might help to prevent a domestic crisis).

If anything, the recent events in Libya confirmed these assumptions. On March 22, 2011, the KCNA—a North Korean official news agency— quoted a spokesman for the DPRK Foreign Ministry as saying:

> The present Libyan crisis teaches the international community a serious lesson. It was fully exposed before the world that "Libya's nuclear dismantlement" much touted by the US in the past turned out to be a mode of aggression whereby the latter coaxed the former with such sweet words as "guarantee of security" and "improvement of relations" to disarm itself and then swallowed it up by force. It proved once again the truth of history that peace can be preserved only when one builds up one's own strength as long as high-handed and arbitrary practices go on in the world.

For a change, the present author believes that this particular KCNA statement makes perfect sense.

Indeed, in 2003 Colonel Gaddafi did exactly what the North Korean rulers had stubbornly refused to consider—surrender his country's nuclear materials in exchange for better relations with the United States and other Western nations. As we have seen, the compromise did not work. When his own people decided to get rid of him, the rebels found willing military support from the West and the eccentric dictator had nothing to deter the mighty West from intervening in the domestic politics of his country. The North Korean leadership must have thought that had Gaddafi not been persuaded to surrender his nuclear program in 2003, the West would never have seriously considered intervening in Libya.

The North Korean regime is thus not going to respond to either pressure or rewards, and this is increasingly obvious to the interested parties. There is therefore a great—and growing—temptation to say that North Korea is better to be forgotten and safely left alone. This is the essence of the "strategic patience" strategy, which has quietly become the mainstream thinking of the US foreign policy establishment after 2009. In essence it says that the United States is willing to talk to North Korea, and maybe even "reward" it with some monetary and political concessions, as long as North Korea does what the United States wants it to do—that is, starts dismantling its nuclear program. If it doesn't do so, the United States should, as strategic patience promoters insist, ignore North Korea's antics, since North Korea isn't going to be all that harmful anyway. A somewhat similar attitude seems to be dominant among the South Korean Right. These people believe that aid and political concessions make sense only if North Korean leaders agree to policies that are seen as "rational" by Seoul.

This reasoning might be attractive, but it seems to be unrealistic. North Korea has not the slightest desire to be left alone. Indeed, they cannot afford to be left alone. In order to compensate for the innate inefficiency of their economy, they need outside help, delivered on their specific conditions. So far, the best way to squeeze this aid has been to appear dangerous, unpredictable, and irrational. Therefore, they will continue to appear thus, attempting to cause more trouble for those countries and international forces from whom they hope to squeeze some resources. The alternative is not really attractive—either to survive on meager and perhaps diminishing returns of their nonfunctioning economy or to become excessively dependent on just one sponsor (China).

The supporters of strategic patience (aka, benign neglect) should understand that whilst being benignly neglected, North Korean leaders will work hard to improve their nuclear and missile arsenal, at the same time trying to proliferate (both as a way to pressurize by being troublesome and as a way to earn extra cash). South Koreans are in an even less enviable situation, as we have argued above, since the refusal to deal with the North Korean regime means that South Korea will face an almost endless chain of provocations. This is bad news for Seoul, since an outbreak of inter-Korean tensions is much more costly for the South than for the North.

Like it or not, the strategic patience of both Washington and Seoul is limited. Sooner or later, they are likely to give in and rejoin the game that is initiated and stage-managed by Pyongyang. The price of not doing so is too costly. It therefore makes sense to be prepared to rejoin the game on the conditions that are—in the long run, at least—more favorable for Seoul, Washington, and, in the final count, the majority of the North Korean population. The North Korean problem has no quick fixes, but this does not mean that it has no solution whatsoever.

THINKING LONG TERM

When we discuss the North Korean problem, it is important to keep in mind that it has three different, if interconnected, dimensions.

For the United States, the major problem is North Korea's willingness to develop and maintain (perhaps, even proliferate) nuclear weapons and other WMD, as well as Pyongyang's inclination to engage in seemingly reckless provocative behavior.

For South Korea, the major issue is North Korea's refusal to initiate any kind of reforms that would bring about economic growth and a political transformation, thus creating better conditions for a manageable unification. The ceaseless brinkmanship of Pyongyang also constitutes a serious problem for Seoul (actually, a significantly greater problem than for the United States, which is lucky to be located thousands of miles away).

There is also another, often unmentioned, dimension of the problem: that of average North Koreans. For them, the continuing existence of the system in its present ossified form means that they are doomed to live lives that are both materially and spiritually impoverished (and full of fear, too). Unable to enjoy the fruits of economic growth that the luckier people in all neighboring countries have experienced, their lives are, essentially, struggles for physical survival. They are deprived of even the theoretical opportunity to become acquainted with more refined forms of culture. Last but not least, they always remember that harsh punishment waits for everybody who deviates from the state's rigidly prescribed forms of behavior. On balance, this waste of human lives and energy might be the greatest consequence of the Kim family's dictatorial rule.

As we have seen above, all of Pyongyang's policies—the nuclear and WMD programs, the unwillingness to reform, the determined efforts to maintain a police state, the penchant for creating regional tensions—are closely connected to the nature of the North Korean regime. Without these strategies, the regime and the ruling elite will be in serious trouble and so they persist with these policies, no matter what the cost to their own population, to outsiders, and even to the long-term future of their country. The only way to alter North Korea's behavior is to change the nature of North Korea's regime. But how?

To answer this question, it makes sense to have a closer look at the not-so-distant history. What brought about the end of Communism in Eastern Europe and the Soviet Union? In the end, it was the ingrained inefficiency of the centrally planned economy, its inability to provide the population with the level of consumption that prevails in the developed West. This is not to deny that the desire for national independence among the ethnic minorities as well as a longing for democracy and political freedoms among the better educated sections of the population also played a significant role in the demise of Communism. However, on balance, the fate of the Communist regimes of Eastern Europe and the Soviet Union was sealed by their economic inefficiency, not their political repressiveness. The author himself was witness to this transformation and hence can assure readers that the decisive impact on the Soviet imagination in the final decades of Communism was produced by the sight of shelves at an American supermarket rather than by the sight of vote counting at an American polling station.

Paradoxically, the less dramatic transformation of China was also a result of similar changes: by the 1970s, the Beijing leaders were aware that China, in spite of the mad experiments of Chairman Mao, was increasingly lagging behind its neighbors, and that its state-planned economy failed to deliver. They concluded that reform was necessary.

However, in order to become a political factor, this economic inefficiency had to first become known to and acknowledged by the majority of the population. Had the Soviet leadership been willing and able to maintain a North Korean level of isolation and repressiveness, the Soviet Union might still be in existence today. But the regimes of Eastern Europe and the Soviet Union were soft on their population (in the post-Stalin era, that is) and did not maintain the level of isolation required. Consequently, the average Soviet and Eastern European citizen gradually became aware that peoples of the developed West were living lives that were both more affluent and less controlled by the authorities. The same is applicable to the Chinese decision makers of the 1970s: they knew that China was lagging behind, and this knowledge prompted them to act.

If anything, North Korea is even more vulnerable to outside information than the Soviet Union and Eastern European countries used to be. After all, in Korea the tremendous economic success is enjoyed by the other half of the same nation, not by some distant countries whose cultures are different and whose languages are incomprehensible. For a long time, Soviet agitprop tried to cushion the impact of the news about Western prosperity by insisting that it was the cruelty of historic fate, and not the ingrained problems of the system, that prevented the Soviet people from enjoying the same consumption levels as Americans. In the 1960s and 1970s the Soviet media argued that the Soviet people should not compare themselves with the lucky inhabitants of North America who had never suffered a foreign invasion and could exploit the entire world for their selfish purposes (references to the slave trade and genocide of American Indians came easily). The argument was not bought by the majority of the Soviet population, but for a while it helped to some extent.

North Korean propagandists face an unenviable situation: they have to explain the stunning prosperity of the area that at the time of the division was an agricultural backwater and is populated by members of the same ethnic group who share the same language and culture as the destitute inhabitants of North Korea. Now, when the information blockade has become more difficult to maintain, North Korean propaganda does its best to explain South Korean success as the fruits of shamelessly selling out to US imperialism. The ruse might work to some degree, but this explanation has less chance of succeeding than the elaborate but plausible constructs of 1960s Soviet propaganda.

There is another peculiarity that makes the North Korean regime vulnerable to the spread of information about the outside world. The personality cult of the Kims has some similarities with a religious cult, but on balance the North Korean ideology is secular, with roots going back to Marxism and further back to the European Enlightenment. Unlike fundamentalist ideologues in some other parts of the world, North Korean propagandists do not promise that the faithful would enjoy eternal happiness in the afterlife in the company of 72 virgins. Instead, they claim that North Korean official ideology knows how to best arrange the economic and political life in this world, how to provide economic growth and general well-being. Unfortunately for the North Korean elite, their system has failed to deliver the promised goods and this failure is made remarkably clear in light of the extraordinary success of South Korea.

The existence of the rich and free South is the major challenge for North Korean leaders, so the spread of knowledge about South Korea is bound to make the status quo untenable.

In order to initiate changes in North Korea, it is necessary to put North Korea's rulers under pressure from its people and the lower echelons of the elite. Only North Koreans themselves can change North Korea. They are the major victims of the current unfortunate situation, and they also will become major potential beneficiaries of the coming change.

The only long-term solution, therefore, is to increase internal pressure for a regime transformation, and the major way to achieve this is to increase North Koreans' awareness of the outside world. If North Koreans learn about the existence of attractive and available alternatives to their regimented and impoverished existence, the almost unavoidable result will be the growth of dissatisfaction toward the current administration. This will create domestic pressure for change, and the North Korean government will discover that its legitimacy is waning even among a considerable part of the elite (largely among those who don't have vested interests in keeping the system unchanged).

This might end in a regime collapse, but it is also possible that facing such pressure, the leadership might attempt some reforms it would not otherwise even contemplate. Reforms might theoretically end in success— that is, in the emergence of a developmental dictatorship, North Korean— style. However, due to the reasons outlined above, it seems to be far more probable that attempts at reforms will simply hasten the collapse of the regime. Either way (a regime collapse or regime transformation), it will be an improvement of the situation for both a majority of the North Korean people as well as for outsiders.

Admittedly, one of the above-mentioned scenarios is almost certain to happen eventually. Due to its innate inability to deliver economic growth, the North Korean government has become the major obstacle to North Korea's economic development. As history has shown countless times, in the modern era an economically inept regime always falls sooner or later. Information about the outside world is spreading anyway, whatever the government does—largely thanks to new technologies (like DVD players), but also due to the slow-motion disintegration of domestic surveillance and control. The measures discussed below will *not* change the course of history, but will merely speed events up to a certain (perhaps quite small) extent—and will also make the coming crisis more manageable.

This outside support for information dissemination will also serve another important purpose that is not well understood. The half-century rule of the Kim dynasty was a social and economic disaster, but its eventual (and, like it or not, unavoidable) collapse might initially mean a disaster of comparable proportions. It is already time to start thinking about a post-Kim future, to undertake measures that will make the future transformation of North Korea less painful.

This policy is unlikely to succeed in a short span of time, so we indeed need serious strategic patience in dealing with North Korea—as long as strategic patience does not mean being idle and doing nothing. Conversely, this policy—or rather set of policies—can be implemented by a number of actors. Efforts aimed at changing North Korea can be carried out by the bureaucracies of the different states who have a stake in the issue. But there is also a great deal of space for NGOs, private foundations, and even individuals. All efforts that increase North Korea's exposure to the outside world should be welcomed. All interpersonal exchanges should work toward the same goal.

Currently, there are three channels that can provide the North Korean populace with unauthorized information about the outside world. First, officially approved academic, cultural, and other interpersonal exchanges, endorsed by the North Korean authorities, will unavoidably bring such potentially dangerous knowledge inside the country. Second, radio broadcasts and digital media might deliver news that is beyond the control of the North Korean regime. Third, the small but growing community of North Korean refugees—currently residing in South Korea but maintaining relations with families and friends in the North—might play a major and important role in disseminating this type of communication.

THE HIDDEN BENEFITS OF ENGAGEMENT

Of all the three channels mentioned above, official exchanges between North Korea and the outside world are especially significant. Since such exchanges will have to be approved by the North Korean authorities, nearly all participants will necessarily come from the country's current elite.

One can expect that conservatives in Washington, Seoul, and elsewhere will question the value of these exchanges. They may say that such exchanges in effect reward the North Korean leadership and its cronies. There is a kernel of truth (actually a rather large kernel) in this point of view. There is no doubt that the top functionaries in Pyongyang and the spoiled brats of the Pyongyang government quarters will be the first to take advantage of international student exchanges or overseas study trips. However, to be frank, they are exactly the type of people who matter most. Changes to North Korea might start from below, but it is more likely that transformation will be initiated by well-informed and disillusioned members of the elite.

There is a historic example that shows the potential power of seemingly controlled and limited exchanges. In 1958 an academic exchange agreement was signed between the Soviet Union and the United States. In the United States, the diehard conservatives insisted that the agreement would merely provide the Soviets with another opportunity to send spies or educate propaganda-mongers. In addition, the critics continued, this would be done on American taxpayers' money.

The first group of exchange students included exactly the people the conservatives were not eager to welcome onto US soil. There were merely four Soviet students selected by Moscow to enter Columbia University for one year of study. One of them, as we know now, was a rising KGB operative whose job was indeed to spy on the Americans. He was good at his job and eventually made a brilliant career in Soviet foreign intelligence. His fellow student was a young but promising veteran of the then-still-recent World War II. After studies in the United States, he moved to the Communist Party central bureaucracy, where in a decade he became the first deputy head of the propaganda department—in essence, a second-in-command among Soviet professional ideologues.

Skeptics seemed to have been proven right—until the 1980s, that is. The KGB operative's name was Oleg Kalugin, and he was to become the first KGB officer to openly challenge the organization from within. He was the first person to criticize the KGB's role as a party watchdog, and initiated a campaign aimed at its transformation into a regular intelligence and counterintelligence service.

His fellow student, Alexandr Yakovlev, was a young party propagandist. In due time, he was to become a Central Committee secretary, the closest associate of Mikhail Gorbachev. He made a remarkable contribution to the collapse of the Communist regime in Moscow (some people even insist that it was Yakovlev rather than Gorbachev himself who could be described as the real architect of perestroika).

Eventually, both men said it was their experiences in the United States that changed the way they saw the world, even if they were prudent enough to keep their mouths shut and say what they were expected to say.

Indeed, academic and personal exchanges seem to be the most efficient way to promote the spread of subversive information. By their nature, such exchanges imply a great deal of immersion into the host society by the visiting North Koreans. As a result of gained access to such a thorough view of everyday South Korean life, the North Koreans will be much less likely to suspect that they are dealing with the sort of staged propaganda show their own country is famous for. Such an approach also targets people who tend to belong to the elite and who, upon their return, will quietly share their impressions with the people who really matter. Last but not least, interpersonal exchanges will also help introduce North Koreans to the knowledge and technology that will be so necessary when the decades-long North Korean stagnation finally ends.

It is unlikely that the North Korean authorities will agree to send a significant number of their students, scientists, and officials to the United States (and it is virtually impossible that such people will ever be allowed to visit South Korea). So in most cases, education programs should be conducted by other countries, including those that are seen as more or less friendly toward North Korea. South Korean and American hard-liners may take issue with this, but they may be proven wrong in this regard: *all* exchanges with the outside world are good for promoting North Korea's transformation.

Naturally, these programs are not going to be paid for by the North Korean government itself. To paraphrase a remark by veteran North Korea expert Aidan Foster-Carter, North Korean leaders are people who never do anything as vulgar as paying their bills. There is, however, a need to financially support academic and interpersonal exchange programs and this is a place where both official agencies of third-party countries and perhaps private foundations will have a role.

This issue might be somewhat difficult politically. From personal experience, I know that diplomats from some developed countries are reluctant to openly support exchanges with North Korea out of fear that such exchanges might be perceived in Washington as a breach of international solidarity with the South and as rewarding a brutal and disgusting regime. Taking into consideration the conservatives' approach to the issue, these fears might be quite justified. This is unfortunate, however, since exchanges are not means to reward the North Korean elite but rather a way to change North Korean society, thus undermining this elite's grip on power.

Apart from academic exchanges, one should encourage all activities that create an environment conducive to contact between North Koreans and foreigners (and especially between North and South Koreans). This is the major reason why the Kaesong Industrial Zone is actually a very good idea: projects where North and South Koreans work together are bound to produce many situations where uncontrolled and unscripted exchanges between them will take place.

Judged from the regime's point of view, Kim Jong Il's decision to tolerate and even encourage the Kaesong Industrial Zone was a grave mistake—perhaps even the greatest mistake ever made by the North Korean oligarchs, whose survival depends on the ability to keep the populace in ignorance of the outside world. The Kaesong Industrial Zone might generate a significant income for the North Korean authorities, but it has also produced a dramatic transformation of the worldview of the 150,000 to 200,000 North Koreans who live in Kaesong and whose family members or friends work in the Industrial Park.

Regarding the political consequences that are likely to result from apolitical interaction at the workplace, I would like to relate an incident that happened a few years ago, when the present author was flying from Seoul to Moscow. In the plane I sat next to a Russian couple in their late 50s. Judging by their dress and behavior, the husband was a moderately successful businessman who had begun his career in the Soviet days as an engineer in my native Leningrad. He told me how, in the mid-1970s, a team of French engineers came to his plant to assist in the installation of newly purchased French equipment. The factory's "first department" (that is, the resident KGB bureau) told Russians that it would be okay to talk to the French about anything as long as politics was avoided. For their part, the French engineers did not touch upon dangerous topics.

One night, the French equipment stopped functioning. It was too late to go home, so the French and Russian engineers had to stay all night drinking tea, talking, and waiting for a repair team. In the middle of their conversation, a French engineer said, "You are so happy here!" Sincerely or not, the Russian engineers gave a patriotic answer: "Thanks to our Socialist System we are happy!" The French engineer, however, did not leave it at that: "Your life is so shitty, but you have no clue how awful it really is and this is why you are so happy!" This exchange was obviously not a life-changing experience for my fellow traveler—but sudden life-changing experiences are more common in B-grade movies than in real life. Nevertheless, this short exchange had a real impact—it was, after all, recollected some 35 years later.

From this perspective, it is unfortunate that in 2008 the Seoul administration postponed and, for all practical purposes, cancelled the plans for a second industrial park that were discussed by the Roh administration in 2007. The more industrial parks there will be around, the better.

An added—but very important!—advantage of the industrial parks and other forms of joint North-South enterprises is the role they play in introducing North Koreans to the modern industrial environment and modern technologies. In effect, they can teach North Korean workers some practical manufacturing skills. These skills are not going to be particularly sophisticated, but in the future even these moderate abilities might make a difference.

Hence, if one wants to change North Korea, all exchanges between the North and the outside world, especially exchanges between North and South Korea, should be actively encouraged—even if ostensibly such exchanges enrich the regime, providing it with money, or benefit members of the current elite. This is the reason why the Sunshine Policy, so much criticized and even vilified by the South Korean Right, was probably not a bad idea. It is true that such a policy was not based on the reciprocity principle. But, one cannot expect reciprocity when dealing with such an impoverished country, anyway (and of course, the goal remains to change North Korea, not make economic gains through cooperation with it).

Unfortunately, at the time of writing, the full-scale revival of the Sunshine Policy does not look likely. Its opponents firmly believe that the policy was at best a waste of resources, at worst the savior of a brutal regime. They also pin much hope on the current approach of, essentially, ignoring the North. This policy line might sell well with ideologically inclined voters, but its actual results are very different from what is intended. Such policy is more likely to extend the life expectancy of the Kim family regime while also maintaining an unnecessary high level of tensions on the Korean peninsula. It is possible that conservatives will never realize that they are wrong on this issue, so they will persist with this pseudo-hard-line approach for a few more years. Their stubbornness is a true waste of time, but much can be done in the meantime and, paradoxically, conservatives seem to be the people best suited to do it.

A FLOWER OF UNIFICATION

In the summer of 1989 Pyongyang was hosting a lavish international event—the 13th World Festival of Youth and Students. Such festivals were essentially gatherings of young left-leaning intellectuals and artists, heavily subsidized by the Soviet Union and the Communist bloc. The Pyongyang festival was meant to be a symbolic reaction to the Olympic Games, which had been successfully hosted by South Korea in 1988. (In those days North Korea still tried hard to compete with the South.)

That summer, North Koreans were exposed to a great number of happenings and personalities, but none left as much an impression as a young girl named Im Su-gyong. Im Su-gyong was a student of Hankook University of Foreign Studies and also an activist from the National Council of Student Representatives, a left-leaning, nationalistic, and generally pro-Northern students' organization in Seoul.

During that era, North Korean sympathizers played an important and even decisive role in the South Korean students' movement, so one should not be surprised that a powerful South Korean students' association decided to dispatch their delegation to Pyongyang. The South Korean government, then still dominated by hard-line anti-Communists from the then recently overthrown military regime, banned the trip. But Im Su-gyong and some other activists ignored the ban and went to Pyongyang nonetheless (they had to go to Pyongyang via third-party countries, since then, as now, there was no direct way to go to the North).

In North Korea, Im Su-gyong was met with the greatest pomp imaginable. North Korean propagandists saw the girl as a gift from heaven: she was beautiful, charming, charismatic, and full of enthusiastic belief in the glories of Stalinism with North Korean characteristics. They did their best to present her as representative of South Korean youth, who if the North Korean official media was to be believed, spent their days and nights secretly studying the works of Kim Il Sung and Kim Jong Il and planning demonstrations in front of US army bases.

There is no doubt that a many South Korean students, at that stage at least, sincerely believed that North Korea was a viable alternative to the capitalist South, which was seen by progressive intellectuals as an "underdeveloped victim of US neo-colonialism." Thus, the Seoul student did not say anything to embarrass her handlers and duly delivered the politically correct statements the authorities wanted to hear.

However, more than 20 years later, one can see that Im Su-gyong's visit to North Korea was a major blunder by the North Korean authorities. Regardless of the subjective beliefs of Ms. Im herself and the calculations of her handlers, her trip to Pyongyang inflicted a major blow to the then officially approved image of South Korea, allegedly a place of destitution and poverty. According to the official media, South Korean workers were starving whilst their kids made a miserable living by working in sweatshops, begging, or polishing the shoes of sadistic American soldiers.

It would have been difficult *not* to believe these stories, since the North Korean public was cut off from the outside world to an extent that would have been unbelievable in any other Communist country, including the Soviet Union of the Stalin era.

But the message was dead wrong. In those decades, North Korea stagnated while South Korea went through an economic miracle, transforming itself into a developed industrial society. Nonetheless, North Koreans knew none of what was happening just a few hundred miles from their villages, towns, and cities.

Nowadays, we would probably describe what happened as "Im Su-gyong mania." The girl was known in official propaganda as "the flower of unification"—the epithet is still remembered by virtually all North Koreans. North Koreans noticed that the girl looked healthy and optimistic and was very well dressed. For a while, she became a trendsetter in the world of North Korean fashion—North Korean women wanted to wear "Im Su-gyong–style trousers" (even though North Korean women at the time were discouraged from wearing trousers outside the workplace), and imitate her short, straight haircut. North Koreans also noted—with some shock—that she often did not wear a bra.

People were also surprised by her willingness to deliver unscripted speeches—something that was quite unusual for North Koreans, who

(continued)

took it for granted that all political statements had to be carefully prepared and rehearsed countless times. Even though she did not say
anything to contradict North Korean slogans, her apparent sincerity
and the ease with which she spoke were striking and so very different
from what the North Korean public was used to.

After a month and a half spent in North Korea, Im Su-gyong and
Mun Ik-hwan, another South Korean leftist/nationalist dissident,
went back to the South. As a way to protest the division of Korea,
on the 15th of August, 1989, on the anniversary of Korea's liberation
from the Japanese colonial regime, they chose to cross the DMZ at
Panmunjom, even though such a move was against South Korean
law.

The duo crossed the border, whereupon they were immediately
arrested. The North Korean public assumed that Im Su-gyong made
a great sacrifice. It was widely believed that she would spend
the rest of her life in the terrible dungeons of the South Korean
dictators.

Im Su-gyong indeed stood trial after her return to the South. The
anachronistic and nondemocratic National Security Law, then and
now still in operation in South Korea, criminalizes any kind of unauthorized visit to the North. As a result, Im Su-gyong was sentenced to five
years in prison (she was released after three-and-a-half years of imprisonment). Needless to say, this was a shameful decision, but it is
not the focus of our story.

North Korean propaganda then miscalculated again. Trying to
capitalize on Im Su-gyong's tremendous popularity, they aired an interview with her parents, who lived in Seoul. This interview is widely
remembered by the North Koreans, since it produced an explosive
impact on their thinking about the South.

North Koreans were surprised to discover that the family members
of a political criminal were allowed to stay in their home in the capital
city, keep their jobs, and talk freely to journalists. Having seen the interview, North Koreans began to suspect that South Korea was not
only far more affluent than they were told: they also came to the conclusion that the "ruling Fascist clique" in Seoul was unusually soft
when dealing with the internal opposition.

I think they would be much more surprised to learn that in 2012, Im Su-gyong—whose views have not changed that much—became a member of the South Korean Parliament. However, from the mid-1990s, her exploits ceased to be reported by the North Korean media.

Im Su-gyong's trip was the beginning of major changes. A few years later in the late 1990s, unauthorized information about the outside world began to filter into North Korea—largely thanks to the spread of videotapes and, later, VCDs and DVDs, as well as the effective collapse of immigration controls on the border with China.

However, the first breaches in the information blockade were inflicted by North Korean authorities themselves. They wanted to show how popular their regime was in the South, but they ended up unwittingly providing proof of South Korean economic success and political freedom.

REACHING THE PEOPLE

Personal exchanges seem to be the best way to put the knowledge of the outside world within the reach of North Koreans. However, apart from such officially approved activities, different channels might be used to reach the same goal—and not all such channels need be to the North Korean government's liking.

Until recently, there was good reason to be skeptical about attempts to reach the North Korean masses over the heads of their masters. In Kim Il Sung's North Korea all possible channels of uncensored interaction were safely sealed by the regime, which maintained a strict policy of self-isolation. However, in recent decades the situation has measurably changed. DVD players are common now, and even computers are not unheard of anymore. Tunable radios, while still technically illegal, are smuggled into the country in growing quantities, together with banned South Korean DVDs. Additionally, North Korean people are less afraid to talk amongst themselves and even sometimes raise politically dangerous topics. Authorities are less willing to enforce old regulations that still remain on the books.

These changes mean that nowadays, for the first time in decades, it is becoming possible to deliver unauthorized knowledge directly to North Koreans. The information blockade can be penetrated, and the North Korean public seems to be more receptive to critical messages than it has ever been since the end of the Korean War.

Of the ways to break through, one has to first mention radio broadcast. The general population and resistance leaders of the post-Communist countries now widely recognize the special role of the radio broadcast during the Cold War era. When Lech Walesa, leader of the Polish democracy movement Solidarity, was asked about the degree of influence Radio Free Europe had on the Polish opposition, he famously replied: "The degree cannot even be described. Would there be Earth without the Sun?"[3]

Fortunately, recent years have been marked by a dramatic increase in broadcasts targeting North Korea. According to a study conducted in the summer of 2009 by the InterMedia Group, at that time there were five radio stations that specifically targeted the North Korean audience—not counting the government-run KBS and some Christian stations in South Korea. The total broadcast time amounted to 20.5 hours a day (once again, excluding KBS). If one takes into account the fact that a few years ago the total broadcast time did not exceed four to five hours, this is a remarkable breakthrough.[4] The scale of the audience is difficult to estimate, but different sources indicate that it is not insignificant. For example, in early 2010 Peter Beck estimated that the number of listeners might have reached one million (or some 5 percent of the total population).[5]

The North Korean audience is currently targeted by large government-owned stations, of which KBS (Korean), Radio Free Asia, and Voice of America play chief roles. There are also a number of smaller defector-based stations staffed by former North Koreans. They gravely lack funds and expertise, but are not short on enthusiasm and often have clandestine networks that collect valuable information from inside North Korea. These stations—both large and small—need more active support.

Another traditional medium is leaflets, which are now delivered exclusively by the refugees' NGOs (a government program was halted a decade ago). This author is somewhat skeptical of the efficacy of the balloon program. The occasional encounter with a short piece of information provided by a printed text is unlikely to seriously change the worldview of a North Korean. Nonetheless, such efforts might be continued.

The digital age has brought new opportunities that have never been utilized. For example, the continuing spread of VCD/DVD players inside North Korea creates manifold opportunities for introducing information about the outside world. It is now possible to produce visual material—essentially, documentaries—specifically designed for North Korean audiences. Such documentaries can rely on the obvious advantage of visual appeal, and thus have the potential to be more effective than radio broadcasts.

Digital technologies also have simplified the process of dissemination of textual material. In the Cold War era, a broadcast reached a far larger audience than text and had a much greater impact, since printed books were unwieldy and difficult to smuggle and copy. In the Communist countries, photocopying machines were closely monitored by security police, so in most cases copying had to be done by typewriter. It took about one week to make four or five copies of an average book, which is the reason why samizdat, the clandestinely published materials so much discussed in the West, was systematically accessed only by a handful of opposition-minded intellectuals.

Things have now changed, however, thanks to the advent of digital technologies. A book can now be easily scanned and/or converted into a text file. Hundreds of such files can easily fit into one USB drive or DVD disk. In the 1970s it would take years of typewriting (or days of photocopying) to reproduce such a large volume of text, but now the job can be done within minutes. A digital book is also easier to hide or destroy than its paper equivalent. The efficiency of digital technologies means that even one copy of a book (or rather a collection of books, a "digital library") once smuggled across the border could continue to proliferate inside North Korea.

By their very nature, the texts will be more appealing to intellectuals and the lower reaches of the elite. Such scanned materials might include textbooks on major social subjects and humanities, as well as purely technical material (and special attention should be given to textbooks and manuals dealing with computers). It is important to introduce books that have different, even mutually exclusive, opinions—as long as the books are well-written and the arguments are sound. North Koreans should not be treated with syrupy propaganda and anti-Communist harangues. Instead, they must become accustomed to intellectual differences and arguments. They should read what was written by the Left and Right, zealous antiglo-balists and stubborn libertarians alike. They should be exposed to the modern world, with all its complexity and uncertainty.

WHY THEY MATTER: WORKING WITH THE REFUGEES IN SOUTH KOREA

When, in the 1970s, Vaclav Havel, the would-be president of the Czech Republic, was talking about the future of his country, he specifically emphasized the special role that might be played by "the second society." He admitted that the Communist regime in Czechoslovakia (ridiculously permissive and liberal by North Korean standards) was repressive to the degree that made organized resistance impossible. So, Havel reasoned, the only way to resist was to minimize and avoid popular involvement with the regime. People could not (and hence should not) protest openly, but instead they should live their lives as if the Central Committee, Party Youth, and political study sessions did not exist.

What Havel described was already in existence in the 1970s Soviet Union and Eastern Europe. Only a tiny minority was directly involved with the dissenters, but many more lived lives that were completely disconnected from the official rhetoric and official ideology. By the late 1970s, among the intellectuals of Moscow (let alone Warsaw and Prague), it became almost suspicious if somebody professed seemingly sincere support for the exist-ing political system. In this milieu, the party rhetoric and party politics were treated as something akin to bad weather. It was tacitly admitted that nothing could be done about it, but rain outside was not a reason to stop one's daily routine or to deprive oneself of small pleasures of life.

This milieu of nonpolitical (or slightly opposition-leaning) intellectuals was the environment that produced active dissenters. It also played an important role when Communism began to crumble in the late 1980s. Many of these people eventually became political activists, journalists, even industrial managers. They were a group from which a significant part of the post-Communist elite emerged. These were people with knowledge, experience, and, in some cases, nationwide fame and moral authority. They were also people who were not compromised by a track record of collaboration with the overthrown Communist governments.

As a rule, the stronger and more influential such a second society was in a particular Communist country, the less painful and more successful the post-Communist transition tended to be. Among other things, it produced a sad paradox—countries where the former Communist apparatchiks fared worst after the Communist collapse were usually the very same countries where Communism itself was least repressive (Hungary, Poland, and Czechoslovakia).

Unfortunately, the North Korean regime has always been the most thorough in its control over its population. As a result, no second society has been able to emerge there. More or less every North Korean with education and experience can be plausibly described as a lifelong regime collaborator. The Kim family does not give its subjects any chance to live lives that would be autonomous from the state—or at least this is the case with socially prominent individuals. Closet opponents of the regime exist amongst educated North Koreans, but they are usually too terrified to share their doubts even among themselves.

This absence of a second society does not merely strengthen the Kim family's regime. It is also bound to create manifold problems in the future, when the regime loses power. Everybody will have some skeletons in his/her closet.

It is therefore important to encourage the emergence of a second society, or an alternative elite. Such an elite is unlikely to emerge inside North Korea, however, even though broadcast and proliferation of digital materials might play a role in bringing modern knowledge within the reach of some educated North Koreans. Hope, therefore, should be pinned on the refugee community in South Korea.

North Korean refugees are very different from those Eastern Europeans who fled West during the Cold War. To start with, they cannot be plausibly described as "defectors" since most of them were driven away from the North by starvation and/or other nonpolitical reasons. Furthermore, Eastern European and Soviet defectors were well educated, while North Korean refugees are largely farmers and manual workers. At first glance, it seems unlikely that from such a group a second society can emerge.

However, the situation is not that hopeless. First, there is a small but not insignificant number of well-educated refugees. Contrary to what is often assumed outside South Korea, they are not actively supported by the South Korean state, so one should not be much surprised by the sight of a former North Korean engineer who makes a living through pizza delivery (well, more likely he will be working at a Chinese eatery, far more common in Seoul). Support systems and jobs for such people are crucial.

Second, there are younger defectors who still see themselves as North Koreans but who can and should be educated. There is an urgent need to introduce scholarships that would specifically target this group.

Scholarships for MA and PhD studies are of special importance, since currently those refugees who are accepted to a university can study for free but this important privilege is granted only to undergraduates. However, nowadays a bachelor's degree alone doesn't stand for much in South Korea, where some 85 percent of high school graduates proceed to colleges and universities. It is advanced degrees that matter, but so far there is no systematic support for aspiring MA and PhD refugee students.

One might expect that such support should be forthcoming from the South Korean government. But unfortunately this is not the case—due to reasons largely related to the domestic situation, the South Korean government is not enthusiastic about providing such support (among other things, such preferential treatment might provoke outrage from South Korean MA and PhD candidates and their families). Therefore, such scholarships must be provided by overseas donors.

There is, of course, a need to support the political and cultural undertakings of this small but growing refugee community—radio stations, newspapers, and artistic groups. We need more North Koreans who will become South Korean journalists, policy analysts, and painters. But there is an even greater need for North Korean professionals—construction engineers, accountants, scientists, water-treatment specialists, and doctors.

These people will play at least three roles in future developments.

First of all, refugees will make an additional—and highly efficient—channel for efforts to reach the average North Koreans. Nowadays, refugees stay in touch with their families and friends back in North Korea—thanks to the Chinese cell phones and a network of "brokers" who deal with people movement, money transfers, and letter exchanges. It is understandable that a defector who has become, say, an accountant, will channel back to the North information of much greater importance and impact than a defector who makes a living by waiting tables at a cheap eatery.

Second, when the eventual collapse and/or transformation of North Korea finally comes, some of these refugee intellectuals will probably go back to their native land north of the DMZ. Some of them will become political and social activists, while many more will apply their technical skills in the reemerging North Korean economy. They will play a major role as educators and instructors, teaching North Koreans how things are done in the South and, broadly speaking, in the modern world.

Third, the emerging refugee professionals and intellectuals will become role models for the North Korean refugee community. This community is bound to grow in whatever direction Korea goes. Right now a North Korean refugee tends to become part of the underclass. As is often the case with other minorities, this low social standing has become self-perpetuating. Being deprived of role models, younger refugees will not strive hard enough to be successful in adjusting to the new society—later paying a bitter price for this. It will be of great help if the mother of some unruly teenager from a refugee family can point to Uncle Kim who has succeeded in becoming a surgeon, or Aunt Park who is now a designer with LG Corporation.

CHAPTER 6

Being Ready for What We Wish For

There is little doubt that in the long run the current North Korean regime is doomed. Its innate—and incurable—economic inefficiency and the resulting inability to decrease the steadily growing income gap with its neighbors (especially South Korea) is its Achilles' heel.

In the long run the outside world and the vast majority of North Koreans themselves will benefit from the likely collapse of the Kim family regime. However, we should not think in the terms that are common for so many freedom fighters, revolutionaries, and idealistic politicians (such politicians might be rare, but they do exist). We should not believe that the demise of the inefficient and brutal regime will herald the sudden, immediate arrival of eternal bliss and happiness. On the contrary, as every historian knows only too well, every revolution fermented, every independence declared, every liberation achieved brings a significant measure of disruption and chaos—and this is applicable even to those revolutions that with the wisdom of hindsight are seen as almost trouble-free. Unfortunately, the future North Korean revolution has little chance of being smooth, and subsequent events will most likely be painful. The regime collapse will mark the beginning of a long, winding road to the recovery of North Korea. It will take decades to clean the mess created by the Kim family regime's long misrule, and some traces of the sorry past might be felt for generations.

Now is the time to start considering what will happen after the Kim family regime passes—and what should be done to make the recovery less tortuous. There are some simple and cheap but potentially efficient measures that can be taken now—for example, policies that aim at creating an alternative elite (discussed above) will clearly help to cushion the pains and shocks of the coming transformation. And, of course, it is now time to start an honest, taboo-free discussion of ways to handle the coming challenges.

A PERFECT STORM

For decades Koreans have believed that the future unification of their country would be a major, cathartic event that would usher in an era of unprecedented happiness, harmony, and prosperity on the Korean peninsula. In the long run this is indeed likely to be the case—if judged from the perspective of a future historian living in, say, the year 2133. However, for those Koreans who will have to live through the decades immediately following unification, it will be a time of dramatic upheaval, social disruption, and profound shock.

Alas, nobody knows when and how unification will happen—and this alone makes preparations difficult. It is likely to come suddenly, too. In all probability, unification will occur as a result of some crisis of political authority and collapse of state control within North Korea. Such a crisis will come more or less out of the blue, so even the presidents and prime ministers of great powers might learn about such a crisis from TV news reports rather than from predictions by their diplomats and reports from their spymasters.

The world has never seen a unification of two societies so different in their economic and technological levels and their respective worldviews. The unification of Germany is clearly a precedent, but the two Germanys were never as far apart as the two Koreas are. More or less every East German family watched West German TV since the late 1960s, and visits by relatives as well as letter exchanges were easy to arrange. This is a far cry from North Korea, where the vast majority knows almost nothing about actual life in South Korea. The average North Korean has access to only two sources of information about life in the South—smuggled syrupy South Korean melodramas and the horror stories of official Pyongyang propaganda. Needless to say, both sources leave much to be desired.

THE COSTS OF UNIFICATION

The last 15 years have seen the emergence of a small cottage industry— people have begun to speculate on how much unification of the Koreas will cost.

This is a highly speculative undertaking to be sure, since nobody knows when (or more precisely—if) unification will happen. Furthermore, reliable statistical information about the North Korean economy is absent. Moreover, comparisons with other unifications like Germany and usually the forgotten Yemen are so different in demographic and economic terms that they are not very useful.

Much depends also on how one defines "costs." Does the "cost of unification" mean the cost of raising the per capita GDP of North Korea to that of contemporary South Korea? Or is it merely the cost of raising it to a respectable but lower level, like half that of current South Korea? Or rather, is it the cost of kick-starting the North Korean economy? All of these assumptions have been used and predictably, depending on which one was used, different studies have produced wildly different cost estimates.

Another problematic issue is the question of the unification benefits. Few would doubt that the costs would be partially upset by, say, decrease in military spending, increase of market size, and other similar factors. However, these factors are difficult to predict. Some researchers try to factor the unification benefit into the calculations, while others ignore them.

Nonetheless, everyone agrees on one thing: unification is going to be very expensive. Estimates range from $0.2 trillion to $5 trillion. Even the lowest amount is roughly quarter of South Korea's annual GDP. The upper figure is, of course, five times that of South Korea's annual GDP.

In 2010 the Federation of Korean Industries conducted a survey of 20 leading South Korean experts who expressed their estimates

(continued)

of the unification cost. The estimate averaged at the impressive level of US$3 trillion. The figure includes the initial costs of stabilizing the situation after unification, as well as of bridging the gap between the two Koreas.[1] It is remarkable that experts were not asked how much it will cost to raise the income of the North to the level of the South, but merely to the level that will ensure that Korea will have a "unified and stable society." This wording is very nebulous and imprecise, but it clearly implies that even with such astronomical investment the North will lag behind the South.

The FKI-selected expert panel was not optimistic about timing, either. One third (35 percent) believed that it would take more than 30 years to close the gap (partially), and an additional 25 percent believed that task would require 20 to 30 years.

A few months later, in early 2011, Nam Sung-wook, director of the Institute for National Security Strategy, an influential government think tank, presented the South Korean Parliament with a report that estimated the costs at a comparable but somewhat lesser level of US$2.1 trillion.[2]

There are more optimistic opinions, of course. For example, in early 2012 the influential Korea Economic Institute, a private think tank, published a report that said the unification—assuming that unification would happen immediately—would cost merely US$0.2 trillion. This seems to be the most sanguine of the recent estimates.[3]

This optimism is not widely shared. In 2009 Credit Suisse estimated the unification cost at US$1.5 trillion. This amount was thought to be necessary to raise North Korea's per capita GDP to 60 percent of that of the South's within 10 years.[4]

In 2010 Peter Beck, at Stanford University at the time, estimated that it would cost US$2 trillion to US$5 trillion to raise the average income in the North to 80 percent of that of the South.[5] This might be the highest of all estimates—but, alas, may be proven accurate.

The figures thus seem to fluctuate greatly and hardly should be taken too seriously. One should not be that surprised about this when taking into consideration the paltry nature of the available data, great level of uncertainty, and lack of historic precedents. Nonetheless, it seems that most estimates—or rather guestimates—are between US$1.5 trillion and US$2.5 trillion. This is significantly larger than the entire GDP of South Korea, which is currently around US$1 trillion.

Bearing in mind the scale of the expenses, one should not be too judgmental about the increasingly cautious attitude toward the unification project among the South Korean public. At the end of the day, this project will have to be supported by the South Koran taxpayers, and they are predictably wary of this.

When people talk about a unification cost (and such talks are very common in South Korea nowadays), they usually mean the financial burden that will fall upon South Korean taxpayers. This burden is likely to be crushing, but Koreas' unification will also produce a vast array of other social problems, many of which will have no attractive solutions. It makes sense to outline some of these likely problems—with the full understanding that many others will pop up as well, completely unexpectedly.

If we look at the experience of the anti-Communist revolutions in Eastern Europe, we can see that educated, urban, white-collar workers, essentially the Eastern European equivalent of the middle class, played the leading role in these movements. It was largely schoolteachers, low-level managers, nurses, engineers, and skilled industrial workers who in the late 1980s went into the streets of Moscow, Prague, and Budapest, demanding democracy and a market economy. If a popular movement plays a role in the collapse of North Korea, the same scenario is likely to be repeated in North Korea as well. However, the North Korean "middle class" are people who—in relative terms—are likely to lose the most after unification.

This does not mean that unification will bring ruin to the medical doctors and sociology teachers of North Korea. Their absolute income is almost certain to increase instantly and dramatically, in fact. However, they will also discover that their skills are of little value in post-unification society.

North Korean professionals generally tend to have a solid background in theory, so it is quite possible that the average North Korean engineer is more confident in using calculus than his or her South Korean peer. But their practical and applied knowledge is usually archaic and/or irrelevant. If a North Korean engineer never worked in missile or nuclear design, he or she has probably never used a modern computer and doesn't know what CAD stands for. He or she also has virtually no command of English, the major language of modern technical manuals, documentation, and reference books. A typical North Korean engineer spends his or her entire career working out how to keep in operation the rusty equipment of the 1960s Soviet vintage. From the point of view of a South Korean employer, such a person has no value as an engineer.

Everyone who worked in North Korea during the famine testifies to the remarkable skills and selflessness of medical doctors. They knew how to make workable drips out of empty beer bottles and how to conduct a complicated heart surgery with equipment straight from the 1930s. However, after unification, North Korean physicians and surgeons will immediately discover that they have never heard of perhaps 90 percent of the drugs and procedures that are now standard in modern medicine.

Even school and college teachers will find themselves in serious trouble. Those who teach theoretical and nonpolitical subjects—like geometry or organic chemistry—will probably be able to maintain professional employment, but what about the rest, especially teachers of humanities? The average North Korean teacher of history knows a lot about events that never actually happened—like, say, the alleged leading role of Kim's family during the March 1, 1919, uprising, or Kim Jong Il's childhood allegedly spent at a nonexistent secret camp on the slopes of Mount Paekdu. He or she has little knowledge, however, about the events that defined the course of Korea's actual history—pretty much all that he or she knows of traditional Korean culture is that it is the "reactionary culture of a feudal ruling class."

It might be argued that these people should be reeducated, but this is easier said than done. Reeducation will require a lot of money and time. Some people (those with exceptional gifts and good luck) will probably master new skills, but for the vast majority of North Korea's "middle class" this will not be possible. In absolute terms, their standard of living is set to rise dramatically: they will have computers and drive cars, will eat meat and fish every day, and will have more time to enjoy sunsets. But at the same time, their relative social standing will decline, and many of them will perceive this as humiliation.

But we should not be too elite-orientated and worry only about the fate of the relatively privileged groups. Many common North Koreans are also bound to have reasons for being disappointed by the "unification by absorption." For a while the citizens of what is now North Korea will enjoy the newfound prosperity, since the post-unification government is likely to instantly deliver what Kim Il Sung once promised: an opportunity to enjoy a meal of meat soup with boiled rice while sitting under a tiled roof. They will appreciate a new individual freedom as well—it is nice to listen to a song you like even though it has no references to the Dear Leader and Great Family. But they will soon inevitably start comparing themselves with their southern compatriots, just to discover that a significant gap continues to exist. The North Korean people will support unification (and perhaps even fight for unification) on the assumption that it will soon deliver the living standards that approximate those of South Koreans. Needless to say, this cannot possibly happen.

Nearly all North Koreans will soon discover that they are not eligible for anything but low-skilled, low-paid work. Some of them will manage to retrain themselves, but a majority will have to spend the rest of their life sweeping floors and working in sweatshops. They will see this as the result of discrimination. Indeed, as the bitter experience of North Korean refugees in the South demonstrates, some discrimination against the Northerners is almost certain to emerge. But to a large extent most of this so-called discrimination will reflect objective disadvantages of the North Korean workers who lack many modern skills.

Some South Korean businesses will rejoice when they discover a reservoir of low-skilled but disciplined and cheap labor in the North. However, most authorities agree that cheap low-skilled labor is not what the South Korean economy needs at present.

Many North Koreans will move to the alluring bright lights of the cities of the South—after all, Seoul lays within merely one day's walk of what is now North Korea. Labor migrants from the North will probably undercut unskilled South Korean workers, driving wages down and further in-creasing mutual distrust between the former citizens of the two Korean states. Some of them will certainly take up criminal activities of all kinds, so after unification, South Korean cities, now remarkably safe at any time day or night, might become dangerous. Younger women from the North will probably contribute toward the revival of the steadily declining sex industry in South Korea—with predictable consequences for the way the two Koreas perceive each other.

The mass migration of Northerners to the South is likely to produce much social friction but on balance it is the much smaller migration of Southerners to the North that will produce greater problems. Rudiger Frank, an East German by birth and a perceptive observer of Korean events, recently put it nicely in a private conversation with the author: "When and if Korean unification comes, it will be necessary to protect Southerners from the Northerners, but it will be far more important to protect Northerners from Southerners—from predatory Southern busi-nesses in particular."

Indeed there are a number of potentially explosive problems, including the attitude toward the 1946 Land Reform Law, which has never been of-ficially accepted by the South Korean government. Unlike, say, China where former landlords were either slaughtered or, if they were lucky, cowed into permanent silence, most North Korean landlords were fortu-nate to escape to the South between 1946 and 1953. They seldom forgot to take their land titles, so nowadays significant parts of the best arable land in North Korea theoretically have "legal owners" who are happily living somewhere in Seoul. As the present author knows from many experiences, these old land titles are carefully preserved by the second and third gener-ation of ex-landowners.

The history of South Korea's economic boom was also the history of obscenely profitable land speculations. In some parts of the Apgujeong ward of southern Seoul, for example, the price of land increased some thousandfold in the years 1963–1990 (this is after the adjustment to the inflation was made!). South Koreans understand the potential value of land, especially if it is located close to a future booming business or industrial center. Unless something is done, the holders of pre-1946 land titles will descend on destitute North Korean villages, using litigation in order to take from North Korean farmers the only potentially valuable asset they have. Unfortunately (for North Korean farmers), the descendants of post-1946 migrants tend to be very successful and powerful in modern South Korea and therefore, if they decide to fight for "their" property, have a chance of succeeding.

Greedy scions of long-dead landlords are not the only people who are going to create trouble in the post-unification real estate market. Investing in North Korean real estate is likely to be tremendously profitable in the long run. At the same time, even though a shadow real estate market is now quietly developing in North Korea, the majority of North Koreans have distorted ideas about the value of real estate. One should not be surprised about this fact—when the present author bought real estate for the first time in his life, in the still (technically) Soviet Leningrad of 1991, a one-bedroom apartment in this second-largest city in the then Soviet Union would cost less than a badly made Lada subcompact car and would be just slightly more expensive than a new IBM desktop computer (IBM PC XT with hard drive of 20 Mb, if you remember such a thing). If South Korean investors are "lucky," they might easily persuade some North Koreans to sell their derelict houses for the price of, say, a shiny new fridge or a Japanese motorbike. Needless to say, urban North Koreans will soon realize that they have been cheated, and this will not make them more enthusiastic about the realities of unification.

The experience of post-Socialist Eastern Europe and the USSR has shown yet another potential vulnerability the ex-Communist populations have. They are ignorant and sometimes very naïve about the workings of markets. They therefore can easily fall prey to con artists who peddle all kinds of get-rich-quick plans. Ponzi pyramid schemes seem to be especially common. In 1994 in Russia, a Ponzi scheme run by the MMM Company wiped out the savings of five million ex-Soviet citizens. The MMM affair led to some political disturbances but it was nothing in comparison to post-Communist Albania. In Albania, a number of Ponzi schemes succeeded in attracting the investment of a quarter to half of all Albanians—some $1.2–1.5 billion, or half of the annual GDP in this country with a population of three million. Their collapse in 1997 led to a short but intense civil war that cost an estimated 500 to 1,500 people dead.[1] Romania—another country that resembled North Korea in many regards—also suffered from the collapse of the Caritas, as a local Ponzi scheme was known, even though this collapse did not lead to much violence.

Unfortunately, similar events are also likely to happen in North Korea. North Koreans might be street-smart in their own ways, but they tend to be remarkably credulous and naïve when it comes to the workings of modern capitalism. Actually, we already have a warning sign: according to recent research, in South Korea one in five Northern refugees has been a victim of fraud, a rate more than 40 times higher than the national average.[2] They will make an easy prey for the predatory outsiders, especially those from the South—and such an outcome is not going to promote better mutual understanding in post-unification Korea.

It is clear that the social transformation of North Korea will be difficult for everybody. There is one group, however, that seems to stand out—the military.

The North Korean military is estimated to be 1.1–1.2 million strong. Most of these people can be seen as soldiers only if you stretch the definition of military service. They are essentially an unpaid labor force, whose members are also taught some basic military skills. But the North Korean armed forces also include a significant minority (perhaps as many as 300,000–400,000 people) of professional warriors, who have spent their entire adult lives mastering ways of low-tech killing. They are soldiers in the special forces, units of the Pyongyang Defense Command and other elite formations.

After unification, they are likely to find themselves in an unenviable situation, since these lifelong professional soldiers usually don't have even those limited skills that can be found among the civilian population. They are also likely to be hit especially hard by the collapse of the official value system: the sudden realization of the emptiness and lies behind the Juche ideology and the Kim family cult. Some of them will find poorly paid jobs as security guards, but many others will opt for more lucrative opportunities in the criminal underworld.

A PROVISIONAL CONFEDERATION AS THE LEAST
UNACCEPTABLE SOLUTION

Let us now consider some ways in which we can mitigate the negative consequences of unification whilst making the most of its numerous advantages.

One of the possible solutions might be the creation of a transitional confederative state where both North and South would maintain a significant measure of autonomy and keep different legal systems as well as, possibly, different currencies. A major task of such a confederation would be to lay the foundations for a truly unified state and to mitigate the more disastrous effects of North Korea's future transformation.

The idea of confederation has been suggested many times before, but in nearly all cases it was assumed that the two existing Korean regimes would somehow agree to create a confederative state. Needless to say, one has to be very naïve to believe that the current North Korean rulers could somehow coexist with South Korea within such a confederative state. Even if they are somehow persuaded to accept such a risky scheme, very soon their own population will become dangerously restive.

In real life, a confederation will become possible only when and if the North Korean regime is overthrown or changes dramatically, so that a new leadership in Pyongyang will have no reason to fear the influence of the South. In other words, only a post-Kim government can be realistically expected to agree to such a provisional confederation. It does not really matter how this government will come to power, whether through a popular revolution, a coup, or something else. As long as this government is genuinely willing to unite with the South, it might become a participant of the confederation regime. If an acute security crisis leads to a South Korean or international peacekeeping operation in the North, the emergence of a provisional confederation still remains a possible—and highly desirable—solution on the way to Korea's reunification.

The length of the provisional confederation regime should be limited, and 10 to 15 years seems like an ideal interval. A longer period might alienate common North Koreans, who will probably see the entire confederation plan as a scheme to keep them from fully enjoying the South Korean lifestyle while using them as cheap labor. On the other hand, a shorter period might not be sufficient for a serious transformation—and a lot of things will have to be done.

One of the tasks of such a provisional system will be to control cross-border movement. The confederation will make it relatively easy to maintain a visa system of some kind, with a clearly stated (and reasonable) schedule of gradual relaxation. For example, it might be stated that for the first five years all individual trips between the two parts of the new Korea will require a visa-type permit and North Koreans will not be normally allowed to take jobs or longtime residency in the South. In following years these restrictions could be relaxed and then finally lifted.

One has to be realistic: this administrative border control is not going to be particularly efficient in stopping North Koreans' exodus to the South. Post-unification border guards are not going to machine-gun illegal crossers, and with South Korea being so rich, so attractive, and so close, fines and mild punishments will have only marginal impacts. After all, the North Korean people have spent the last two decades boldly flouting countless regulations that were supported by an exceptionally severe system of sanctions and punishments. Thus, immigration between the two countries can be reduced only if life in North Korea itself will become sufficiently attractive within a suitably short period of time.

To achieve this goal, the North Koreans also should be protected from the less scrupulous of their newfound brethren. The provisional confederation regime, while encouraging other kinds of investment, should strictly control (or even ban) the purchase of arable land and housing in the North by South Korean individuals and companies, thus reducing the risks of a massive land rip-off being staged by greedy real estate dealers from the South.

It will be important to explicitly acknowledge the 1946 land reform, declaring the property claims null and void. To placate former owners, some partial compensation might be considered, even though the present author is not certain whether grandchildren of former landlords, usually rich and successful men and women, are in dire need of such compensation (especially when one takes into account that many of these families got their land by being remarkably deferential to their Japanese overlords in the colonial era).

The property of the state-run agricultural cooperatives should be distributed among the villagers. As a first step, it might be preferable to give the land of the cooperatives to the farmers who currently farm on them—not as property, but rather on a free rent basis. In five to ten years, those families who continuously toil on their land plots, producing food and paying taxes, should be accorded full ownership rights. This will discourage some North Koreans from rushing South while also contributing to the revival of North Korean agriculture. By the end of the confederation period, land and real estate in North Korea should be safely privatized, with North Korean residents (and, perhaps, recent defectors) being major or, better still, sole participants in this process. Incidentally it is conceivable that North Korean farmers will do what many East German farmers did after unification—reestablish agricultural cooperatives. But, these will be genuine cooperatives, and not the state-run farms thinly disguised as voluntary communal farmer's organizations.

The confederation regime will help to mitigate the problems of the North Korean middle class and professionals—essentially, by shielding them from competition for the most difficult initial years. During the confederation regime period, special efforts could be made to reeducate those people, preparing them for a new environment, helping them to master modern techniques and skills. Most of the North Korean doctors, teachers, and engineers will be unable to adjust, unfortunately, but at least the 10- or 15-year leniency period will give a chance to the lucky and determined, while also providing others with time to find alternative ways to make a living. During this leniency period they should be allowed to practice their professions, even though some minimal retraining might be strongly encouraged or even made mandatory.

The military of the two Koreas should be integrated, with large (perhaps, disproportionately large) quotas reserved for former North Korean servicemen in the united army. If former military officers are given commissions in the post-unification forces, their remarkable skills and their sincere nationalist zeal will find a useful and safe outlet.

The confederation also should execute some policies ensuring that North Koreans will not remain the source of "cheap labor," to be used (and abused) by the rich South. Encouragement of trade unions might be one such activity.

Naturally, the rich South will have to provide North Korea with large and consistent aid. Fixed transfers plus direct investment (the more the better) and fixed-purpose aid grants will be necessary. However, it probably will make sense not to repeat the German mistake of merging currencies overnight—for a while at least, keeping two separate currency systems seems to be a better option.

It will make sense to give North Koreans a fixed admission quota in the most prestigious universities in Seoul. In South Korea the top positions in management, politics, and culture are nearly monopolized by the graduates of the top four to five schools, which are all located in Seoul. This situation might be regrettable, but it is not going to change anytime soon. Since North Korean students normally cannot be pushed through an extremely demanding system of pre-exam cramming, they are not going to be competitive in the entrance exams. The only way to get them into places like Seoul National University and Yonsei University is some kind of affirmative action system. Such an affirmative action system is going to be unpopular with South Korean parents who are very sensitive to any hint at region- or class-based preferences in admission policy. But, such sacrifices are necessary preconditions for reforging a unified Korean society.

Politics in the post-unification confederation will be tricky and highly contentious. Currently it seems that there are two possible solutions.

First, it is possible that for the entire length of the transitional period, or at least a few initial years, North Korea would be run by some outside government. Such a government might be appointed by Seoul, but some kind of UN-mandated international administration might also emerge from a future crisis. Unfortunately, such an administration is likely to be full of greedy and ignorant carpetbaggers who take every opportunity to enrich themselves before running away. Alternatively, some of the bureaucrats in a "Viceroyalty of North Korea" will be younger, idealistic officials from the South, who might be personally clean and devoted, but also remarkably naïve.

Alternatively, immediately after the crisis, a democracy might be introduced into the North. This seems to be an attractive option, but assuming that the alternative elite is either absent or very weak, such a democracy will most likely be dominated by minor officials of the Kim family era—or at least their children and close relatives. These natural-born opportunists may instantly change their colors and claim themselves to have been lifelong closet democrats (like their peers in Eastern Europe and the USSR once did).

Their children will fare even better—as a matter of fact, the second generation of the elite is bound to succeed even in the (unlikely and undesirable) case of their parents being ousted from the positions of power. One can easily imagine the choice that will be made by recruiters of a major international (or, for that matter, South Korean) corporation when, in the post-Kim North Korea, they deal with two candidates—a charming girl with a degree from the best Pyongyang college, passable English, and great social skills, and a young girl of the same age from the countryside with no working knowledge of the English language, a very basic picture of the outside world, and little understanding of how the modern economy works.

The choice seems obvious, but one should remember that the former in our thought experiment is almost certain to be the daughter of a party cadre (perhaps an efficient interrogator from the political police or a senior guard in a prison camp). This is principally because usually only well-connected people—in the case of North Korea, people who get their hands dirty (most of the time at least)—can give their children the opportunity to acquire the aforementioned education. Even her great looks might hint that she had the rare privilege of being exempt from annual labor mobilizations (such stints of hard work in the open air are really bad for the skin, and physically age participants). Meanwhile, nearly all the children and grandchildren of the people who once were unlucky to fall victim to Kim Il Sung's wrath and spend their youth in camps or in exile in the countryside will look like the second girl in the above example—being exiled to the countryside, she would have not the slightest chance to acquire the education and skills that could make her successful in the post-Kim world.

The present author is a historian, and this makes him immune to the ideas of "triumphant justice"—most injustices of history have never been avenged, and many injustices have paid off handsomely, both to perpetuators and their descendants. But even pushing moral issues aside, one has to admit that there are serious problems with the Kim-era ex-elite: those people will retain their old habits, including, in all probability, a remarkable appetite for kickbacks. Their knowledge of modern economics and technology, while superior to that of the "lower orders," still leaves much to be desired. To further complicate things, a Northern democratic government would be prone to populist decisions, responsive to pressure from below. Ordinary North Koreans are likely to hold particularly naïve views on how their society and economy can and should operate, and some mistakes introduced via popular vote might become ruinous and costly.

Ultimately, both solutions appear to be flawed. Whichever road will be taken out of the current situation, one must expect a great deal of mistakes, demagoguery, mutual accusations, wild populism, and, alas, official corruption. Nonetheless, on balance one should prefer a corrupt and inefficient democracy (run by the local turncoats) over an inefficient and corrupt viceroyalty (run by the carpetbagging outsiders). It is better to give North Koreans an opportunity to sort out their problems themselves— and if they make mistakes, they will suffer consequences and, hopefully, learn something. It is also important that they see less reason to blame outsiders for such mistakes. North Korea is their country—not a country of foreigners (even those foreigners who sincerely wish them best) and not even the country of South Koreans—so they must be empowered as soon as possible.

One of the thorniest issues is the post-unification fate of medium- and high-level bureaucrats as well as the small army of enforcers who once ensured the survival of the Kim family regime. It is quite possible (and indeed highly probable) that many people in both South and North will loudly demand justice be served to the former security police officers, secret informers, and prison guards. The graphic exposure of the horrors of the North Korean prisons and camps will greatly strengthen such demands. This approach is noble and understandable but, unfortunately, unrealistic.

My acquaintances from the North Korean security police say that such police usually have one informer for every 40 to 50 adults. This claim seems plausible since it comes from a number of people who do not know one another—and do not have a particular reason to lie about the figure. This means that roughly 200,000 to 300,000 North Koreans are now active police informers. There is no doubt that some informers have been dropped from the roster, so the total number of informers and ex-inform-ers might be well over half a million. On top of that, some quarter to half million North Koreans might have been on the payroll of the security police at certain periods of their lives. Unless the entire justice system of post-unification Korea is going to spend years dealing with former in-formers and political police personnel, no honest and fair investigation of their deeds is possible.

In North Korea, the managerial and professional elite maintain much closer connections with the ruling bureaucracy than was once the case in the Soviet Union or countries of Eastern Europe. The closeness of these con-nections means that any honest and systematic efforts at "de-Kimification" (analogous to post-1945 German "de-Nazification") will mean that virtually all North Koreans with managerial and professional skills will have to be removed from the professional scene. It will be great if the efforts aimed at creating an alternative elite (as outlined above) produce a sufficient number of skilled and ethically untainted personnel by the time of unification. How-ever, we should not be that optimistic—even if the second elite emerges soon, it is likely to remain small.

One must be honest: no justice is likely to be possible in dealing with the former agents of the Kim family dictatorship. There are far too many of them, and their crimes, committed over long decades, are now almost impossible to investigate thoroughly. Most of their victims became statis-tics long ago. Sadly enough, the rejection of the regime's henchmen and collaborators will also mean the rejection of nearly all people with useful experience and education. Thus, the justice is not merely impossible: it might be very damaging.

There is also another important reason why there should be no rush to punish Kim's people. One of the major reasons why the Kim family regime has been so stubborn in rejecting reforms is the widespread perception among the Pyongyang elite that regime collapse (a highly probable outcome of such reforms) would lead to the political demise and perhaps even physical slaughter of the current elite. This fear of persecution is not merely the major reason why these people have refused to switch to more rational methods in running their country. It is also the reason why the North Korean elite and its supporters (a significant minority of the total population) are likely to fight in order to protect the system if and when the final crisis comes. A clear and unequivocal promise of general amnesty for all former misdeeds will perhaps help to prevent a full-scale civil war. In order to be taken seriously, such an offer should be made in no uncertain terms, thus making its eventual retraction less likely. And of course, such an offer, once made, should be kept.

This does not necessarily mean that misdeeds of the Kim regime should be neglected and glossed over. A possible—and very partial—solution is the Truth and Reconciliation Commission, an approach once pioneered by South Africa, where crimes and human rights abuses under apartheid were investigated but no judgments were passed and no punishments administered.

Another possible device is the lustration system, akin to what was used in post-Socialist Eastern Europe. According to this system, the more prominent collaborators of the Communist governments—secret police officers, mid- to high-level party officials, and so on—were deprived of the right to occupy important administrative positions or to serve in the judiciary and law enforcement agencies. The same policy might be acceptable in North Korea as well, but it should not target too many members of the old elite. In a sense, for at least a few decades every educated North Korean could be plausibly described as a regime collaborator, so this definition should be applied only to those who were actively involved with the most repulsive and obvious forms of police terror—like prison camp administrators. We should leave it to the investigative journalists and historians of later generations (and, perhaps, even descendants of some of the culprits) to fully investigate their crimes.

The Kim family should not become an exception. Ideally, it makes sense to let these people (and there are a few dozen of them) leave the country and proceed to comfortable exile somewhere—perhaps in Macao, where they can be controlled and protected by China, which can also deny direct responsibility for sheltering the dictatorship's first family. Let these people do what they are rumored to be best at: devour impressive quantities of delicacies, while also enthusiastically chasing after women. Perhaps some of them will also write memoirs where they will persuasively explain how they would have brought unbelievable prosperity to their homeland had their plans not been sabotaged by corrupt officials and a "complicated" international environment (this is what the overthrown politicians always do).

Even confiscation of the Kim family assets, now rumored to be hidden in Switzerland, Hong Kong, and Macao, might not be such a good idea. The couple of billion they have managed to steal will make little difference in the mammoth task of post-Kim reconstruction and might be a price worth paying for a relatively bloodless transition. And of course we should not forget that if you live a billionaire's lifestyle, it is much more difficult to present oneself as a martyr and victim of unjust persecution.

The proposals discussed above are going to be seen as controversial and, if implemented, are bound to be described by many a future historian as "ethically dubious compromises" or even as "backroom deals between the North and South Korean elites" and thus "anti-democratic" and even "immoral." As a historian myself, I do not mind letting future historians feel self-righteous. But in real life, the policy decisions tend to be choices between bad and worse. In this case, the alternative seems far worse: North Korean secret police machine-gunning civilians in the belief that by doing so they are saving their families; risky and even suicidal brinkmanship by generals who see themselves as cornered; an alienated, bitter, but large and influential underclass of former regime collaborators who will be united with common Northerners in their disgust at South Korean carpetbaggers. And, after all, one should also keep in mind that the choice of the alternative route will not make future historians happy: decisive and thorough (and seriously counterproductive) cleansing of former regime collaborators will be branded as a "witch hunt" in their writings.

SOMETHING ABOUT PAINKILLERS . . .

We have seen that neither diplomatic concessions nor military and economic pressure are likely to influence the North Korean regime. One
has to wait until history takes its course while speeding up developments through persistent and patient policies. The wait might be long. It
is not impossible that Kim Jong Un's succession may trigger a chain of
events that will bring the regime down in the next few years. But it is at
least equally possible that the Kim family regime will survive this and
other challenges and will remain essentially unchanged until, say, 2020
or even 2030.

We therefore face a persistent problem whose solution will take a long
time—probably, decades. But what should be done in the meantime? Due
to the democratic nature of the United States, South Korea, and most of
the governments involved in the region, we can be certain that at regular
intervals a new group of decision makers will pop up just to repeat the
same mistakes their predecessors once made. The pendulum is likely to
keep moving between overly optimistic hopes for engagement and overly
bullish hopes for pressure—as has been the case for the last 20-odd years.
But even if cold-minded realists and pragmatists prevail somehow, they
still have to do something about North Korea as it exists now. They need
to reduce the security risks created by its nuclear program, its brinkmanship, and its risky, if cynically rational, international behavior.

The North Korean issue cannot be simply dealt with using one set of
long-term policies, outlined above. It also requires a set of shorter-term
policies aimed at preventing (or mitigating) excessive provocative behavior, reducing proliferation threats, and diminishing the sufferings of
ordinary North Koreans. However, one should never forget that these
short-term policies are essentially palliative, akin to a painkiller that
masks the symptoms and makes life bearable until the illness itself can be
treated—but does not solve the problem itself.

The first of such shorter-term policies might be a de facto acceptance of
the North Korean nuclear program. Admittedly, this is exactly what North
Korean strategists want. They don't talk about freezing their program for

monetary rewards anymore, but they have indicated a number of times that they might be ready to stop further development of their nuclear capabilities if the rewards are sufficiently high.

The "complete, verifiable, and irreversible" denuclearization is doomed to remain unattainable as long as the Kim family regime is in control. Due to the manifold reasons outlined above, North Korea will keep at least a part of its modest nuclear arsenal. The North Korean leaders might compromise on certain things (if they are paid handsomely enough), but this is the nonnegotiable bottom line—and after the second nuclear test the Washington mainstream came to understand it.

Nevertheless, the North Koreans have expressed their interest in the solution recently proposed by Siegfried Hecker, the former head of the US Department of Energy laboratories in Los Alamos, known as the "three no's": "No more nukes, No better nukes, No proliferation." This means that North Korea is expected to halt its nuclear research and production, while keeping the existent nukes—in exchange for some concessions and compensations from the outside world (which, for all practical reasons, means the United States).

This proposal might be acceptable for Pyongyang—if the fee is good, that is. After all, North Korea does not need its old rusty reactors any more. Yongbyon, the North Korean nuclear research center, cannot possibly outproduce Los Alamos in the United States or Arzamas-16 in Russia, and it does not make much political sense to increase the North Korean nuclear arsenal further. The Yongbyon laboratories have already produced enough plutonium for a few nuclear devices, and this is more than sufficient for the dual political purposes of deterrence and blackmail. If North Koreans use these facilities to increase their nuclear armory from the five to ten devices they are suspected of possessing now to, say, 50 or even 100 devices, their ability to deter and/or blackmail will not increase five- or tenfold. As a matter of fact, it will not increase much at all. Consequently, these research and production facilities have outlived their usefulness and thus can be dismantled.

Perhaps the North Koreans will agree to accept measures that will make proliferation less likely, thus addressing another major US concern. It is open to question which types of measures will be acceptable, but perhaps surprise inspections of ships and airport facilities will be allowed (once again, North Korea's diplomats will require a high price for such a major concession, which in effect infringes their sovereignty).

Even a partial surrender of existent nukes might be negotiable. Perhaps North Korea can be bribed into giving up part of its plutonium and/or a few nuclear devices. However, this denuclearization is not going to be either "complete" or "verifiable." Actually, it has to be very partial. North Korea's leaders will need to at least maintain a high level of ambiguity about their nuclear capabilities or, ideally, receive an explicit or implicit admission that they will be allowed to keep a stockpile of weapons-grade plutonium and/or enriched uranium as well as a couple of nuclear devices. The stockpile and nuclear devices will be safely hidden somewhere in its underground facilities, to serve as a deterrent and also a potential tool for diplomatic blackmail.

Of course, the "three no" proposal is not without serious downsides. From the US point of view, such a deal would mean that North Korea is rewarded for its nuclear blackmail. Indeed, North Korea is so far the world's only state that first signed the Nuclear Non-Proliferation Treaty (NPT), then withdrew from the NPT and successfully developed a workable nuclear device. If it is not only allowed to keep its nuclear arsenal but also manages to squeeze some monetary aid from the United States, this will clearly create a dangerous precedent. Control—especially in regard to proliferation—is also a difficult issue because few would doubt that the North Korean side would use every opportunity to cheat. Last but not least, it is important to keep in mind that signed treaties have virtually no binding power in the North Korean leaders' frame of mind, so we can be sure that the North Korean side will keep its obligations only as long as they receive a steady supply of aid and other payments.

However, although these problems and concerns are real, it nonetheless might make sense to accept the "three no" approach. The alternatives are even less attractive. The North Korean government is not going to remain idle while Washington ignores it. North Korean engineers will work hard to produce more uranium and plutonium, to perfect available technologies while the North Korean diplomats quietly but persistently explore possible markets for nuclear weapons. Meanwhile, missile engineers will continue their work as well, and sooner or later they will develop a sufficiently reliable long-range delivery system that is quite capable of hitting the continental United States. In January 2011 the US Secretary of Defense Robert Gates said that North Korea is "within five years of being able to strike the continental United States with an intercontinental ballistic missile."[3] As head of the US military establishment, Robert Gates might have an instinct for exaggerating threats—and some people have assumed that he exaggerated the Soviet missile threat as the CIA head in the 1980s.[4] Chances are, then, that it will probably take longer than five years—but it will happen sooner or later if the Kim family regime stays in control long enough. And there is little doubt that, while their engineers and spies are working hard, North Korean politicians will stage occasional confrontations, just to remind the world that they are capable of inflicting damage if their demands are ignored.

In order to prevent such developments, it might make sense to seriously consider the "three no" approach—in spite of its only too obvious shortcomings. But, even if such an approach is accepted, one should enter the deal without any illusions. This is merely the way to buy time—and quite an imperfect way at that.

Another possible and useful palliative is the maintenance of the six-party talks that are currently in yet another hibernation period. Ostensibly these talks were once initiated in order to bring about the complete denuclearization of North Korea. This stated goal is unachievable (or, to be more precise, talks will not contribute much in achieving this goal). However, this does not necessarily mean that the six-party talks are of little or no value.

There are at least two important functions the six-party talks serve well. First, the very existence of negotiations contributes toward stability in and around North Korea; the six-party talks marginally reduce the likelihood of military confrontation in the region.

That said, it is the second function that is of special importance. The six-party talks create a convenient venue for diplomats of all interested countries to discuss North Korea-related problems. The six-party talks are not going to reach their stated goal of denuclearization, but they are a natural place to agree on positions and actions in case of a major crisis. When a new crisis comes (and it will come sooner or later), interested parties will have precious little time to discuss manifold challenges, so speedy and reliable interactions between all major stakeholders will be vital. Neither the unwieldy UN bureaucracy nor standard diplomatic channels are efficient and fast enough in addressing such an emergency; and the stakes in a grave crisis may be very high.

It is therefore a good idea to keep the six-party talks in place—partially as a way to mitigate tensions and handle the ongoing problems but largely as a place where future North Korea—related issues can be dealt with quickly and decisively. Taking into account the possible political and diplomatic consequences of regime collapse in the North, this is a cheap and efficient measure. It is important, however, not to lose sight of the main goal: waiting for (and, to an extent, promoting) regime transformation inside North Korea. The measures outlined above should be seen realistically. Short-term policies are painkillers—not antibiotics.

Conclusion

What to say in concluding this book? Perhaps we should start with two pieces of bad news: first, North Korea is a problem; and second, this problem has no fast or easy solution.

Who is responsible for the North Korean tragedy? Starry-eyed West European intellectuals who in the 1840 and 1850s, surrounded by gross injustices and inequalities, suggested an alternative to the nascent capitalist system? Or young East Asian idealists who in the 1920s enthusiastically embraced the Marxist (or, rather, Leninist) recipes as a way for national salvation? Or battle-hardened Soviet commanders who in the 1940s wanted to "liberate" the Korean people while creating a friendly government in a neighboring country? Or the North Koreans who in the 1950s came to believe that the Soviet (or, rather, Stalinist) model would provide them with a blueprint for building a new Korean nation, powerful, prosperous, and proud? The sad part of the North Korean story is that most of its key players—or key culprits, should we say?—were decent human beings, often driven by noble and admirable motivation. They made decisions that seemed logical at the time. The accumulated result is, however, a complete mess, with no easy and universally acceptable solution in sight.

North Korea remains a problem for the outside world because in order to survive, its decision makers have no choice but to live dangerously. Real or alleged proliferation attempts, nuclear and missile tests, and occasional shoot-outs do not reflect the insane bellicosity or irrationality of the North Korean leadership. On the contrary, these actions are manifestations of a quite rational survival strategy that might have no viable alternative if judged from the point of view of Pyongyang's tiny elite.

We should bear in mind the fact that we outsiders are not the primary victims of North Korea's situation. The greatest suffering is borne by the North Korean people who are the major victims of the North Korean tragedy. While other nations of East Asia enjoy an era of unprecedented improvement in living standards, educational achievement, and life expectancy, North Koreans are stuck with a system that is both repressive politically and grotesquely inefficient economically. Many of them have found ways to cope, but on balance the current situation has brought ruin to countless lives and has led to a great waste of human creative force and energy—and continues to do so.

At the same time, the North Korean problem does not have any easy solution. So far the policies of Seoul and Washington have oscillated between a hard- and soft-line approach. But neither is going to produce much impact on the international and domestic behavior of the North Korean elite. These people cannot be bribed into changing themselves and their country, nor can they be blackmailed into reform.

Nonetheless, there is also good news. The North Korean regime is not sustainable in the long run. Subtle and spontaneous change is gradually eroding the ideological, political, and even economic foundations of the regime. The government understands how dangerous these spontaneous changes are, but cannot do much about the situation; the erosion cannot be halted, let alone reversed. It is not impossible that Kim Jong Un and his future confidants (yet to be seen at the time of writing) will take risks and initiate reforms, hoping to create a North Korean version of a "developmental dictatorship." One can wish them some luck, since gradual evolution is usually better than dramatic and violent upheaval, but—perhaps unfortunately—such a reformist regime has little chance of remaining stable in the presence of an affluent South that is so near.

So what can the outside world do? Frankly, not all that much. It can in some ways attempt to speed up the slow-motion erosion of the Kim family dictatorship, creating forces that will demand change, while also ensuring that the coming crisis will be less chaotic and painful. It makes some sense to speed things up somehow—after all, if the inevitable happens a few years earlier it will mean that fewer people will die in prison camps and more people will have the chance to live, work, and raise children in a more decent society. For the outside world, it means one or two fewer major crises. Nonetheless, one should not become too enthusiastic about these attempts to speed up the inevitable: such efforts, however admirable and useful, will have a relatively moderate impact on the situation.

It is even more important to prepare for the post-unification mess because it will bring difficult and often unforeseen challenges (and the North Korean crisis is bound to be messy). Admittedly the potential threats associated with North Korea's collapse are widely understood, but usually it makes people fantasize about a gradual transformation of the regime along Chinese lines as the way to deliver a "soft landing." Unfortunately, a soft landing, while not completely impossible and indeed desirable, is not very probable. Instead, we are likely to face either of two scenarios: either a hard landing or the extended survival of the regime in its existing form followed, in due time, by an even harder landing. Thus, the only way to achieve the desirable soft landing is to make the hard landing as soft as possible—or, speaking less metaphorically, to find ways to mitigate the social and economic disasters that will be brought about by the likely collapse of the regime.

There is one problem we should keep in mind, however—the policies that might help to change North Korea eventually are not going to sell well in the countries that have the largest stakes in promoting such a change—above all, in the United States and South Korea. This is not because these policies are expensive or difficult to implement or might lead to unnecessary complications. On the contrary, these policies are cheap—so cheap, actually, that in some cases contributions by individuals might make a difference. But there is a serious problem with all of these policies—they require long-term commitments to goals that are likely to be achieved well after the next election cycle. These are not the types of policies that sell well in a democracy, at least as long as official bureaucracies and political decision makers are involved.

Even though such programs as support for broadcasting or providing scholarships for refugees will hardly cost more than a few million dollars a year, one cannot expect them to win the ringing endorsement of professional politicians once they realize that the impact is likely to be felt by the next generation and that it will be quite difficult to attribute the success to their policies.

Alas, the hawkish approach sells well when the regime under consideration is a repulsive hereditary dictatorship. It is very good for both politicians' self-esteem and election results to insist that "We don't negotiate with evil; we defeat it," even when such lofty statements are nonsensical and have no impact on the world outside polling stations.

The sales pitch of the doves is equally powerful. Indeed, it is appealing to say that North Korean decision makers are also "humans who love their families," so sufficient kindness in dealing with them will help to bring about a wonderful world of mutual harmony. There is no doubt that North Korean leaders are humans who love their families—actually this wonderful and noble feeling might be one of the major reasons behind what they doing. After all, as we have seen, they believe that not only their future but that of their loved ones is contingent on the continued existence of their regime and this regime can be maintained only through skillful diplomatic brinkmanship and the generous application of terror within state borders.

This is the sorry reality of modern democratic politics, once described by Winston Churchill as "the worst form of government." Churchill later added, however, that "except all those other forms that have been tried from time to time," we should not despair. If government bureaucracies are not particularly interested, part of the work can and should be done by private foundations and individuals. Everything that improves interactions between North Koreans and the outside world should be welcomed and supported.

North Korean history is another sad example of how lofty ideals and good intentions can turn sour. The founding fathers of North Korea might be brutal and shrewd, but they were neither cold-minded killers nor power-hungry politicos. Rather, they were sincere—if ruthless—idealists who wanted to bring about a perfect world. They made the wrong choice, however, and in due course their children and grandchildren found themselves captives of a brutal and inefficient system. This wasn't anybody's intention, since most of the key participants in the North Korean tragedy were rational and often well-meaning human beings. Nevertheless, the result was and remains a disaster, and this disaster is likely to continue for a few more years or even decades—and its consequences are likely to haunt Koreans for generations.

NOTES

CHAPTER 1

1. For those who want to learn about North Korean history in some depth, the best introduction is a short book by Adrian Buzo (its main emphasis is on the 1965–1995 events, however).

   Adrian Buzo, *The Guerilla Dynasty: Politics and Leadership in North Korea* (Boulder, Colo.: Westview Press, 1999).

2. Chay Jongsuk, *Unequal Partners in Peace and War: The Republic of Korea and the United States, 1948–1953* (Westport, Conn.: Praeger, 2002), 32–33.

3. On the factions in the North Korea leadership and the complicated domestic politics of the 1940s see: Andrei Lankov, *From Stalin to Kim Il Sung: the Formation of North Korea, 1945–1960* (New Brunswick: Rutgers University Press, 2002).

4. The best biography of Kim Il Sung was written by Dae-Sook Suh in the 1980s, before the Soviet archives were opened and provided a wealth of additional material. However, most of what he wrote in the 1980s managed to stand such a hard test surprisingly well. See Dae-Sook Suh, *Kim Il Sung: The North Korean Leader* (New York: Columbia University Press, 1988).

5. For a detailed discussion of these instructions (complete with referrals to archival material and lengthy quotes) see: Andrei Lankov, *From Stalin to Kim Il Sung: the Formation of North Korea, 1945–1960* (New Brunswick: Rutgers University Press, 2002), 42–47.

6. For a detailed description of the meeting (based on the evidence of the surviving diary of Shtykov) see: Chŏn Hyŏnsu. *"Swittŭikkop'ŭ ilki"ka malhanŭn pukhan chŏngkwŏn-ŭi sŏngrip kwachŏng [Shytykov's diary and the formation of North Korea]* // yŏksapip'yŏng 1995nyŏn vol. 32 (1995).

7. In English, plentiful evidence of such support can be found in a well-researched study of Charles Armstrong, who drew on the wealth of the original North Korean document captured by the US forces during the Korean War. See Charles Armstrong, *The North Korean Revolution, 1945–1950* (Ithaca, N.Y.: Cornell University Press, 2003).

8. For the most up-to-date review on the emerging evidence on the Korean War origin, see materials (bulletins and working papers) of the Cold War International History Project. Of special importance is the working paper by Kathryn Weathersby. Kathryn Weathersby, *"Should We Fear This?" Stalin and the Danger of War with America* (Washington, D.C.: Woodrow Wilson International Center for Scholars, 2004).

9. For a detailed description of the 1956 crisis and its consequences, see Andrei Lankov, *Crisis in North Korea: The Failure of De-Stalinization, 1956* (Honolulu: University of Hawai'i Press, 2005).

   Of special importance is a well-researched work by Balázs Szalontai, who used Eastern European documents to carefully trace the formation of Kim Il Sung's peculiar version of "national Stalinism." See Balázs Szalontai, *Kim Il Sung in the Khrushchev Era: Soviet-DPRK Relations and the Roots of North Korean Despotism, 1953–1964* (Stanford: Stanford University Press, 2005).

10. Research on the educational background of the Manchurian guerrillas was done by Wada Haruki. Wada Haruki, *Kim Il Sŏng-wa Manchu hangil chŏnchaeng [Kim Il Sung and anti-Japanese resistance in Manchuria]* (Seoul: Ch'angjak-kwa pip'yŏngsa, 1992), 303.

11. Bernd Schaefer, *North Korean "Adventurism" and China's Long Shadow, 1966–1972* (Washington, D.C.: Woodrow Wilson International Center for Scholars, 2004), 9.

    This working paper by Bernd Schaefer provides a wealth of new information on the tense relations between China and North Korea in the era of China's "Cultural revolution."

12. Ibid., 5.

13. Ibid., 2.

14. Ibid., 7–9.

15. Not much is written about the debt debacle of the 1970s. For some basic information, see Sophie Roell, "For North Korean Exposure Try Buying Its Debt," *Dow Jones Newswires*, Pyongyang, May 7, 2001.

16. For a comprehensive review of the nonclassified material in regard to North Korea's involvement with smuggling, see Sheena Chestnut, "Illicit Activity and Proliferation: North Korean Smuggling Networks," *International Security* vol. 32, iss.1 (2007): 80–111.

17. There are a large number of publications on the abductions of Japanese citizens. For example, see Patricia Steinhoff, "Kidnapped Japanese in North Korea: The New Left Connection," *Journal of Japanese Studies*, vol. 30, (Winter 2004): 123–142.

18. For a detailed study of the politics behind the transfer of the ethnic Koreans to the DPRK, see Tessa Morris-Suzuki, *Exodus to North Korea: Shadows from Japan's Cold War* (Lanham, Md.: Rowman & Littlefield, 2007).

19. In 1969 Chad and Central African Republic became the first two states to maintain full diplomatic relations with both Koreas. See Barry Gills, *Korea Versus Korea: A Case of Contested Legitimacy* (London and New York: Routledge, 1996), 132.

20. Mitchell Lerner, *Kim Il Sung, the Juche Ideology, and the Second Korean War* (Washington, D.C.: Woodrow Wilson International Center for Scholars, 2011).

21. For a comprehensive overview of the PDS since its inception and until its collapse in the 1990s, see No Yong Hwan and Yŏn Ha Ch'ŏng, *Pukhan-ŭi chumin saenghwal pochang chŏngch'aek p'yŏngka [Evaluation of the welfare policies in North Korea]* (Seoul: Hankuk pokŏnsahoeyŏnkuwŏn, 1997), 47–62.

22. For more information, see Viola Lynne (ed.), *Contending with Stalinism: Soviet Power and Popular Resistance in the 1930s* (Ithaca, N.Y.: Cornell University Press,

2002), 173; Alex Dowlah, and John Elliot, *The Life and Times of Soviet Socialism* (Westport, Conn.: Praeger Publishers, 1997), 168.

23. Chad Raymond, "No Responsibility and No Rice: The Rise and Fall of Agricultural Collectivization in Vietnam," *Agricultural History* 1 (2008), iss. 1: 49.

24. Michael Nelson, *War of the Black Heavens: The Battles of Western Broadcasting in the Cold War* (Syracuse, N.Y.: Syracuse University Press, 1997), 163.

25. Yonhap news report, January 18, 2011.

26. For the most detailed description of the North Korean prison system in English, see David Hawk, *Hidden Gulag, Second Edition* (Washington, D.C.: U.S. Committee for Human Rights in North Korea, 2012).

27. Ibid., 30.

28. See prison memoirs by Kang Ch'ŏl-hwan: Kang Chol-hwan and Pierre Rigoulot, *The Aquariums of Pyongyang: Ten Years in a North Korean Gulag* (New York: Basic Books, 2001).

29. Kang Chŏl-hwan. "Pukhan kyogwasŏ sok-ŭi Namhan" [South Korea in North Korean textbooks], *Chosŏn ilbo*, December 7, 2001, 54.

30. Yi Hyo-bŏm and Ch'oe Hyŏn-ho, "Pukhan kyokwasŏ-rŭl t'onghan chŏngsonyŏn kach'igwan yŏngu: Kodŭng chunghakkyo kongsanjujŭi todok 3,4 haknyŏn chungsim-ŭro. Pukhan yŏngu hakhoebo. [A study of the youth value system through North Korean textbooks: centered around the textbooks for "Communist Morality" for years 3 and 4 in high school]," *Pukhan yŏngu hakhoebo*, 2000, iss. 2, 250.

31. *DPR Korea 2008 Population Census. National Report* (Pyongyang: Central Bureau of Statistics, 2009).

32. *World Health Statistics 2011* (Geneva: World Health Organization, 2011), 116–122.

33. Brian Myers, "The Watershed That Wasn't: Re-evaluating Kim Il Sung's 'Juche speech' of 1955," *Acta Koreana*, 2006, iss. 9: 89–115.

34. Kim Jong Il, *On the Juche Idea of Our Party* (Pyongyang: Foreign Languages Publishing House, 1985), 7.

35. The life story of Kim Jong Il has been a topic of many works, but due to the nature of his regime it is often difficult to distinguish between facts and unsubstantiated rumors. So far, the most comprehensive Kim Jong Il biography in English is Michael Breen, *Kim Jong-il: North Korea's Dear Leader* (Singapore and Hoboken, N.J.: Wiley, 2004).

36. George McCune, *Korea* (Cambridge, Mass.: Harvard University Press, 1950), 56–57.

37. Historical statistics compiled by Angus Maddison and his research team. Available for download at: www.ggdc.net/maddison/Historical_Statistics/horizontal-file_02-2010.xls.

38. On the scale of the North Korean military, see Nicholas Eberstadt, *Korea Approaches Reunification* (Armonk, N.Y.: M. E. Sharpe, 1995), 51–72.

CHAPTER 2

1. For trade statistics, see Kongdan Oh and Ralph Hassig, *North Korea Through the Looking Glass* (Washington, D.C.: Brookings Institution Press, 2000), 44–45.

2. Daniel Goodkind and Loraine West, "The North Korean Famine and Its Demographic Impact," *Population and Development Review*, vol. 27 (2001), iss. 2: 219–238.

3. Pak Keong-Suk, "Economic Hardship and Famines since the 1990s and Their Impact on Population Dynamics in North Korea," Presentation at the 51 Asia Seminar at Waseda University, Tokyo, Japan, December 2010.

4. Daniel Goodkind, Loraine West, and Peter Johnson, "A Reassessment of Mortality in North Korea, 1993–2008," Paper presented at the annual meeting of the Population Association of America March 31–April 2, 2011, Washington, D.C.

5. Kim Byung-Yeon and Song Dongho, "The Participation of North Korean Households in the Informal Economy: Size, Determinants, and Effect," *Seoul Journal of Economics*, vol. 21 (2008), iss. 2, 373.

6. Kim Pyŏn Yŏn and Yang Mun Su, *Pukhan kyŏngche-esŏŭi sichangkwa chŏngpu [The government and market in North Korean economy]* (Seoul, Sŏul taehakkyo ch'ulp'anmunhwawŏn, 2012), 124.

7. Ibid., 124.

8. The decrease in official-sponsored drug production was reported by the AFP (Agence France-Presse), which cited the US State Department. See "US says N. Korea's State Drug Trafficking on Wane," *Asiaone News*, March 4, 2011, accessed at news.asiaone.com. This agrees quite well with the observations of the present author.

9. Yi Yŏng-guk told his own story in a recently published book: Yi Yŏng-guk, *Na-nŭn Kim Chŏng-il kyŏnghowon iŏssta [I was the bodyguard of Kim Jong I])* (Seoul: Sidae chŏngsin, 2004).

10. P Tumankang-ŭl kŏnnŏon saramtŭl [People who have crossed the Tumen River] (Seoul: Chŏngdo ch'ulp'an, 1999), 27.

11. For a review of the existent research on the number of North Korean refugees in China, see Stephan Haggard and Marcus Noland, *Witness to Transformation: Refugee Insights Into North Korea* (Washington, D.C.: Peterson Institute for International Economics, 2011), 2.

12. For a description of such VIP defection (arranged for an aged woman by her daughter), see Barbara Demick, *Nothing to Envy: Ordinary Lives in North Korea* (New York: Spiegel & Grau, 2010), 239–247. In her informative and highly recommended book, Demick also provides detailed descriptions of far more common, cheap defections.

13. Some rough estimates of the scale of remittances have been made in 2009–11 by a number of people, including the present author. These estimates lay in the $5–20 million range.

14. International Crisis Group, *Strangers At Home: North Koreans in the South Report N°208* (Brussels: International Crisis Group, 2011), 14–15. This report is the latest (and arguably the best) of a small number of English-language materials dealing with the refugee problem in South Korea. There is a large number of Korean-language material, however.

15. The spread of videos was widely reported by refugees and the media. For a detailed account of the North Korean "video revolution," see Yi Chu-chol, "Pukhan chuminui oepu chongpo suyong taeto pyonhwa" [The Research of Changes in North Koreans' Attitudes toward the Outside World Information], *Hankuk tongpuka nonchong*, vol. 46 (2008): 245–248.

16. InterMedia, "International Broadcasting in North Korea: North Korean Refugee/ Traveler Survey Report," April–August 2009.

17. Remarks about the role of the computer as a status symbol: Kim Po-kŏn. "The 5 storages and 6 contraptions which serve as symbols of prosperity in North Korea," *T'ongil Hankuk [Unified Korea]* vol. 27 (2009), iss. 1: 80. I would add that in my own talks with defectors this new symbolic significance of the computer was mentioned frequently.

CHAPTER 3

1. Surjit Bhalla, *Imagine There's No Country: Poverty, Inequality, and Growth in the Era of Globalization* (Washington, D.C.: Institute for International Economics, 2002), 16.

2. According to the calculations of Angus Maddison, the most respected economic historian of our days, in 1960 the per capita GDP was: $1,226 for South Korea, $1,277 for Somalia, $1,353 for Taiwan, $1,445 for Senegal (measured in 1990 International Geary-Khamis dollars).

3. Chad Raymond, "No Responsibility and No Rice: The Rise and Fall of Agricultural Collectivization in Vietnam," *Agricultural History*, vol.82 (2008), iss.1: 54–55.

4. Sang T. Choe, "North Korea Moving from Isolation to an Open Market Economy: Is It time to Invest or to Continue Observing?" *Competitiveness Review*, vol. 13 (2003), iss.2: 60–69.

5. Terence Roehrig, "Creating the Conditions for Peace in Korea: Promoting Incremental Change in North Korea," *Korea Observer*, vol. 40 (2009), iss.1: 222.

6. For details on the ongoing argument over the actual size of the North Korean GDP, see I Chong-sok, "Pukhan kukmin sotuk chaepyongka" [Reassessment of the National Income of North Korea], *Chongsewa chongchaek* 3 (2008): 1–4.

     For the most recent estimates of the North Korean GDP see: 2011 *Pukhan-ŭi chuyo t'onggye chip'yo [Major Statistical Indicators for North Korea, 2011]* (Seoul: National Statistics Office, 2012).

7. Richard Vinen, *History in Fragments: Europe in the Twentieth Century* (London: Abacus, 2002), 513.

8. There is, actually, an ongoing debate on the reasons behind this relative success of the former nomenklatura and, more broadly speaking, Communist Party members in the post-Communist societies. Majority opinion is that it was brought about by the survival of institutions and networks, while the minority believes it is due to their personal qualities—opportunism, ambitions, organizational skills. There is no need, however, to go into excessive details: the continuing domination of the former elite is an undisputable and widely recognized fact. See Akos Rona-Tas and Alya Guseva, "The Privileges of Past Communist Party Membership in Russia and Endogenous Switching Regression," *Social Science Research* 30 (2001): 641–652.

9. *Tokyo Shimbun*, February 2, 2011.

10. Nicholas Eberstadt once aptly described North Korean diplomacy as a "chain of aid-seeking stratagems."

11. For a detailed study of the "food diversion problem," see Stephan Haggard and Marcus Noland, *Famine in North Korea: Markets, Aid and Reform* (New York: Columbia University Press, 2007), 108–125.

12. Seen as the beginning of a long-awaited Chinese-style reform program, the 7.1 measures have been treated at great length by numerous scholars. For the best summary in English, see Young Chul Chung, "North Korean Reform and Opening: Dual Strategy and 'Silli (Practical) Socialism,'" *Pacific Affairs*, vol. 77 (2004), iss. 2: 283–305. For Korean, see Kang Il-chon and Kong Son-yong, "7.1 kyongche kwanri kaeson chochi 1 nyonui pyongkawa chaehaesok" [The First Anniversary of the 7.1 Economy Management Improvement Measures: The Analysis and Appraisal], *Tongil munche yonku*, vol. 15 (2003): 131–146.

13. See, respectively, *Wall Street Journal*, June 20, 2004; Victor Cha and Chris Hoffmeister, "North Korea's Drug Habit," *New York Times*, June 3, 2004; Howard W. French, "North Korea Experiments, with China As Its Model," *New York Times*, March 28, 2005.

14. Yim Kyong-hun, "Pukhansik kyongche kaehyok-e taehan pyongka-wa chonmang: 7.1 kyongche kwanri kaeson chochirul chungsim-uro" [The Appraisal and Prospects of an Economic Reform, North Korean Style; Centered around 7.1 Economy Management Improvement Measures], *Hankuk chongchi yonku*, vol. 16 (2007): 290, 295–391.

15. Nam Song-uk, "Nongop punyaui kaehyok tanhaengkwa paekupche chaekae" [Execution of Reforms in Agriculture and Revival of the Rationing System], *Pukhan* 2005, iss.12: 81.

16. Between May and June of 2005 rice at Hamhung market cost 950 won per kilo. See Kim Yong-chin, "Hampuk Musan chiyok ssalkaps sopok harak" [Rice Prices in Dramatic Decline in Musan and North Hamgyong], *Daily NK*, July 17, 2007.

17. Kim Yong-chin, "Paekŭp 700g taesangŭn motu chikchang chulkŭnhara" [Those Who Are Eligible for 700 g Rations Must Go to the Workplace], *Daily NK*, December 7, 2006.

18. The coming of this ban was reported in October when rumors began to spread. The ban went into effect on December 1, 2007. See *Onŭl-ŭi Pukhan sosik*, December 6, 2007, 2.

19. *Onŭl-ŭi Pukhan sosik*, March 12, 2008, 2–3.

20. *Onŭl-ŭi Pukhan sosik*, November 6, 2008, 1–2.

21. Regarding the number of North Korean defectors hiding in China from 2006 to 2008, there are still large estimates, but the author tends to agree with Yun Yo-sang. See Yun Yo-sang, "Haeoe talpukcha siltaewa taechaek" [The Current Situation of North Korean Defectors Overseas and Policy toward Them], *Pukhan* 2008, iss.5: 70. Yun concludes that in 2007 there were between 30,000 and 50,000 North Koreans hiding in China. In May 2007 NGO representatives operating in China also agreed that the number of refugees was close to 30,000. See "Talpuk haengryol 10 nyon . . . suscha chulko kyechung tayang" [Ten Years of Defections from the North . . . Numbers Go Down, Social Variety Increases], *Daily NK*, May 14, 2007. These estimates agree with what the present author himself heard on trips in 2007 and 2008 to the borderland areas both from Chinese officials and from independent researchers.

22. The interview was widely reported in the media. For example, see "Kim Jong Il's Son Talks Succession," *CNN World*, October 12, 2010.

23. As quoted by Yonhap Agency report, January 28, 2011.

CHAPTER 4

1. Gregory Schulte, "Stopping Proliferation Before It Starts," *Foreign Affairs* (July/ August 2010): 83.

2. On Syria—North Korea nuclear cooperation, see, for example: Gregory Schulte, *Uncovering Syria's Covert Reactor* (Carnegie Endowment for International Peace, 2010).

3. For a description of South Korea's short-lived nuclear weapons program, see Don Oberdorfer, *The Two Koreas: A Contemporary History* (New York: Basic Books, 2001), 68–74.

4. Walter Clemens, "North Korea's Quest for Nuclear Weapons: New Historical Evidence," *Journal of East Asian Studies*, vol.10 (2010), iss.1: 127.

5. The United States' near obsession with the nuclear program produced an impressive volume of literature dealing with the topic—dozens of books, hundreds of research papers. For a short and document-based introduction into the early history of the North Korean nuclear project, see a collection of articles edited by James Clay Moltz and Alexandre Y. Mansourov: *The North Korean Nuclear Program: Security, Strategy, and New Perspectives from Russia* (New York: Routledge, 2000). For more up-to-date information, a report by the Congressional Research Service might be of great help: Larry Niksch, *North Korea's Nuclear Weapons Development and Diplomacy* (Washington, D.C.: Congressional Research Service, 2010). For a short and highly professional review of the North Korean nuclear program, see an article by Siegfried Hecker, the former director of the Los Alamos Laboratories: Siegfried Hecker, "Lessons Learned from the North Korean Nuclear Crises," *Daedalus* 139 (2010): 44–56.

6. Korean Peninsula Energy Development Organization, *2005 Annual Report* (New York: KEDO, 2005), 13.

7. For a short but comprehensive review of KEDO's history, see Yoshinori Takeda, "KEDO Adrift," *Georgetown Journal of International Affairs*, vol. 6 (2005), iss. 2: 123–131. The article might be seen as an unintended obituary for the KEDO, which ceased operations soon after it was published.

8. Jeffrey Smith, "U.S. Accord with North Korea May Open Country to Change," *Washington Post*, October 23, 1994, A36. Expectations of imminent collapse were widely—albeit privately—shared with the journalists at the time. See, for example, Jim Hoagland, "The Trojan Horse at North Korea's Gate," *Washington Post*, August 2, 1995, A25.

9. The World Food Program INTERFAIS database. Available at www.wfp.org/fais.

10. For a detailed description of the monitoring regime, see Stephan Haggard and Marcus Noland, *Famine in North Korea: Markets, Aid and Reform* (New York: Columbia University Press, 2007), 92–102.

11. Siegfried Hecker, "Lessons Learned from the North Korean Nuclear Crises," *Daedalus* 139 (Winter 2010): 47.

12. The Kosis, the database of the National Statistics Office, is available at nso.go.kr.

13. *2010 T'ongil ŭisik chosa [2010 Survey of unification opinion]* (Seoul: Sŏultaehakkyo t'ongilp'yŏnghwayŏnkuso, 2010), 22–23.

14. Aidan Foster-Carter, "Towards the Korean Endgame," *The Observer*, December 1, 2002.

15. The World Food Program INTERFAIS database. Available at www.wfp.org/fais.

16. T'ongkyechŏng, *Pukhanŭi chuyot'ongkyechip'yoo [North Korea's main statistical indicators]* (Seoul: National Statistical Office, 2010), 35, 87.

17. Statistics for the Kŭmgang project can be found at "Kŭmkangsan kwankwang 10 chunyŏn kwanlyŏn charyo," *Pukhan kyŏngche ripyu*, 2008, iss. 11: 78–95.

18. For the best available summary on the KIZ situation in English, see Dick Nanto and Mark Manyin, *The Kaesŏng North-South Korean Industrial Complex*. RL 34903 (Washington, D.C.: Congressional Research Service, 2011).

19. Hahm Chaibong, "South Korea's Miraculous Democracy," *Journal of Democracy* 19 (2008): 138.

20. Kando, known in Chinese as Jiandao, is an area located on the western bank of the Tuman River. The exact borders of the area are disputed, but more radical Korean nationalists include a large part of Manchuria in Kando.

21. Hangyore, September 4, 2004.

22. For a detailed treatment of the history wars between China and the Koreas, see Terence Roehrig, "History as a Strategic Weapon: The Korean and Chinese Struggle over Koguryo," in *Korean Studies in the World: Democracy, Peace, Prosperity, and Culture*, ed. Seung Ham Yang, Yeon Sik Choi, and Jong Kun Choi (Seoul: Jimoon-dang, 2008); Peter Hays Gries, "The Koguryo Controversy, National Identity, and Sino-Korean Relations Today," *East Asia*, vol. 22 (2005), iss.4: 3–17; Andrei Lankov, "The Legacy of Long-Gone States: China, Korea and the Koguryo Wars." *Japan Focus*, September 2, 2006.

23. For 2010 data, see Chungang Ilbo, May 27, 2011; for other data, see Dick Nanto and Mark E. Manyin, *China-North Korea Relations* (Washington, D.C.: Congressional Research Service, 2010), 15. For 2011 data, see: *2011nyŏnto Pukhan-ŭi taeoe kyŏngche silchŏk punsŏk-kwa 2012 nyŏnto chŏnmang [2011 North Korea's domestic an international economic performance and 2012 outlook]* (Seoul: Taeoe kyŏngche chŏngch'aek yŏnkuwŏn, 2012), 4.

24. "China, South Korea Start Talks on Free-Trade Pact," *Bloomberg News*, May 2, 2012.

25. For a detailed review of the current state of Chinese economic advances into North Korea, see Jaewoo Choo, "Mirroring North Korea's Growing Economic Dependence on China: Political Ramifications," *Asian Survey* 48 (2008): 343–372.

INTERLUDE

1. "North Korea: 6 Million Are Hungry," *Reuters*, March 26, 2011; Charles Clover, "Catastrophe in North Korea; China must pressure Pyongyang to allow food aid to millions threatened by famine," *The Times*. March 22, 2010. 2; Blaine Harden, "At the Heart of North Korea's Troubles, an Intractable Hunger Crisis," *Washington Post*, March 6, 2009, A.1; Reuters, "Food Shortage Looms in North Korea," *International Herald Tribune*, April 17, 2008, 3.

2. 2009nyŏn pukhan kyŏngchesŏngchangryul ch'uchŏng kyŏlkwa [Results from estimates of North Korea's 2009 growth rates] (Seoul: Hankuk ŭnhaeng, 2010), 1.

CHAPTER 5

1. Wade L. Huntley, "Sit Down and Talk," *Bulletin of the Atomic Scientists* 59 (2003): 28.
2. Wade L. Huntley, "Threats All the Way Down: U.S. Nuclear Initiatives in a Unipolar World," *Review of International Studies* 32 (2006): 49–67.
3. Lee Edwards, *Mediapolitik: How the Mass Media Have Transformed World Politics* (Washington, D.C.: Catholic University of America Press, 2001), 126.
4. InterMedia, *International Broadcasting in North Korea: North Korean Refugee/ Traveler Survey Report April–August 2009* (Washington, D.C.: InterMedia, 2009).
5. Peter Beck, "North Korea's Radio Waves of Resistance," *Wall Street Journal*, April 16, 2010.

CHAPTER 6

1. On the MMM scheme in Russia, see William Rosenberg, *The Democratic Experience in the Transitional Russia. In Extending the Borders of Russian History: Essays in Honor of Alfred Rieber* (Budapest and New York: Central European University Press, 2003), 525–526. On the Albanian civil war of 1997, see Dirk Bezemer (ed.), *On Eagle's Wings: The Albanian Economy in Transition* (New York: Nova Science, 2008), 22–24.
2. International Crisis Group, *Strangers at Home: North Koreans in the South Report N°208*, (Brussels: International Crisis Group, 2011), 17.
3. Elisabeth Bumiller and David Sanger, "Gates Warns of North Korea Missile Threat to U.S.," *New York Times*, January 11, 2011.
4. Doug Waller, "The Second Time Around for Bob Gates," *Time*, December 4, 2006.

BOX 13

1. "Korean Unification Will Cost Over US$3 Trln, Experts Say," *Asia Pulse*, September 14, 2010. Original report available at the website of the FKI, www.fki.or.kr.
2. "Think-Tank Estimates Unification Cost for Koreas at $2.14 tln," *Korea Herald*, February 27, 2011.
3. Kim Hee-jin, "Post-Kim Unification Cost Estimates Keep Rising," Korea Joongang Daily, January 12, 2012.
4. The report is not publicly available, but Credit Suisse funding was reported at the time. See, for example, "Peace Worries Some Korea Watchers More than War," *China Post*, October 28, 2009.
5. Peter Beck, "Contemplating Korean Reunification," *Wall Street Journal*, January 4, 2010.

INDEX

The abbreviations N.K. and S.K. stand for "North Korea" and "South Korea."